4

College Reading

HOUGHTON MIFFLIN
ENGLISH FOR ACADEMIC SUCCESS

Cheryl Benz
Georgia Perimeter College

Cynthia M. Schuemann
Miami Dade College

SERIES EDITORS

Patricia Byrd

Joy M. Reid

Cynthia M. Schuemann

Houghton Mifflin Company

Boston   New York

Publisher: Patricia A. Coryell
Director of ESL Publishing: Susan Maguire
Senior Development Editor: Kathy Sands Boehmer
Editorial Assistant: Evangeline Bermas
Senior Project Editor: Kathryn Dinovo
Manufacturing Assistant: Karmen Chong
Senior Marketing Manager: Annamarie Rice

Cover graphics: LMA Communications, Natick, Massachusetts

Photo credits: © Patrik Giardino/Corbis, p. 1; © Bill Varie/Corbis, p. 1; © Bill Eichner, p. 2; © Michael S. Yamashita/Corbis, p. 39; © James Mitsui, p. 42; © Charles Gupton/Corbis, p. 50; © Dave Ellis, p. 52; © Royalty-Free/Corbis, p. 73; © Royalty-Free/Corbis, p. 89; © Ronnie Kaufman/Corbis, p. 101; © Royalty-Free/Corbis, p. 104; © Ariel Skelley/Corbis, p. 106; © Darrell Gulin/Corbis, p. 125; © Corbis, p. 139; © Ed Kashi/Corbis, p. 139; © Charles Mauzy/Corbis, p. 142; © Kevin Schafer/Corbis, p. 142; © Ray Bird; Frank Lane Picture Agency/Corbis, p. 150; © Lester V. Bergman/Corbis, p. 156; © Ted Spiegel/Corbis, p. 165; © Ben Benschneider, p. 159; © Paul A. Souders/Corbis, p. 162; © Seattle Times staff, p. 163; © Jose Luis Pelaez, Inc./Corbis, p. 176; © Houghton Mifflin Company/Boston, p. 179; © Reuters/Corbis, p. 217; © Michael S. Yamashita/Corbis, p. 223; © Houghton Mifflin Company/Boston, p. 227; © Bettmann/Corbis, p. 228; © Bettmann/Corbis, p. 231; © Giraudon/Art Resource, NY, p. 253; © Gianni Dagli Orti/Corbis, p. 256

Acknowledgments appear on pp. 267–268 which constitutes an extension of the copyright page.

Printed in the U.S.A.

Library of Congress Control Number: 2004112259

ISBN: 0-618-23023-8

123456789-CRW-08 07 06 05 04

Contents

Houghton Mifflin English for Academic Success Series

Houghton Mifflin English for Academic Success Series

SERIES EDITORS

Patricia Byrd, Joy M. Reid, Cynthia M. Schuemann

☐ What Is the Purpose of This Series?

The Houghton Mifflin English for Academic Success series is a comprehensive program of student and instructor materials. For students, there are four levels of student language proficiency textbooks in three skill areas (oral communication, reading, and writing) and a supplemental vocabulary textbook at each level. For both instructors and students, a useful website supports classroom teaching, learning and assessment. In addition, for instructors, there are four Essentials of Teaching Academic Language books (*Essentials of Teaching Academic Oral Communication, Essentials of Teaching Academic Reading, Essentials of Teaching Academic Writing,* and *Essentials of Teaching Academic Vocabulary*). These books provide helpful information for instructors who are new to teaching and for experienced instructors who want to reinforce practices or brush up on current teaching strategies.

The fundamental purpose of the series is to prepare students who are not native speakers of English for academic success in U.S. college degree programs. By studying these materials, students in English for Academic Purposes (EAP) programs will gain the academic language skills they need and learn about the nature and expectations of U.S. college courses.

The series is based on considerable prior research as well as our own investigations of students' needs and interests, instructors' needs and desires, and institutional expectations and requirements. For example, our survey research revealed what problems instructors feel they face in their classrooms and what they actually teach; who the students are and what they know and do not know about the "culture" of U.S. colleges; and what types of exams are required for admission at various colleges.

Student Audience

The materials in this series are for college-bound ESL students at U.S. community colleges and undergraduate programs at other institutions. Some of these students are U.S. high school graduates. Some of them are long-term U.S. residents who graduated from a high school before coming to the U.S. Others are newer U.S. residents. Still others are more typical international students. All of them need to develop academic language skills and knowledge of ways to be successful in U.S. college degree courses.

All of the books in this have been created to implement the Houghton Mifflin English for Academic Success competencies. These competencies are based on those developed by ESL instructors and administrators in Florida, California, and Connecticut to be the underlying structure for EAP courses at colleges in those states. These widely respected competencies assure that the materials meet the real world needs of EAP students and instructors.

All of the books focus on . . .

- Starting where the students are, building on their strengths and prior knowledge (which is considerable, if not always academically relevant), and helping students self-identify needs and plans to strengthen academic language skills
- Academic English, including development of Academic Vocabulary and grammar required by students for academic speaking/listening, reading, and writing
- Master Student Skills, including learning style analysis, strategy training, and learning about the "culture" of U.S. colleges, which lead to their becoming successful students in degree courses and degree programs
- Topics and readings that represent a variety of academic disciplinary areas so that students learn about the language and content of the social sciences, the hard sciences, education, and business as well as the humanities

All of the books provide . . .

- Interesting and valuable content that helps the students develop their knowledge of academic content as well as their language skills and student skills
- A wide variety of practical classroom-tested activities that are easy to teach and engage the students

■ Assessment tools at the end of each chapter so that instructors have easy-to-implement ways to assess student learning and students have opportunities to assess their own growth

■ Websites for the students and for the instructors: the student sites provide additional opportunities to practice reading, writing, listening, vocabulary development, and grammar. The instructor sites provide instructor's manuals, teaching notes and answer keys, value-added materials like handouts and overheads that can be reproduced to use in class, and assessment tools such as additional tests to use beyond the assessment materials in each book.

☐ What Is the Purpose of the Reading Strand?

The four books in the Reading strand focus on the development of reading skills and general background knowledge necessary for college study. These books are dedicated to meeting the academic needs of ESL students by teaching them how to handle reading demands and expectations of freshman-level classes. The reading selections come from varied disciplines, reflecting courses with high enrollment patterns at U.S. colleges. The passages have been chosen from authentic academic text sources, and are complimented with practical exercises and activities that enhance the teaching-learning process. Students respond positively to being immersed in content from varied disciplines, and vocabulary and skills that are easily recognized as valuable and applicable.

Because of the importance of academic vocabulary in both written and spoken forms, the Reading strand features attention to high-frequency academic words found across disciplines. The books teach students techniques for learning and using new academic vocabulary, both to recognize and understand the words when they read them, and to use important words in their own spoken and written expressions. In addition to language development, the books provide for content and academic skill development. They include appropriate academic tasks and provide strategies to help students better understand and handle what is expected of them in college classes. Chapter objectives specified at the beginning of each chapter include some content area objectives as well as reading and academic skills objectives. For example, student work may include defining key concepts from a reading selection, analyzing the use of facts and examples to support a theory, or paraphrasing information from a reading as they report back on points they have learned. That is, students are not taught to work with the reading selections for some abstract reason, but to learn to make a powerful connection between working with the exercises and activities and success with teacher-assigned tasks from general education disciplines. The chapter objectives are tied to the series' competencies which were derived from a review of educator-generated course expectations in community college EAP programs. The objectives also reflect a commitment to sound pedagogy.

Each book has a broad "behind-the-scenes" theme to provide an element of sustained content. These themes were selected because of their high interest for students; they are also topics commonly explored in introductory college courses and so provide useful background for students. Materials were selected that are academically appropriate but that do not require expert knowledge by the teacher. The following themes are explored in the Reading strand—Book 1: Society; Book 2: Enduring Issues; Book 3: Diversity; and Book 4: Memory and Learning.

The series also includes a resource book for teachers called *Essentials of Teaching Academic Reading* by Sharon Seymour and Laura Walsh. This practical book provides strategies and activities for instructors new to the teaching of reading and for experienced instructors who want to reinforce their practices or brush up on current teaching strategies.

The website for each book provides additional teaching activities for instructors and study and practice activities for students. These materials include substantial information on practical classroom-based assessment of academic reading to help teachers with the challenging task of analysis of student learning in this area. And, the teacher support on the series website includes printable handouts, quizzes and overhead transparency forms, as well as teaching tips from the authors.

☐ What Is the Organization of *College Reading 4*?

College Reading 4 prepares high-intermediate to advanced level students for the demands of college-level academic reading.

Themes

Six chapters of readings in literature, study skills, psychology, environmental science, economics, and education present concepts and language that many students will encounter in future courses. The academic disciplines have been chosen to match courses which ESL students most often take in U.S. colleges and universities.

Competencies

College Reading 4 develops the reading competencies listed in this book and referred to as objectives at the start of each chapter. Additional content specific objectives are also listed there. These competencies are developed and reinforced in logical sequence based on reading assignments and hierarchical task complexity.

Reading Development

- Chapters 1 and 2 revisit fundamental reading skills—identifying details that support themes or examples that support theories, recognizing inferences and cultural references, and outlining and paraphrasing.
- Chapters 3 through 5 present students with reading opportunities that include interpreting charts and graphs, assessing problems and generating solutions, exploring personal beliefs, and recognizing and evaluating sources.

Academic Success

Special feature elements include reading strategy boxes and Master Student Tips to highlight important advice for students. Power Grammar notes draw attention to grammar shifts that influence meaning. Rather than "grammar in context," *College Reading 4* exploits "grammar from [the] context," of the readings.[1] For example, through reading, students learn to examine parts of speech, explanation or definition markers, and language features that characterize different writing styles found in academic passages.

---

1. Byrd, P. and Reid, J. (1998) *Grammar in the Composition Classroom.* Boston: Heinle.

Content Knowledge

- Several readings per chapter theme facilitate sustained content reading.
- Content skill building is present in every chapter: from understanding tone and figurative language in literature from Chapter 1 to case studies and reported research in Chapters 3 and 4, and to historical contrasts in Chapter 6.

Vocabulary Development

Vocabulary development is a key feature of *College Reading 4*, so each reading selection was analyzed for its Flesch-Kincaid Grade Level, and other factors to ensure that readings were appropriate for this level. The reading selections represent readings actually assigned to college students taking freshman-level coursework.

The Web Vocabulary Profiler[2] was used to identify academic[3] and high-frequency[4] vocabulary items in each selection. These analyses aid teachers tremendously in determining which vocabulary items should be stressed in pre- and post-reading activities. *College Reading 4* features a range of vocabulary-building activities aimed at student retention of academic and high-frequency words.

Academic vocabulary words in the reading selections are unobtrusively marked with dotted underlines and a footnoted glossary provides extra help for students when needed.

Chapter Organization and Exercise Types

Each chapter is clearly divided into sections marked Reading Assignment 1, 2, etc. The reading assignment sections include common features which indicate pre-reading, reading, and post-reading activities. Following the reading assignment sections, each chapter has a final component called Assessing Your Learning at the End of a Chapter.

2. The Web Vocabulary Profiler, maintained by Tom Cobb, analyzes a reading to identify academic and high-frequency vocabulary words within the text. A link to his site can be found by visiting our site at www.college.hmco.com/esl/instructors/
3. *Academic* words refers to the Academic Word List compiled by Dr. Averil Coxhead of Victoria University of Wellington. These 570 word families are commonly found in academic texts from all subjects. A link to her site with the complete list can be found by visiting our website.
4. *High-frequency* vocabulary words refers to the 2,000 most frequently used words, the General Service List of English words, also known as the West List (1953).

Getting Ready to Read

Schema-building activities—photographs, group discussions, etc.—activate students' prior knowledge before reading. Students also study potentially unfamiliar vocabulary and key concepts and terms in the academic discipline before they read.

Reading for a Purpose

In this section, readers are guided to read for specific information through pre-reading tasks such as prediction of ideas, formation of pre-reading questions responding to short pre-test items, and other exercises. These activities focus readers' attention on a particular purpose for reading: finding key ideas.

Demonstrating Comprehension   Instead of monotonous comprehension exercises, *College Reading 4* features a variety of interest-peaking activities to monitor comprehension. After each reading, there is not just one or two, but multiple opportunities to assess comprehension. Main idea, major points, supporting ideas, text organization, and confirmation of pre-reading tests and other activities provide repeated checks of students' understanding of reading.

Questions for Discussion   Once students demonstrate a basic understanding of a reading selection, they delve more deeply into its content and language through group and pair discussions. Students write complete sentence answers to the questions after their discussions to exploit the language gained from reading in developing writing skills.

Reading Journal   The reading journal feature also facilitates the reading-writing link. Students express reactions to key ideas in reading or write extended answers to discussion questions. Journal writing also serves as another way to check reading comprehension.

Learning Vocabulary   Each chapter includes directed vocabulary learning exercises and strategy suggestions for students.

Focusing on [Subject Area]   Here students are exposed to more in-depth exercise types that focus on content learning expectations or assignments from the different discipline areas associated with each chapter.

Linking Concepts   In this section, readers synthesize information gained from two or more sources and transfer ideas from reading to their experiences. Students express these connections in discussion and writing.

Assessing Your Learning at the End of a Chapter

This final section of each chapter asks students to revisit the chapter objectives in a reflective manner, and review for a test. Then, a practice self-test tied to the objectives is provided. Students can test themselves on their understanding and retention of important content and language features in the readings. The items in the student practice tests are similar to items included on the sample tests provided for instructors to use. (Visit the series website at www.college.hmco.com/esl/instructors.) Finally, academic vocabulary from the chapter is also revisited, and a For Further Study web link reminder is provided for students.

Acknowledgments

At Houghton Mifflin Company, we would like to thank ESL director Susan Maguire, who made the project a reality, and developmental editor Kathy Sands Boehmer who kept our large team of at times unwieldy writers on track. Co-series editors Patricia Byrd, Georgia State University; Joy Reid, University of Wyoming, as well as the all the team members, lent an enormous store of insight and theoretical and pedagogical knowledge to the series. They were a constant source of support.

We are indebted to our family members who always believed in us. They were there for us whenever the light at the end of the tunnel dimmed.

Also, Steven Donahue, Patricia Killian, and Mary Goodman served us as advisors, and helped guide this book through its early stages. The following reviewers also contributed practical comments:

Harriet Allison, Gainesville College
A. Mara Beckett, Glendale Community College
Anne Bachmann, Clackamas Community College
David Dahnke, North Harris College
Amy Drabek, Queens College
Mark Ende, Onandaga Community College
Duffy Galda, Pima Community College
Daryl Kinney, Los Angeles City College
Pat LaRose, Queens College
Linda Linn, San Jacinto College
Melanie Majeski, Nagatuck Valley Community College
Marilyn Mirman, Baltimore City Community College
Jane Perry, Norwalk Community College
Geraldine Shelton, Prince George's Community College
Colleen Weldele, Palomar College

Finally, students are the core reason that teachers strive to improve methods and materials. Our students at Miami Dade and Georgia Perimeter Colleges have also greatly influenced our work. Above all, we dedicate these materials to them and wish them success in their academic pursuits.

☐ What Student Competencies Are Covered in *College Reading 4*?

Houghton Mifflin English for Academic Success Competencies
College Reading 4

Description of Overall Purposes

Students develop the ability to comprehend and interpret authentic college-level texts in content areas by applying appropriate reading strategies.

Materials in this textbook are designed with the following minimum exit objectives in mind:

Competency 1:
(level/global focus)
The student will demonstrate comprehension of academic texts with general education content from a range of disciplines. (Text sources may include materials from Houghton Mifflin college "essentials" sources and college freshman level textbooks.)

Competency 2:
(flexibility)
The student will adjust reading strategies according to textual demands (e.g., varying reading rate, interpreting charts or graphs) and reading purposes (e.g., test preparation, searching an appendix.)

Competency 3:
(components)
The student will analyze the use of facts and examples to support and explain generalizations, statements of theory, and implicit main ideas or assumptions. These distinctions will aid the student in prioritizing what to learn for test-taking purposes (e.g., distinguishing more relevant from less relevant or irrelevant pieces of information.)

Competency 4:
(organization)
The student will use a wide range of textual clues to compare meaning, structure, and style of academic materials.

Competency 5:
(vocabulary)
The student will develop vocabulary by applying effective strategies to clarify, analyze, and learn the meaning of new words in nonliterary text, and the student will interpret the use of figurative language in literary text.

Competency 6:
(vocabulary)
The student will discriminate, select, learn and use important words pertinent to specific academic reading contexts.

Competency 7:   The student will apply the following critical thinking
(critical thinking)   skills through reading. The student will:

a. Make plausible inferences or interpretations.
b. Develop perspectives through exploration of beliefs,
    arguments, and theories.
c. Ask significant questions.
d. Clarify understanding of issues raised in texts.
e. Articulate plausible implications or consequences.
f. Generate or assess solutions.
g. Explain and justify opinions in response to readings.
h. Apply knowledge gained from readings to other
    contexts and academic tasks such as discussion,
    writing, and test taking.
i. Extrapolate and manipulate facts and examples.
j. Evaluate the level or degree of credibility of sources.
k. Interpret an author's purpose, point of view, or tone
    when reading literary text.

Competency 8:   The student will demonstrate familiarity with common
(culture)   cultural schema.

Competency 9:   The student will apply effective study skills.
(study strategies)

☐ What Are the Features of the Reading Books?

The Houghton Mifflin English for Academic Success series is a comprehensive program of student and instructor materials. The fundamental purpose of the program is to prepare students who are not native speakers of English for academic success in U.S. college degree programs.

The Reading strand of the Houghton Mifflin English for Academic Success series focuses on the development of reading skills and general background knowledge. It is dedicated to meeting the academic needs of students by teaching them how to handle the reading demands and expectations of freshman-level college classes. The four books provide reading selections from authentic academic text sources and practical exercises and activities that enhance the teaching-learning process. Students respond positively to being immersed in vocabulary, content, and skills that are easily recognized as valuable and applicable.

Authentic Academic Reading Selections: The reading selections come from varied disciplines reflecting freshman-level courses with high enrollment patterns at U.S. colleges. The selections represent true reading demands college students face.

---

32   Chapter 1 The Global Melting Pot

Reading Selection 3

THE ROOTS OF OLD AND NEW WORLD FOODS

By Fodil Fellag

1   When the Spanish first conquered the New World in the late 1400s, their goal was to find gold and silver, which they did in enormous quantities. Although these metals were important to the Spanish and world economies of the times, they probably did not have an immediate, noticeable impact on the lives of common people. Much less desired, but infinitely more important in the everyday life of the world today, is the variety of new foods the New World explorers uncovered. Since that time, a wide range of foods first grown by indigenous[1] Americans has taken the world by storm.[2]

2   Imagine you went to an Italian restaurant, and it had no tomatoes available. Would the restaurant have anything you could eat that would be Italian? Yet, just a few centuries ago, tomatoes were totally unknown outside Central and South America. The list certainly does not stop there. For example, Indian and Pakistani cooking are known to the rest of the world as very spicy, yet the spicy part comes mostly from different varieties of peppers, all of which come from the New World. Indeed, almost all the cuisines of the world would be far different and far poorer without the food stuffs that originated in the Americas.[3]

3   Imagine a world without any sorts of beans, squash, zucchini, or pumpkins, all originally American. One might say that humanity can survive without them, and that is probably true. But now picture a world without potatoes. If the production of potatoes was suddenly stopped for some reason, much of the world would be distressed. When that happened in Ireland in the mid nineteenth century,[4] millions of people died or were forced to emigrate

1. *indigenous* = native
2. *take something by storm* = to suddenly become very successful and admired in a particular place
3. *the Americas* = North America, Central America, and South America considered together as a whole
4. The failure of the potato crops that caused mass starvation in Ireland occurred from 1845 to 1850.

Reading Assignment 2   A Slave's Journey in Sudan   225

Reading Selection 2

A SLAVE'S JOURNEY IN SUDAN

By Nicholas D. Kristof

1   April 23, 2002, KHARTOUM, Sudan—Abuk Achian was 6 years old when Arab raiders[1] attacked her village in southern Sudan, carried her off on horseback, and turned her into a slave.

2   Ms. Achian, now a pretty woman of 18, is one of many thousands of Sudanese women and children who have been kidnapped and enslaved over the last 20 years. Stopping this slavery will require international pressure.

3   Originally the Sudanese government excused the slave raids, as a way to reward Arab soldiers fighting on the government side in Sudan's civil war. Lately it has begun to crack down on[2] the tribal[3] raiding, although it still tends to deny that slavery exists here.

4   Ms. Achian was one of about 30 former slaves whom I met in Sudan (despite the efforts of the government, which did just about everything it could to limit my reporting here). Her story is typical: She is a member of the Dinka tribe, black Africans who are Christians or animists,[4] while the kidnappers are Baggara, or Muslim Arab herdsmen.[5]

5   "I was so scared," she recalled of her first few weeks in captivity.[6] "I couldn't understand the language that they spoke, and I was crying. But they beat me until I stopped crying and started to learn their language."

6   Her duties were to sleep outside with the camels, milk them, and make sure they did not run off. Her master beat her regularly and prohibited her to ever talk to other Dinka.

1. *raiders* = a small group of armed persons who make a sudden, forcible attack
2. *crack down on* = to make an effort to stop bad or illegal behavior by being strict and determined
3. *tribal* = relating to a *tribe*, a group made up of families, clans, or other groups with a common ancestry, culture, and leadership
4. *animists* = persons who believe that individual spirits live in animals and other natural objects
5. *herdsmen* = people whose job is to keep animals of a single kind feeding and moving together in a *herd*, or group
6. *captivity* = the state of being imprisoned, confined, or enslaved

Content and Academic Skill Development: In addition to language development, the books provide for content and academic skill development with the inclusion of appropriate academic tasks and by providing strategies to help students better understand and handle what is expected of them in college classes.

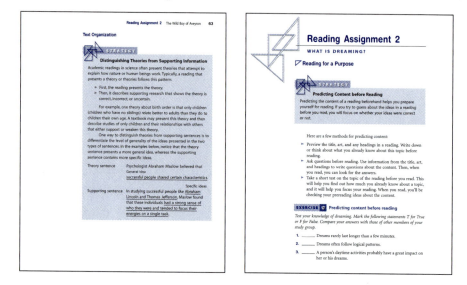

Academic Vocabulary: Academic vocabulary is important in both written and spoken forms, so the Reading strand features attention to high-frequency academic words found across disciplines. The books teach students techniques for learning and using new academic vocabulary and provide many practice exercises.

Integrated Review and Assessment: Each chapter closes by revisiting objectives and vocabulary and provides a practice test.

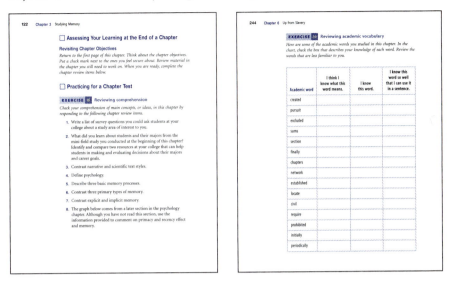

Master Student Tips: Master Student Tips throughout the textbooks provide students with short comments on a particular strategy, activity, or practical advice to follow in an academic setting.

Power Grammar Boxes: Students can be very diverse in their grammar and rhetorical needs so each chapter contains Power Grammar boxes that introduce the grammar structures students need to be fluent and accurate in academic English.

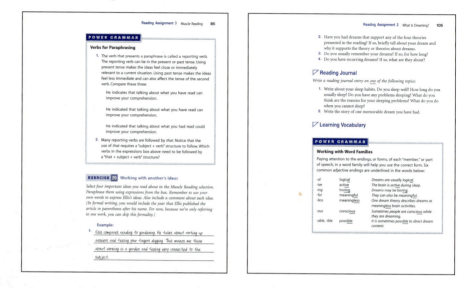

Ancillary Program: The following items are available to accompany the Houghton Mifflin English for Academic Success series Reading strand:

- Instructor website: Additional teaching materials, activities, and robust student assessment.
- Student website: Additional exercises and activities.
- The Houghton Mifflin English for Academic Success series Vocabulary books: You can choose the appropriate level to shrinkwrap with your text.
- The *Essentials of Teaching Academic Reading* by Sharon Seymour and Laura Walsh is available for purchase. It gives you theoretical and practical information for teaching reading.

Remembering Our Lives

ACADEMIC FOCUS: LITERATURE

Academic Reading Objectives

After completing this chapter,
you should be able to:

✓ Check here as you
master each objective.

1. Improve your reading comprehension ☐
2. Increase your reading speed ☐
3. Recognize inferences ☐
4. Identify details and examples that support themes ☐
5. Increase your vocabulary ☐

Literature Objectives

1. Interpret tone ☐
2. Recognize descriptive language ☐
3. Identify figurative language and idioms ☐
4. Relate ideas from texts to personal life experiences ☐
5. Understand common American cultural references ☐
6. Identify similarities and differences between two texts ☐

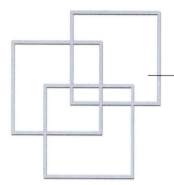

Reading Assignment 1

LA GRINGUITA

☐ Getting Ready to Read

EXERCISE **1** **Participating in class discussion**

Before you read, discuss the following questions with a partner and then with the rest of your classmates.

1. A memoir is an account of the personal experiences of an author. Have you ever read a memoir before? Who was the memoir about? Where and when was the memoir set?

2. The name of this memoir is *La Gringuita*. Do you know what this phrase means in Spanish? (If possible, find someone in your class who speaks Spanish.)

3. Read the introductory paragraph for Selection 1 that tells about Julia Alvarez.

La Gringuita

By Julia Alvarez

Julia Alvarez (1950–) came to the United States from the Dominican Republic as a young teenager. She explores the themes of loss of native land, language, culture, and extended family in her works, including *How the Garcia Girls Lost Their Accents*, *In the Time of Butterflies*, a National Book Critics Circle Award finalist, and *Yo!* Selection 1 is from *Something to Declare* (1998), a collection of essays and reminiscences. In it, Alvarez describes the effect of language and culture in defining the woman she would become.

4. What do you think this memoir is about?

5. Have you ever regretted not taking an opportunity when it presented itself to you? Describe the opportunity and what you did about it.

EXERCISE 2 **Previewing vocabulary**

Sometimes when read you come across unfamiliar words. Previewing vocabulary before you read can help you read more quickly and with better understanding.

*Below are some words you will see in Selection 1. Remember that you will understand the pieces better when you read the complete text. For now, try to guess the meanings of the **bold** words that may be unfamiliar to you.*

1. My mother gave him an **indignant** look, stood up, and went in search of the conductor to report this fresh man.
   a. helpful   **b.** angry   **c.** sad   **d.** interested

2. Decades later, hearing the story, my father, ever **vigilant** and jealous of his wife and daughters, was convinced—no matter what my mother said about idiomatic expressions—that the sailor had made an advance.
   a. watchful   **b.** quiet   **c.** certain   **d.** tired

3. At school, there were several incidents of name-calling and stone-throwing, which our teachers claimed would stop if my sisters and I joined in with the other kids and quit congregating together at recess and **jabbering** away in Spanish.
   a. arguing   **b.** playing   **c.** translating   **d.** talking

4. In fact, they felt my studying Spanish was equivalent to taking a
"**gut course**." Spanish was my native tongue, after all, a language I
already had in the bag and would always be able to speak whenever I
wanted.
   a. anatomy class   **b.** language class   **c.** easy class   **d.** bad class

5. Dilita and I **yakked**, back and forth, starting first in Spanish out of
consideration for our boyfriends, but switching over into English as
we got more involved in whatever we were talking about.
   a. talked   **b.** went   **c.** flirted   **d.** looked

6. Still, when I tried to talk to Mangú about something of substance,
the conversation **floundered**. I couldn't carry on in Spanish about
complicated subjects, and Mangú didn't know a word of English.
   a. became monotonous   **b.** became influential   **c.** became easy
   d. became confusing

7. "To have a lover whisper things in that language **crooned** to babies,
that language murmured by grandmothers, those words that
smelled like your house . . ."
   a. repeated   **b.** whistled   **c.** sung   **d.** explained

8. And, as I spoke, that old **yearning** came back. What would my life
have been like if I had stayed in my native country?
   a. reasoning   **b.** desire   **c.** fear   **d.** happiness

STRATEGY

Focusing on General Ideas: Memoirs

A memoir is a story a person writes about her or his own life. When
reading a memoir, focus on the **main ideas** or **themes** the writer is
trying to illustrate. In other words, it is more important to focus on
general ideas than specific details. When you read Selection 1, a
memoir, read it fairly quickly. Do not worry too much if you do not
understand every word at first. Try to understand the main themes or
ideas. Read all the way through once. Then, as you read again,
concentrate on the details that support the theme.

EXERCISE 3 **Developing reading fluency and speed**

Use this simple test to determine your reading speed. Your instructor can time your reading for exactly one minute. When your instructor says "start," begin reading this passage. When your instructor says "stop," circle the last word you read. Use the numbers at the right side of the chart to calculate your reading speed. (You can do this by counting the number of words on the last line you read and adding it to the number at the end of the last full line you read.)

LA GRINGUITA

The inevitable, of course, has happened. I now speak my	10
native language "with an accent." What I mean by this is that I	23
speak perfect childhood Spanish, but if I stray[1] into a heated	34
discussion or complex explanation, I have to ask "Por favor.	44
¿Puedo decirlo en inglés?" Can I please say it in English?	55
How and why did this happen?	61
When we emigrated to the United States in the early sixties,	72
the climate was not favorable for retaining our Spanish. I	82
remember one scene in a grocery store soon after we arrived. An	94
elderly shopper, overhearing my mother speaking Spanish to her	103
daughters, muttered[2] that if we wanted to be in this country, we	115
should learn the language. "I do know the language," my mother	126
said in her boarding school English, putting the woman in her	137
place. She knew the value of speaking perfect English. She had	148
studied for several years at Abbot Academy, flying up from the	159
Island to New York City, and then taking the train up to Boston.	172
It was during the war, and the train would sometimes fill with	184
servicemen, every seat taken.	188

One time, a young sailor asked my mother if he could sit in the   202

empty seat beside her and chew on her ear. My mother gave him an   216

indignant look, stood up, and went in search of the conductor to   228

report this fresh man. Decades later, hearing the story, my father,   239

ever vigilant and jealous of his wife and daughters, was convinced   250

—no matter what my mother said about idiomatic[3] expressions—   259

that the sailor had made an advance. He, himself, was never   270

comfortable in English. In fact, if there were phone calls to be made   283

to billing offices, medical supply stores, Workman's compensation,   291

my father would put my mother on the phone. She would get better   304

results than he would with his heavy, almost incomprehensible   313

accent.   314

Write your reading speed: _____ wpm (words per minute)

Master Student Tip

▼ To be successful in college, you will have to do a lot of reading. The average student reads 250 words per minute (wpm). More efficient readers read 400 wpm. How do you compare?

STRATEGY

Improving Reading Speed

Here are some things you can do to improve your reading speed:

1. **Avoid pronouncing words as you read**. If you say the words aloud, you can read only as fast as you can say the words. You should be able to read most materials at least two or three times faster silently than orally.

2. **Avoid rereading.** Rereading words and phrases is a habit that will slow you down.

3. **Try to guess the meanings of unfamiliar words.** You usually do not have to know the exact meaning of a word in order to understand the meaning of the sentence it's in. If it is important to learn the exact meaning of a word, underline it, but don't stop reading. Later, look up all the underlined words at once. Looking up words in the dictionary while you read can really slow you down. In Selection 1, some words that may be unfamiliar to you are defined in the footnote at the bottom of the page. Using the footnote definitions can also save you time.

4. **Increase the number of words you read at one time.** This will give you a wider eye span. Written material is more difficult to understand if you read one word at a time. Increasing the number of words you read will help you learn to read by phrases or thought units.

☐ Reading the Selection

Julia Alvarez (1950–) came to the United States from the Dominican Republic as a young teenager. She explores the themes of loss of native land, language, culture, and extended family in her works, including How the Garcia Girls Lost Their Accents, In the Time of Butterflies, *a National Book Critics Circle Award finalist, and* Yo! *Selection 1 is from* Something to Declare *(1998), a collection of essays and reminiscences. In it, Alvarez describes the effect of language and culture in defining the woman she would become.*

As you read this selection, remember to focus on the central theme Alvarez is trying to illustrate through the story of her life. You may notice that some words have a dotted underline. These are words found in many academic texts. We will work with them later. You may also notice less common (and some Spanish) words with footnoted definitions to help you. All reading selections in this textbook come from authentic sources and have not been modified or adapted. For your first reading of La Gringuita, focus on the global theme.

Reading Selection 1

LA GRINGUITA

By Julia Alvarez

1   The inevitable, of course, has happened. I now speak my native language "with an accent." What I mean by this is that I speak perfect childhood Spanish, but if I stray¹ into a heated discussion or complex explanation, I have to ask "Por favor. ¿Puedo decirlo en inglés?" Can I please say it in English?

2   How and why did this happen?

3   When we emigrated to the United States in the early sixties, the climate was not favorable for retaining our Spanish. I remember one scene in a grocery store soon after we arrived. An elderly shopper, overhearing my mother speaking Spanish to her daughters, muttered² that if we wanted to be in this country, we should learn the language. "I do know the language," my mother said in her boarding school English, putting the woman in her place. She knew the value of speaking perfect English. She had studied for several years at Abbot Academy, flying up from the Island to New York City, and then taking the train up to Boston. It was during the war, and the train would sometimes fill with servicemen, every seat taken.

4   One time, a young sailor asked my mother if he could sit in the empty seat beside her and chew on her ear. My mother gave him an indignant look, stood up, and went in search of the conductor to

---

1. **stray** (strā) *intr.v.* To wander about or roam, especially beyond established limits.
2. **mut·ter** (mŭt´ər) *intr.v.* To speak in low, unclear tones.

report this fresh man. Decades later, hearing the story, my father, ever vigilant and jealous of his wife and daughters, was convinced— no matter what my mother said about idiomatic[3] expressions— that the sailor had made an advance. He, himself, was never comfortable in English. In fact, if there were phone calls to be made to billing offices, medical supply stores, Workman's compensation, my father would put my mother on the phone. She would get better results than he would with his heavy, almost incomprehensible accent.

5   At school, there were several incidents of name-calling and stone-throwing, which our teachers claimed would stop if my sisters and I joined in with the other kids and quit congregating together at recess and jabbering away in Spanish. Those were the days before bilingual education or multicultural studies, when kids like us were thrown in the deep end of the public school pool and left to fend for ourselves. Not everyone came up for air.

6   Mami managed to get us scholarships to her old boarding school where Good Manners and Tolerance and English Skills were required. We were also all required to study a foreign language, but my teachers talked me into taking French. In fact, they felt my studying Spanish was equivalent to my taking a "gut course." Spanish was my native tongue, after all, a language I already had in the bag and would always be able to speak whenever I wanted. Meanwhile, with Saturday drills and daily writing assignments, our English skills soon met school requirements. By the time my sisters and I came home for vacations, we were rolling our eyes in exasperation at our old-world Mami and Papi, using expressions like *far out*, and *What a riot!* and *outta sight*, and *believe you me* as if we had been born to them.

3. i•di•om (ĭd´ē-əm) *n.* A phrase or expression with a special meaning that cannot be understood from the individual meanings of its words. To "chew on her ear" is an idiomatic expression that means to have a conversation.

7   As rebellious adolescents, we soon figured out that conducting
our filial[4] business in English gave us an edge over[5] our strict,
Spanish-speaking parents. We could spin circles around my mother's
absolutamante no by pointing out flaws in her arguments, in English.
My father was a pushover[6] for pithy[7] quotes from Shakespeare, and a
recitation of "The quality of mercy is not strained" could usually get
me what I wanted. Usually. There were areas we couldn't touch with a
Shakespearean ten-foot pole: the area of boys and permission to go
places where there might be boys, American boys, with their mouths
full of bubblegum and their minds full of the devil.

8   Our growing distance from Spanish was a way in which we were
setting ourselves free from that old world where, as girls, we didn't
have much say about what we could do with our lives. In English, we
didn't have to use the formal usted[8] that immediately put us in our
place with our elders. We were responsible for ourselves and that
made us feel grown-up. We couldn't just skirt culpability[9] by using
the reflexive;[10] the bag of cookies did not finish itself, nor did the
money disappear itself from Mami's purse. We had no one to bail us
out of American trouble once we went our own way in English. No
family connections, no tío[11] whose name might open doors for us. If
the world was suddenly less friendly, it was also more exciting. We
found out we could do things we had never done before. We could
go places in English we never could in Spanish, if we put our minds
to it. And we put our combined four minds to it, believe you me.

4. **fil•i•al** (fĭl´ē-əl) *adj.* Of or relating to a son or daughter.
5. **give an edge over** *idiom* Have an advantage over.
6. **push•o•ver** (po͝osh´ō´vər) *n.* A person or group that is easy to defeat or take
   advantage of.
7. **pith•y** (pĭth´ē) *adj.* Precisely meaningful; forceful and brief.
8. *usted* = You, formal. In Spanish, the speaker must decide whether to use formal
   or informal "you." When a child addresses a parent or adult, he or she uses the
   formal form. Parents would use the informal form in response.
9. **skirt culpability** *idiom* To avoid blame.
10. **re•flex•ive** (rĭ-flĕk´sĭv) *n.* In Spanish, sentences can be formed with reflexive
    verbs, so they are passively constructed. In these sentences, we do not know who
    ate the cookies or took the money.
11. *tío* = Spanish for uncle

9   My parents, anxious that we not lose our tie to our native land, and no doubt thinking of future husbands for their four daughters, began sending us "home" every summer to Mami's family in the capital. And just as we had once huddled in the school playground, speaking Spanish for the comfort of it. My sisters and I now hung out together in "the D.R.,"[12] as we referred to it, kibitzing[13] in English on the crazy world around us: the silly rules for girls, the obnoxious behavior of macho guys, and deplorable situation of the poor. My aunts and uncles tried unsuccessfully to stem this tide of our Americanization, whose main expression was, of course, our use of the English language. "Tienen que hablar in español,"[14] they commanded. "Ay, come on," we would say as if we had been asked to go back to baby talk as grown-ups.

10   By now, we couldn't go back as easily as that. Our Spanish was full of English. Countless times during conversation, we were corrected, until what we had to say was lost in our saying it wrong. More and more we chose to answer in English even when the question was posed in Spanish. It was a measure of the growing distance between ourselves and our native culture—a distance we all felt we could easily retrace with just a little practice. It wasn't until I failed at first love, in Spanish, that I realized how unbridgeable that gap had become.

11   That summer I went down to the Island by myself. My sisters had chosen to stay in the States at a summer camp where the oldest was a counselor. But I was talked into going "home" by my father, whose nephew—an older (by twenty years) cousin of mine had been elected the president of El Centro de Recreo, the social club of his native town of Santiago. Every year at El Centro, young girls of fifteen were "presented" in public, a little like a debutante ball.[15] I was two years past the deadline, but I had a baby face and could easily pass for five years younger than I was—something I did not like to hear. And my father very much wanted for one of his daughters to represent la familia among the crème de la crème[16] of his hometown society.

12. *D.R.* = Dominican Republic
13. **kib•itz** (kĭb´ĭts) *v.* Chatting.
14. "*Tienen que hablar en español.*" = "They have to speak Spanish."
15. **deb•u•tante ball** (dĕb´yo͞o-tänt´bôl) *n.* A party for the formal presentation of a young woman to society.
16. **crème de la crème** (krĕm´də lä krĕm´) *n.* Something superlative.

12   I arrived with my DO-YOUR-OWN-THING!!! T-shirt and
bell-bottom pants and several novels by Herman Hesse, ready to
spread the seed of the sixties revolution raging in the States.
Unlike other visits with my bilingual cousins in the capital, this
time I was staying in a sleepy, old-fashioned town in the interior
with Papi's side of the family, none of whom spoke English.

13   Actually I wasn't even staying in town. Cousin Utcho, whom I
called tío because he was so much older than I was, and his wife,
Betty—who, despite her name, didn't speak a word of English
either—lived far out in the countryside on a large chicken farm
where he was the foreman. They treated me like a ten-year-old, or
so I thought, monitoring phone calls, not allowing male visitors,
explaining their carefulness by reminding me that my parents had
entrusted them with my person and they wanted to return me in
the same condition in which I had arrived. Out there in the
boonies,[17] the old-world traditions had been preserved full strength.
But I can't help thinking that in part, Utcho and Betty treated me
like a ten-year-old because I talked like a ten-year-old in my halting,
childhood Spanish. I couldn't explain about women's liberation and
the quality of mercy not being strained, in Spanish. I grew bored
and lonely, and was ready to go back to New York and call it quits
on being "presented," when I met Dilita.

14   Like me, Dilita was a hybrid.[18] Her parents had moved to Puerto
Rico when she was three, and she had lived for some time with a
relative in New York. But her revolutionary zeal[19] had taken the turn
of glamour girl rather than my New England-hippy variety. In fact,
Dilita looked just like the other Dominican girls. She had a teased
hairdo;[20] I let my long hair hang loose in a style I can only describe
as "blowing in the wind." Dilita wore makeup; I did a little lipstick
and maybe eyeliner if she would put it on for me. She wore outfits;
I had peasant blouses, T-shirts, and blue jeans.

17. **the boo•nies** (boo′nēz) *pl.n. Slang* An unflattering name for an isolated place;
    the countryside. (Shortening and alteration of BOONDOCKS.)
18. **hy•brid** (hī′ brĭd) *n.* Something of mixed origin or composition.
19. **zeal** (zēl) *n.* Great interest in or dedication to a cause, ideal, or goal.
20. **teased hairdo** A hairstyle fashionable in the 1960s in which the ends of the hair
    are combed toward the head to make a high, airy effect.

15   But in one key way, Dilita was more of a rebel than I was; she did exactly what she wanted without guilt or apology. She was in charge of her own destino,[21] as she liked to say, and no one was going to talk her into giving that up. I was in awe of Dilita. She was the first "hyphenated" person[22] I had ever met whom I considered successful, not tortured as a hybrid the way my sisters and I were.

16   Dilita managed to talk Utcho into letting me move into town with her and her young, married aunt, Carmen. Mamacán, as we called her, was liberal and lighthearted and gave us free rein to do what we wanted. "Just as long as you girls don't get in trouble!" Trouble came in one denomination, we knew, and neither of us were fools. When the matron in town complained about our miniskirts or about our driving around with boys and no chaperons, Mamacán threw up her hands and said, "!Pero si son americanas!" They're American girls!

17   We hit it off with the boys. All the other girls came with their mamis or tías in tow; Dilita and I were free and clear. Inside of a week we both had boyfriends. Dilita, who was prettier than I, landed the handsome tipo,[23] tall Eladio with raven-black hair and arched eyebrows and the arrogant stance of a flamenco dancer, whereas I ended up with his chubby sidekick, a honey-skinned young man with wonderful dimples and a pot belly that made him look like a Dominican version of the Pillsbury doughboy. His name was Manuel Gustavo, but I affectionately named him Mangú, after a mashed plantain dish that is a staple of Dominican diet. A few days after meeting him, Mangú's mother sent over an elaborate dessert with lots of white frosting that looked suggestively like wedding cake. "Hint, hint," Dilita joked, an expression everyone was using at her school, too.

18   Every night the four of us went out together: Dilita sat up front with Eladio, who had his own car, and I in the backseat with Mangú—a very cozy boy-girl arrangement. But actually, if anyone had been listening in on these dates, they would have thought two American girlfriends were out for a whirl around the town. Dilita and I yakked, back and forth, starting first in Spanish out of

---

21. *destino* = destiny; fate
22. "**hy•phen•at•ed**" **person** = A person from the United States whose origin is shown in hyphenated words, as in German-American, Mexican-American.
23. *tipo* = guy

consideration for our boyfriends, but switching over into English as we got more involved in whatever we were talking about. Every once in a while, one of the guys would ask us, "¿Y qué lo que ustedes tanto hablan?" For some reason, this request to know what we were talking about would give us both an attack of giggles. Sometimes, Eladio, with Mangú joining in, sang the lyrics of a popular song to let us know we were obnoxious:

19   Las hijas de Juan Mejía
son bonitas y bailan bien
pero tienen un defecto
que se rien de tó el que ven.
(The daughters of Juan Mejia
dance well and are so pretty
but they've got one bad quality,
they make fun of everybody.)

20   Las gringuitas, they nicknamed us. Dilita didn't mind the teasing, but Mangú could always get a rise out of me when he called me a gringa.[24] Perhaps, just a few years away from the name-calling my sisters and I had experienced on the school playground, I felt instantly defensive whenever anyone tried to pin me down with a label.

21   But though he teased me with that nickname, Mangú made it clear that he would find a real gringa unappealing. "You're Dominican," he declared. The litmus test[25] was dancing merengue, our national, fast-moving, lots-of-hip-action dance. As we moved across the dance floor, Mangú would whisper the lyrics in my ear, complimenting my natural rhythm that showed, so he said, that my body knew where it came from. I was pleased with the praise. The truth is I wanted it both ways: I wanted to be good at the best things in each culture. Maybe I was picking up from Dilita how to be a successful hybrid.

22   Still, when I tried to talk to Mangú about something of substance, the conversation floundered. I couldn't carry on in Spanish about complicated subjects, and Mangú didn't know a word of English. Our silences troubled me. Maybe my tías were right. Too much education in English could spoil a girl's chances in Spanish.

24. *gringa* = a sometimes offensive name for a female person from the United States or Canada
25. **lit•mus test** (lĭt'məs) *n.* A figurative test for truth or sincerity.

23   But at least I had Dilita to talk to about how confusing it all was. "You and I," she often told me as we lay under the mosquito net in the big double bed Mamacán had fixed for us, "we have the best of both worlds. We can have a good time here, and have a good time there."

24   "Yeah," I'd say, not totally convinced.

25   Down on the street, every Saturday night, the little conjunto[26] that Eladio and Mangú had hired would serenade us with romantic canciones.[27] We were not supposed to show our faces, but Dilita and I always snuck out on the balcony in our baby dolls[28] to talk to the guys. Looking down at Mangú from above, I could see the stiffness of the white dress shirt his mother had starched and ironed for him. I felt a pang of tenderness and regret. What was wrong with me, I wondered, that I wasn't falling in love with him?

26   After the presentation ball, Dilita left for Puerto Rico to attend a cousin's wedding. It was then, when I was left alone with Manuel Gustavo, that I realized that the problem was not me, but me and Manuel Gustavo.

27   Rather than move back to the lonely boonies, I stayed on in town with Dilita's aunt for the two weeks remaining of my visit. But without Dilita, town life was as lonely as life on a chicken farm. Evenings, Mangú would come over, and we'd sit on the patio and try to make conversation or drive out to the country club in a borrowed car to dance merengue and see what everyone else was doing. What we were doing was looking for people to fill up our silence with their talk.

28   One night, Mangú drove out towards Utcho's chicken farm and pulled over at a spot where often the four of us had stopped to look at the stars. We got out of the car and leaned against the side, enjoying the breeze. In the dark, periodically broken by the lights of passing cars, Mangú began to talk about our future.

26. *conjunto* = musical group
27. *canciones* = songs
28. **baby dolls** *n.* A type of pajamas, popular in the 1960s, characterized by short pants and lots of lace.

29   I didn't know what to say to him. Or actually, in English, I could have said half a dozen ambivalent[29] soothing things. But not having a <u>complicated</u> vocabulary in Spanish, I didn't know the fancy, smooth-talking ways of delaying and deterring. Like a child, I could just blurt out what I was thinking.

30   "Somos diferente, Mangú." We are so different. The <u>comment</u> came out sounding inane.[30]

31   "No, we're not," he argued back. "We're both Dominicans. Our families come from the same hometown."

32   "But we left," I said, looking up at the stars. From this <u>tropical perspective</u>, the stars seemed to form different constellations in the night sky. Even the Big Dipper, which was so easy to spot in New England, seemed to be misplaced here. Tonight, it lay on its side, right above us. I was going to point it out to Mangú—in part to distract him, but I could not remember the word for dipper—la cuchara grande, the big spoon?

33   But Mangú would not have been interested in the stars anyway. Once it was clear that we did not share the same feelings, there was nothing much left to say. We drove back to Mamacán's house in silence.

34   I don't know if that experience made Mangú forever wary with half-breed Dominican-York girls; gringuitas, who seem to be talking out of both sides of their mouth, and in two different languages, to boot. I myself never had a Spanish-only boyfriend again. Maybe the opportunity never presented itself, or maybe it was that as English became my <u>dominant</u> tongue, too many parts of me were left out in Spanish for me to be able to be intimate with a <u>potential</u> life partner in only that language.

35   Still, the yearning remained. How wonderful to love someone whose skin was the same honey-dipped, sallow-base color; who said concho[31] when he was mad and cielito lindo[32] when he wanted to butter you up! "!Ay! to make love in Spanis . . . ," the Latina narrator of Sandra Cisneros's story, "Bien Pretty," exclaims. "To have a lover

29. **am•biv•a•lent** (ăm-bĭv' ə-lənt) *adj.* Showing or having conflicting feelings about somebody or something.
30. **in•ane** (ĭn-ān') *adj.* Lacking sense or meaning.
31. *concho* = an unflattering term
32. *cielito lindo* = my pretty, heavenly, or angelic one

whisper things in that language crooned to babies, that language murmured by grandmothers, those words that smelled like your house . . ." But I wonder if after the Latina protagonist[33] makes love with her novio, she doesn't sit up in bed and tell him the story of her life in English with a few palabritas[34] thrown in to capture the rhythm of her Latin heartbeat?

36   As for Manuel Gustavo, I met up with him a few years ago on a visit to the Island. My husband, a gringo from Nebraska, and I were driving down the two-lane autopista[35] on our way up to the mountains on a land search. A pickup roared past us. Suddenly, it slowed and pulled onto the shoulder. As we drove by, the driver started honking. "What does he want me to do?" my husband shouted at me. I looked over and saw that the driver was still on the shoulder, trying to catch up with us. I gestured, what do you want?

37   "Soy yo,"[36] the man called out, "Manuel Gustavo."

38   Almost thirty years had passed. He had gotten heavier; his hairline had receded; there was gray in his hair. But the dimples were still there. Beside him sat a boy about seven or eight, a young duplicate of the boy I had known. "Mangú!" I called out. "Is that really you?"

39   By this time my husband was angry at the insanity of this pickup trying to keep up with us on the narrow shoulder while Mack trucks roared by on the other lane. "Tell him we'll stop ahead, and you guys can talk!"

40   But the truth was that I didn't want to stop and talk to Manuel Gustavo. What would I have to say to him now, when I hadn't been able to talk to him thirty years ago? "It's good to see you again, Mangú," I shouted. I waved good-bye as my husband pulled ahead. In my side mirror, I watched as he signaled, then disappeared into the long line of traffic behind us.

41   "Who was that?" my husband wanted to know.

---

33. **pro•tag•o•nist** (prō-tăg′ə-nĭst) *n.* The main character in a drama or other literary work.
34. *palabritas* = little Spanish words
35. *autopista* = freeway
36. *"Soy yo"* = "It's me."

42   I went on to tell my husband the story of that summer; the presentation; Utcho and Betty; my worldly-wise friend Dilita; Eladio, who looked like a flamenco dancer; the serenades; the big double bed Dilita and I slept in with a mosquito net tied to the four posts. And of course, I told him the story of my romance with Manuel Gustavo.

43   And, as I spoke, that old yearning came back. What would my life have been like if I had stayed in my native country? The truth was I couldn't even imagine myself as someone other than the person I had become in English, a woman who writes books in the language of Emily Dickinson and Walt Whitman, and also of the rude shopper in the grocery store and of the boys throwing stones in the schoolyard, their language, which is now my language. A woman who has joined her life with the life of a man who grew up on a farm in Nebraska, whose great-grandparents came over from Germany and discouraged their own children from speaking German because of the antipathy[37] that erupted in their new country towards anything German with the outbreak of World War I. A woman who is now looking for land in the Dominican Republic with her husband, so that they can begin to spend some time in the land she came from.

44   When we took the turnoff into the mountains, we rolled up our windows so we could easily hear the cassette player. My husband had ordered Spanish-language tapes a while back from the Foreign Service Institute so that he could keep up with my family in the capital. Recently, he had dusted them off and started listening to them to prepare himself for our land hunt. I had decided to join him in these lessons, in part to encourage him, but also because I wanted to regain the language that would allow me to feel at home again in my native country.

37. **an • tip • a • thy** (ăn-tĭp´ə-thē) *n.* A strong feeling of aversion or repugnance.

☐ Assessing Your Learning

Demonstrating Comprehension

EXERCISE **4** **Checking comprehension**

Check your understanding of the memoir by choosing the correct answer. When you finish, compare your answers with a partner's.

1. The elderly woman in the store
   a. was polite.
   b. wanted to teach Julia and her sisters English.
   c. didn't know that Julia's mother could speak English.
   d. owned the store.

2. Mami thought the sailor
   a. was prejudiced against Dominicans.
   b. was trying to start a relationship with her.
   c. was trying to embarrass her.
   d. wanted to see the conductor.

3. Julia was persuaded to take French classes by her
   a. mother.
   b. sisters.
   c. teachers.
   d. father.

4. Julia and her sisters
   a. usually won arguments with their parents in English.
   b. usually tried to argue with their parents in Spanish.
   c. could convince their father, but not their mother.
   d. could convince their mother, but not their father.

5. Julia went to the Dominican Republic that summer because
   a. she did not want to go to summer camp.
   b. her father wanted her to go.
   c. her mother wanted her to go.
   d. she wanted to get away from the United States.

6. Julia was
   a. satisfied staying with Utcho and Betty.
   b. able to spread the seed of the sixties.
   c. lonely with Utcho and Betty.
   d. tired of working on the chicken farm.

7. Dilita and Julia were similar because they
   a. wore the same kinds of clothes.
   b. had the same kind of hairdo.
   c. both spoke English better than Spanish.
   d. both liked being called *gringuitas.*

8. Dilita and Julia were popular with the boys because they
   a. could speak English.
   b. were both the same age.
   c. were both going to be presented at the social club.
   d. didn't have chaperones like the other girls.

9. The boys sang the song about the daughters of Juan Mejia because
   a. they wanted to impress the girls with their singing voices.
   b. they wanted to teach the girls Spanish.
   c. they wanted the girls to stop speaking English.
   d. it was the most popular song at that time.

10. Dilita felt that being a hybrid was
    a. an advantage.
    b. unfortunate.
    c. her destiny.
    d. confusing.

11. Mangú
    a. liked Julia more than she liked him.
    b. wanted to move to the United States.
    c. didn't like to look at the stars.
    d. thought Julia was rude.

12. Julia's husband
    a. is from New York.
    b. is Dominican.
    c. was jealous of Mangú.
    d. was worried about a car accident.

EXERCISE 5   Recognizing inferences

Sometimes we can make a logical conclusion based on information in a reading selection. This is called making an inference. Read each statement below. Select (a) for statements that can be inferred as probably true. Select (b) for statements that can be inferred as probably false. Select (c) for statements that cannot be inferred because you do not have enough information from the reading to know. Note the facts in the text that support the inferences. (See paragraph number indicated at the end of each statement.) Number 1 has been done for you as an example.

1. Papi was a protective husband and father. (¶ 4)
   a. probably true   **b.** probably false   **c.** cannot be inferred

   We can infer this because paragraph 4 says: "my father, ever vigilant and jealous of his wife and daughters."

2. Many of the students at the school could not swim. (¶ 5)
   a. probably true   **b.** probably false   **c.** cannot be inferred

3. Family connections are important in the Dominican Republic. (¶ 8)
   a. probably true   **b.** probably false   **c.** cannot be inferred

4. The sisters liked the responsibility and independence that speaking in English gave them. (¶ 8)
   a. probably true   **b.** probably false   **c.** cannot be inferred

5. Chaperons were a part of dating customs in the Dominican Republic. (¶ 16)
   a. probably true   **b.** probably false   **c.** cannot be inferred

6. Manuel Gustavo disliked the nickname Mangú. (¶ 17)
   a. probably true   **b.** probably false   **c.** cannot be inferred

7. Julia was a good dancer. (¶ 21)
   a. probably true   **b.** probably false   **c.** cannot be inferred

8. Mangú had more English-speaking girlfriends after Julia. (¶ 34)
   a. probably true   **b.** probably false   **c.** cannot be inferred

9. Julia likes the writing of Sandra Cisneros. (¶ 35)
   a. probably true   **b.** probably false   **c.** cannot be inferred

10. Julia was surprised to see Mangú after 30 years. (¶ 37)
    a. probably true   **b.** probably false   **c.** cannot be inferred

11. Julia's husband thought that driving beside the pickup truck was dangerous. (¶ 39)
    a. probably true   **b.** probably false   **c.** cannot be inferred

12. Julia feels that she is more American than Dominican. (¶ 43)
    a. probably true   **b.** probably false   **c.** cannot be inferred

13. Julia's husband speaks Spanish better than she does. (¶ 44)
    a. probably true   **b.** probably false   **c.** cannot be inferred

☐ Focusing on Literature

The study of literature is more than just reading for pleasure. It is a disciplined reading of prose, poetry, or drama with attention to form, language, and ideas. The essay *La Gringuita* is an example of prose in narrative form. A literary narrative includes a plot, a conflict, and a theme that is developed through the characters, events, and dialogue. Reading literature helps us grow and develop compassion as we identify with human struggles and dreams. It helps us shape personal goals and values and clarify identity and understanding of cultural context.

EXERCISE 6 **Exploring a theme**

In La Gringuita, *the theme the author wants to express to the reader is supported by details or examples.* ***A main theme of this reading selection is that Alvarez regrets she does not speak Spanish as well as she speaks English.***

Find ideas in Selection 1 that support the theme of yearning and regret. Reread the selection quickly, and note "M.I." for main idea in the margins next to evidence of the theme. Then, list some details or examples from the selection that support the main idea.

1. Julia wishes she had had another Spanish-speaking boyfriend after Mangú.

2. _____

3. _____

4. _____

Master Student Tip

Develop a personal "word bank" system to store information on new words you want to learn. You could carry a small vocabulary notebook, prepare word cards, or store them in a word file on your computer.

☐ Learning Vocabulary

STRATEGY

Many strategies exist for learning the meanings of new words. Throughout this book, you are encouraged to work with words in various ways to help you learn. Common strategies for learning meaning include the following:

- Look for information in the context surrounding a word that could help you understand it.
- Look for repeated occurrences of the word.
- Think about the meaning of word parts (root, prefix, suffix).
- Think about the meaning of different forms of the word you might already know.
- Look up the word in a dictionary—this could be a bilingual, monolingual, electronic, or special dictionary for language learners.
- Look up the word in the book's index or appendix if available.
- Ask someone else about the meaning of the word.

Academic Vocabulary

Researchers have found that certain words appear over and over again in academic readings. These same words appear across academic disciplines, from textbooks in sociology and world history to articles on business and computer science, so they are important words to learn and remember. As mentioned earlier, common academic words are marked in the reading selections in this textbook with dotted underlines. You may already know some of these words, but others may be new. Develop a system for recording new words and definitions so that you can study and remember them. Make learning unfamiliar academic vocabulary words a priority, and you will not only expand your vocabulary *but also* perform better in academic courses. The identified words are found on the Academic Word List (AWL). To view the complete AWL, visit our website at http://esl.college.hmco.com/students.

EXERCISE **7** Understanding academic vocabulary

Listed in the following chart are some AWL words found in La Gringuita.
*Complete the chart by checking one box for each word. Then, discuss your
results with a classmate. Do you know the same words? Can you explain
the words you know that your classmate doesn't know?*

	Don't know at all	Recognize but don't know well	Know well	Use in my own writing
inevitable (¶ 1)				
complex (¶ 1)				
retaining (¶ 3)				
decade (¶ 4)				
convince (¶ 4)				
compensation (¶ 4)				
incident (¶ 5)				
required (¶ 6)				
equivalent (¶ 6)				
quote (¶ 7)				
pose (¶ 10)				
revolution (¶ 12)				
despite (¶ 13)				
liberation (¶ 13)				
version (¶ 17)				

	Don't know at all	Recognize but don't know well	Know well	Use in my own writing
periodically (¶ 28)				
complicated (¶ 29)				
perspective (¶ 31)				
dominant (¶ 34)				
potential (¶ 34)				
Similar tables for learning AWL words are available at our website, http://esl.college.hmco.com/students.				

EXERCISE **8** **Working with academic vocabulary**

Learn the meaning of the words from the chart in Exercise 7. Then, test your knowledge of the words by completing this crossword puzzle with words from the list.

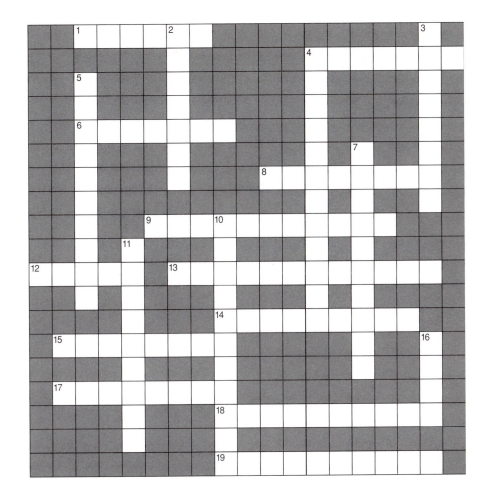

Crossword Puzzle Clues

Across

1. 10 years
4. not simple
6. description from one side
8. persuade
9. like 4 across
12. to repeat the words of someone else
13. once in a while
14. having possibility
15. having the most influence
17. event
18. impossible to avoid
19. the same as

Down

2. in spite of
3. absolutely necessary
4. something like money given as payment
5. a sudden change; overthrow a government
7. freedom
10. point of view
11. keeping
16. ask; as in _____ a question

EXERCISE 9   **Recognizing less common word meanings**

Often, words in English can have more than one meaning. We can tell which definition of a word an author means only by the context of the word. Look at these sentences from the story. Write a definition or synonym for the word in this context.

1. When we emigrated to the United States in the early sixties, the **climate** was not favorable for retaining our Spanish. (¶ 3)

   In this sentence, **climate** means _____.

2. My mother gave him an indignant look, stood up, and went in search of the conductor to report this **fresh** man. (¶ 4)

   In this sentence, **fresh** means _____.

3. Decades later, hearing the story, my father, ever vigilant and jealous of his wife and daughters, was convinced—no matter what my mother said about idiomatic expressions—that the sailor had made an **advance**. (¶ 4)

   In this sentence, **advance** means _____.

4. We couldn't just **skirt** culpability by using the reflexive: the bag of cookies did not finish itself, nor did the money disappear itself from Mami's purse. (¶ 8)

   In this sentence, **skirt** means: _____.

☐ Focusing on Literature

EXERCISE 10 **Identifying tone**

Tone is the way an author or a character in a literary work feels toward something. Tone conveys an attitude and creates feelings within a reader. Tone may be formal or informal, serious or humorous, optimistic or pessimistic, objective or subjective. In several places, Alvarez uses an informal tone in her memoir. Such as in the beginning when she writes:

> The inevitable, of course, has happened. I now speak my native language "with an accent." What I mean by this is that I speak perfect childhood Spanish.

This sentence is written with the same language the author might use if she were sitting in her kitchen with a cup of coffee while she told you the story of her first love. Phrases like "of course" and "what I mean" make the writing seem more like a conversation than a strictly academic text. Writing in this informal way gives the feeling of a more personal relationship between the reader and the writer. How do you feel when you read a passage with a tone like this?

_____

_____

Write three additional sentences or phrases from Selection 1 that convey an informal tone.

1. _____

2. _____

3. _____

Why do you think Alvarez uses an informal tone for this memoir?

_____

_____

More about Tone

Here are some other tones that authors may use. Read through this list of words and their explanations. Discuss with your classmates the meanings of words that are unclear to you. Your instructor can help you clarify words you do not understand. (Visit our website at http://esl.college.hmco.com for additional adjectives that express tones.)

Adjectives expressing tone	
objective, factual, straightforward	using facts without emotion
subjective, opinionated, emotional	expressing opinions and feelings; opposite of objective
formal	having a conventional, structured style
informal	having a style that reflects everyday verbal interactions
cheerful, joyous, happy	feeling good about the topic
optimistic, positive, hopeful, encouraging, lighthearted	focusing on the positive, good side
angry, bitter, hateful	feeling bad or upset about the topic
pessimistic, negative, discouraging	focusing on the negative, bad side; opposite of optimistic
sad, depressing	feeling unhappy
annoyed, irritated, disturbed	feeling bothered or troubled
teasing, mocking, belittling, scornful, ridiculing, sarcastic, caustic	making fun of someone or something; treating with contempt
ironic	contrary to what was expected; surprising in a complex way
nostalgic, sentimental	remembering the past; hoping to return to a time in the past
sympathetic, empathic, compassionate	feeling affinity; identifying with another's feelings

EXERCISE 11 **Practicing with tone**

Reread these sentences from La Gringuita. *Choose the word that best reflects the tone of the sentence or phrase.*

1. An elderly shopper, overhearing my mother speaking Spanish to her daughters, muttered that if we wanted to be in this country, we should learn the language.
   a. encouraging   **b.** ridiculing   **c.** ironic   **d.** sympathetic

2. They treated me like a ten-year-old, or so I thought, monitoring phone calls, not allowing male visitors …
   a. joyous   **b.** annoyed   **c.** sentimental   **d.** sad

3. I grew bored and lonely, and was ready to go back to New York and call it quits on being "presented."
   a. sentimental   **b.** lighthearted   **c.** pessimistic   **d.** objective

4. A few days after meeting him, Mangú's mother sent over an elaborate dessert with lots of white frosting that looked suggestively like wedding cake. "Hint, hint," Dilita joked …
   a. mocking   **b.** optimistic   **c.** cheerful   **d.** discouraging

5. As we moved across the dance floor, Mangú would whisper the lyrics in my ear, complimenting my natural rhythm that showed, so he said, that my body knew where it came from. I was pleased with the praise.
   a. irritated   **b.** straightforward   **c.** happy   **d.** teasing

6. I felt a pang of tenderness and regret. What was wrong with me, I wondered, that I wasn't falling in love with him?
   a. sarcastic   **b.** sad   **c.** angry   **d.** hopeful

7. "No, we're not," he argued back. "We're both Dominicans. Our families come from the same hometown."
   a. bitter   **b.** optimistic   **c.** nostalgic   **d.** mocking

8. I don't know if that experience made Mangú forever wary with half-breed Dominican-York girls; gringuitas, who seem to be talking out of both sides of their mouth, and in two different languages, to boot.
   a. mocking   **b.** pessimistic   **c.** sentimental   **d.** formal

9. Still, the yearning remained. How wonderful to love someone whose skin was the same honey-dipped, sallow-base color; who said concho when he was mad and cielito lindo when he wanted to butter you up! "!Ay! to make love in Spanish …," the Latina narrator of Sandra Cisneros's story, "Bien Pretty," exclaims. "To have a lover whisper things in that language crooned to babies, that language murmured by grandmothers, those words that smelled like your house …"
   a. formal   **b.** joyous   **c.** nostalgic   **d.** scornful

10. By this time my husband was angry at the insanity of this pickup trying to keep up with us on the narrow shoulder while Mack trucks roared by on the other lane. "Tell him we'll stop ahead, and you guys can talk!"
    a. pessimistic   **b.** caustic   **c.** sad   **d.** disturbed

11. I went on to tell my husband the story of that summer; the presentation; Utcho and Betty; my worldly-wise friend Dilita; Eladio, who looked like a flamenco dancer; the serenades; the big double bed Dilita and I slept in with a mosquito net tied to the four posts. And of course, I told him the story of my romance with Manuel Gustavo.
    a. empathic   **b.** sad   **c.** sentimental   **d.** angry

EXERCISE 12   **Studying language choices**

Alvarez uses some Spanish words in Selection 1. Review the selection, and notice when she uses Spanish words. Does there seem to be a reason why she sometimes uses Spanish words? List three possible reasons why she sometimes uses Spanish words in particular places.

1. _____

   _____

2. _____

   _____

3. _____

   _____

Compare answers and discuss your reasons with your classmates.

EXERCISE 13 **Studying description**

Alvarez writes rich descriptions of the characters in her memoir. Find the descriptions of each of the following characters. List words and phrases that Alvarez uses to describe each person.

Dilita (¶ 14 & 15)	Eladio (¶ 17)	Mangú (¶ 17)
hybrid		

Figurative Language

Writers sometimes use figurative language to make descriptions more lively and vivid. They represent ideas in an artistic and creative manner. For example, in paragraph 12 Alvarez describes the town where her family came from as "sleepy and old-fashioned." We all know that *people* sleep, not towns. We can also understand, however, that Alvarez is trying to tell us that this is a quiet town without much excitement.

EXERCISE 14   Interpreting figurative language

The following chart presents other examples of figurative language from Selection 1. For each example, guess what Alvarez is trying to say. Refer to the paragraphs indicated if you need more context.

Figurative language	Your guess—a more common way of expressing the idea
sleepy, old-fashioned town (¶ 12)	*a quiet town without much excitement*
arrogant stance of a flamenco dancer (¶ 17)	
Dominican version of the Pillsbury doughboy (¶ 18)	
attack of giggles (¶ 18)	
as lonely as life on a chicken farm (¶ 27)	
to fill up our silence (¶ 27)	
talking out of both sides of their mouths (¶ 34)	
those words that smelled like your house (¶ 35)	
antipathy that erupted (¶ 43)	

EXERCISE 15   Reviewing categories of figurative language

As mentioned above, when using figurative language an author represents ideas in an artistic and creative manner. Examples of figurative speech are often classified in different categories. Three common categories are metaphor, simile, and personification. *Personification* means thinking of or representing ideas or objects as having human qualities or human form. An example of a personification is It is a <u>happy</u> little <u>valley</u>. Valleys cannot have emotions like being happy, but "happy" in this case has the meaning "sunny and pleasant."

Review the examples of figurative language in the chart above. Which one is an example of personification?

1. _____

Another special class of figurative language is simile. A *simile* is a comparison of unlike things, often in a phrase introduced by the word *like* or *as*. An example of a simile is I felt <u>as if I had just won the lottery</u>. This example is figurative language because the writer did not really just win the lottery but did want you to know that he or she felt very lucky about some good fortune. Another example of a simile is <u>Like diamonds</u>, the sunlight sparkled on the gently moving water. Sunlight and diamonds are two unlike things, but the reflection of the sunlight on the water reminded the writer of diamonds. *Metaphors* are similar to similes, but a direct comparison is made without the words *like* or *as*—for example, <u>That boy is an early bird</u>.

Review the examples of figurative language from the previous chart. Which two are examples of similes?

1. —————————————————————————————————————

2. —————————————————————————————————————

Work with a partner. Write two examples of personification and two examples of similes. For each personification, give an element of nature human qualities or feelings and actions associated with feelings. For each simile, compare a thing or person to something you are reminded of. When finished, share your examples with your classmates.

Personification

1. —————————————————————————————————————

2. —————————————————————————————————————

Similes

1. —————————————————————————————————————

2. —————————————————————————————————————

EXERCISE 16 **Studying idiomatic expressions**

Alvarez describes a misunderstanding her mother had because she did not understand the idiomatic expression "chew on one's ear." The chart presents other idiomatic expressions from La Gringuita. *Work with a partner to complete the chart. Guess the meaning of each expression. Refer to the paragraphs indicated if you need more context. When you finish, check your answers with your instructor.*

Idiomatic expression	What feeling or idea is Alvarez trying to convey? Explain it in a more common way.
1. One time, a young sailor asked my mother if he could sit in the empty seat beside her and **chew on her ear**. (¶ 4)	*He wanted to talk with her.*
2. Those were the days before bilingual education or multicultural studies, when kids like us were **thrown in the deep end** of the public school pool and left to fend for ourselves. (¶ 5)	
3. Not everyone **came up for air**. (¶ 5)	
4. Spanish was my native tongue, after all, a language I already **had in the bag** and would always be able to speak whenever I wanted. (¶ 6)	
5. By the time my sisters and I came home for vacations, we **were rolling our eyes** in exasperation at our old-world Mami and Papi. (¶ 6)	
6. There were areas we couldn't **touch with** a Shakespearean **ten-foot pole**: the area of boys … (¶ 7)	
7. We had no one **to bail us out of** American trouble once we went our own way in English. (¶ 8)	
8. It wasn't until I failed at first love, in Spanish, that I realized how **unbridgeable** that **gap** had become. (¶ 10)	
9. I felt instantly defensive whenever anyone tried to **pin me down with a label**. (¶ 20)	
10. My husband had ordered Spanish-language tapes a while back from the Foreign Service Institute so that he could keep up with my family in the capital. Recently, he had **dusted them off**. (¶ 44)	

☐ For Review and Discussion

EXERCISE 17 Participating in a small-group brainstorm

Julia Alvarez explains that, in the Dominican Republic, "young girls of fifteen were 'presented' in public, a little like a debutante ball." This presentation is a way to show that a girl is moving from childhood to adulthood.

Work with two or three other students. Brainstorm a list of several examples of events that mark the passage from childhood to adulthood in different cultures. For example, in the United States, 16-year-olds are allowed to get a driver's license. Getting a driver's license is an event that marks the passage from childhood to adulthood. Share your group's list with the whole class to compare findings.

Rites of Passage		
Event	**Age**	**Country or Culture**
Getting driver's license	16	U.S.

EXERCISE 18 Participating in class discussion

Discuss the following questions with your classmates:

1. In paragraph 8, Alvarez describes how she feels different when speaking Spanish than when speaking English. Do you "feel" different in different languages or cultures? Explain the differences.
2. Describe possible challenges of being a "hyphenated" person.
3. Dilita is an example of a person who took the challenge of being a "hybrid" and turned it into something positive. Write additional examples (from either your own experience or the experiences of others) of someone taking a challenge and turning it into something positive.

☐ Linking Concepts

STRATEGY

Keeping a Reading Journal

A *reading journal* is a notebook in which you write about ideas in your reading. With this textbook, you will use a reading journal to express your thoughts about what you have read. Putting these thoughts into writing can help you clarify and remember ideas from your reading. Purchase a thin notebook or a "blue book" from your college bookstore to use for your reading journal.

EXERCISE 19   Writing in your reading journal

Choose one of the following topics, and write about it in your journal.

1. Write about one of the topics from the group discussion above.

2. In paragraph 33, Alvarez expresses a feeling of regret about not being able to be intimate in Spanish with a potential life partner. Do you regret something about your life up to now? Do you, like Alvarez, yearn for something to be different?

3. *La Gringuita* is Alvarez's memory of her "first love." What do you remember about your first love?

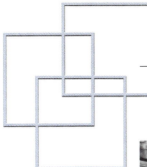

Reading Assignment 2

☐ Getting Ready to Read

EXERCISE 20 **Participating in class discussion**

Before you read Selection 2, discuss the following questions with a partner and then with the rest of your classmates.

1. Reading Selection 2 is a poem. Can you remember a poem you have read in your first language? Have you ever read a poem in English? What are some characteristics of poetry?

2. Selection 2 is titled "My Mother Juggling Bean Bags." What does *juggling* mean? Do you know anyone who can juggle?

3. This poem begins with an epigraph by Victor Borge. An *epigraph* is a short quote from a famous person that sets the theme for a piece of literature. The epigraph of this poem is "Laughter is the shortest distance between two people." What does this epigraph mean?

4. Read the following introductory paragraph for this selection that tells about James Mitsui.

My Mother Juggling Bean Bags

By James Masao Mitsui

James Masao Mitsui (1940–) grew up in Odessa, a small wheat-farming community in eastern Washington State. His parents were from Japan. He and his sister were the only minority students in the school system. A teacher in the Renton, Washington, public schools for thirty-four years, Mitsui published his first volume of poetry, *Journal of the Sun*, in 1974. His most recent book, *From a Three-Cornered World*, was published in 1997 and includes this poem.

5. From the introduction, we learn that James and his sister were in the only Japanese family in a small town. How do you think that circumstance affected his life as he was growing up?

EXERCISE 21 **Previewing vocabulary: cultural references**

One characteristic of poetry is that it usually uses few words to express an idea. One way the poet James Mitsui does this in Selection 2 is by using words that most Americans have experienced. This way, he can use a few words to express a feeling or idea that is common to many Americans. Words or concepts that have special meaning to a particular culture are called **cultural references**. *Below are some cultural references that Mitsui uses. First look at just the words or phrases. How many do you know already? Which ones are new to you?*

bean bag	a small cloth bag filled with pellets or dried beans and used for throwing in games.
low-income apartment	an apartment reserved for people who are retired, on government assistance, or don't have enough money to afford to live somewhere else.
7-Up	a well-known brand name for a sweet, clear, carbonated soft drink.
British jelly cookies	cookies with jelly made in a British style.
Montgomery Ward	a discount retail store that used to sell inexpensive goods through a mail-order catalog.
first-base glove	a special baseball glove used by the player who plays the position of first base.

class of '59	Many times teenagers identify themselves by the year they graduate from high school. Class of '59 means someone who graduated from high school in 1959.
short-sheet *v.*	to fold a bed sheet on a bed in such a way that the bed looks made properly, but when a person gets into the bed, he or she cannot extend his or her legs; used as a kind of practical joke or trick played to make a person feel embarrassed or uncomfortable.
trash burner	a kind of wood-burning stove that poor people used to use to burn their garbage and thus heat their homes.
parlor	an old-fashioned word for the main living room of a house.
swear words	taboo or obscene words.

Definitions adapted from *The American Heritage English as a Second Language Dictionary*. (1998). Boston: Houghton Mifflin Company.

STRATEGY

Reading Poetry

Reading poetry is different from reading other kinds of text. The poet chooses each word carefully. The sound of the words is as important as their meaning. Poetry is meant to be read aloud. First read the poem to yourself two or three times, and then practice reading the poem aloud.

☐ Reading the Selection

James Masao Mitsui (1940–) grew up in Odessa, a small wheat-farming community in eastern Washington State. His parents were from Japan. He and his sister were the only minority students in the school system. A teacher in the Renton, Washington, public schools for thirty-four years, Mitsui published his first volume of poetry, Journal of the Sun, *in 1974. His most recent book,* From a Three-Cornered World, *was published in 1997 and includes this poem.*

James Masao Mitusui

Reading Selection 2

MY MOTHER JUGGLING BEAN BAGS

By James Masao Mitsui

Laughter is the shortest distance between two people.
Victor Borge

At 71, my mother juggled three,
even four bean bags
while shouting "yeeaaat"[1] and "yoi-cho"[2] between her gold
front teeth. My children
stooped to pick up

---

1. *yeeaaat* = an excited expression in Japanese that is like saying "Y-y-yes!" when we do something well.
2. *yoi-cho* = a Japanese expression associated with exerting an effort, especially as part of a group. It is similar to saying "one, two, three!" in English.

her mistakes. They watched,
mouths shaped like little o's,
as "Little Grandma"

laughed in a language
anyone could understand.
On visitation weekends

we visited her low-income apartment
and shared 7-Up, too many
British jelly cookies

and potato chips.
Now, over twenty years later,
I value my mother's humor.

As a child I had one-present
Christmases, but there was always
roast turkey on holidays,

jeans with no holes, and a first-base
glove from Montgomery Ward
that they really couldn't afford.

I remember the night when two girls
from the Class of '59
had driven ten miles from Odessa

just to show my mother how to
short-sheet my bed. I can still hear
her laughter in the dark.

I can also remember my mother
chasing me with a stick of firewood
around the trash burner in the parlor,

using my father's railroad swear words.
She always managed not
to catch me. Now I warn my children—

when I turn 71, I may turn from poetry
to juggling oranges. I owe it to my mother;
I owe it to my six grandchildren.

☐ Assessing Your Learning

Demonstrating Comprehension

EXERCISE 22 **Recognizing inferences**

As before, sometimes we can make a logical conclusion or inference based on information in a reading selection. Read each statement below. Select (a) for statements that can be inferred as probably true. Select (b) for statements that can be inferred as probably false. Select (c) for statements that cannot be inferred because you do not have enough information from the reading. Note the facts in the text that support the inferences.

1. James' mother could not speak English very well.
   a. probably true   **b.** probably false   **c.** cannot be inferred

2. The "mistakes" in line 7 of the poem are dropped bean bags.
   a. probably true   **b.** probably false   **c.** cannot be inferred

3. James' mother was a small woman.
   a. probably true   **b.** probably false   **c.** cannot be inferred

4. James' children thought their grandmother was strange.
   a. probably true   **b.** probably false   **c.** cannot be inferred

5. Grandma lived with James and his children.
   a. probably true   **b.** probably false   **c.** cannot be inferred

6. James' family was poor when he was growing up.
   a. probably true   **b.** probably false   **c.** cannot be inferred

7. James' mother was strict.
   a. probably true   **b.** probably false   **c.** cannot be inferred

8. James' mother enjoyed practical jokes.
   a. probably true   **b.** probably false   **c.** cannot be inferred

9. James admires his mother for her ability to laugh.
   a. probably true   **b.** probably false   **c.** cannot be inferred

10. James' father probably worked for the railroad.
    a. probably true   **b.** probably false   **c.** cannot be inferred

11. James is 71 years old.
   a. probably true   **b.** probably false   **c.** cannot be inferred

12. James wants to embarrass his children by juggling oranges.
   a. probably true   **b.** probably false   **c.** cannot be inferred

13. James wants to make his grandchildren laugh the same way his mother made her children laugh.
   a. probably true   **b.** probably false   **c.** cannot be inferred

☐ Learning Vocabulary

EXERCISE 23   **Matching**

Match the words from the poem with their meanings.

1. stooped   _____ wood from a cut tree used to burn

2. visitation   _____ to have enough money

3. value   _____ bent over

4. afford   _____ believe something is important

5. firewood   _____ the act of spending time with someone

☐ Focusing on Literature

EXERCISE 24   **Identifying tone**

Review the section on tone from earlier in this chapter. What do you think

is the main tone of this poem? _____

Compare your answer with your classmates'.

Poetry

Many times, we think of poetry as rhyming verses. *My Mother Juggling Bean Bags* is not a rhyming poem. It is called free verse. One reason many poems in English are free verse is that English doesn't have as many rhyming words as some other languages do. It is a popular style. Even without rhyming, *My Mother Juggling Bean Bags* does have a form. Each stanza (group of words divided by a double space) has three lines. James Mitsui breaks the lines in the middle of some sentences. Read the poem again, noticing on which words each line ends. How do these breaks affect your reading of the poem?

EXERCISE 25   **Working with language**

Rewrite the poem in a sentence-by-sentence format on separate paper. Then, read it aloud. How do the new breaks affect your reading of the poem?

1. At 71, my mother juggled three, even four bean bags while shouting "yeeaaat" and "yoi-cho" between her gold front teeth.

2. My children . . .

☐ For Review and Discussion

EXERCISE 26   Comparing texts

La Gringuita *and* My Mother Juggling Bean Bags *are both memoirs. Work with a partner. Compare the texts and explain how they are similar and how they are different. Make a list of three similarities and three differences.*

Three similarities:

_____

_____

_____

Three differences:

_____

_____

_____

EXERCISE 27   Participating in class discussion

Discuss the following questions with your classmates.

1. Sometimes a joke is funny in one language but not in another. Do you think humor is culture-specific or universal (the same things are funny in all cultures)? Support your opinion by giving examples of times when "humor doesn't translate," or times when something can be funny in more than one language.
2. In the poem, James's mother plays a practical joke on him by "short-sheeting" his bed. Have you ever played a practical joke? Have you ever had a practical joke played on you? Tell your classmates about the best practical joke you have ever heard of.
3. Why do you think it has taken James Mitsui more than twenty years to value his mother's humor?
4. Why is laughter important?
5. James and his mother grew up under very different cultures. How do you think family ties can remain strong through generations when family members grow up in different cultures? How can parents and grandparents preserve cultural values and traditions?

☐ Linking Concepts

EXERCISE 28   Writing in your reading journal

Write about the following topics in your reading journal:

1. Do you know a person who is really fun to be around—someone who enjoys laughing and joking? Describe the person, and tell why he or she is so much fun to be around.
2. Have you ever tried to write poetry (in any language)? How is writing poetry different from other types of writing?
3. Think of an event in your life, and write a memoir poem about that event.

☐ Assessing Your Learning at the End of a Chapter

Revisiting Objectives

Return to the first page of this chapter. Think about the chapter objectives. Put a check mark next to the ones you feel secure about. Review material in the chapter you still need to work on. When you are ready, answer the chapter review questions below.

☐ Practicing for a Chapter Test

EXERCISE 29   Reviewing comprehension

Check your comprehension of main concepts, or ideas, in this chapter by answering the following questions:

1. What is a memoir? Describe an effective strategy for reading a memoir.
2. Identify three things you should do or should avoid doing to increase your reading speed.
3. Explain what figurative language is, and provide examples.
4. Explain what idioms are, and provide examples.
5. Describe the physical and mental characteristics of one character in *La Gringuita.*
6. What is the tone of the poem *My Mother Juggling Bean Bags*?
7. Identify one similarity between *La Gringuita* and *My Mother Juggling Bean Bags.* Support your answer with examples from each selection.
8. Explain what cultural references are, and provide examples.

EXERCISE 30   Reviewing academic vocabulary

Review the academic vocabulary words you learned in this chapter. Return to Selection 1, La Gringuita, *and look at the words with a dotted underline. Select ten newly learned words you want to know very well and be able to use in your own writing and speaking. On separate paper, write ten original sentences with these AWL words.*

☐ For Further Study

As mentioned earlier, reading literature helps us grow and develop compassion as we identify with human struggles and dreams. It helps us shape personal goals and values and clarify our identities and cultural contexts. Challenge yourself to read a novel. Find out if your college or community is currently sponsoring the reading of a selected book. Join a reading group to discuss the recommended book as you read together.

WEB POWER

Go to http://esl.college.hmco.com/students to view more literary selections, plus exercises that will help you study the selections and the academic words in this chapter.

Reading and Learning

ACADEMIC FOCUS: STUDY SKILLS

Academic Reading Objectives

After completing this chapter, you should be able to:

✓ Check here as you master each objective.

1. Use facts and examples to support and explain statements of theory ☐
2. Outline ☐
3. Paraphrase ☐
4. Improve reading comprehension ☐
5. Increase vocabulary by selecting important words to study and learn ☐

Study Skills Objectives

1. Explain and apply textbook reconnaissance strategy ☐
2. Complete and discuss a self-report survey ☐
3. Evaluate current abilities as a student ☐
4. Define muscle reading ☐
5. Identify the nine steps of muscle reading ☐
6. Demonstrate appropriate selection and application of muscle reading strategies ☐

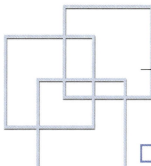

Reading Assignment 1

TEXTBOOK RECONNAISSANCE

☐ **Getting Ready to Read**

*One popular college course for new students is a **study skills**, or **student life**, course. Frequently this class is required for freshmen-level students. Listed below are some investigative questions about study skills courses. First, go over these questions together as a whole class. Then, distribute the investigation tasks (by question number) among student teams. As teams, visit the appropriate places on campus to find answers to the questions. Set a time limit. Later, groups can report back team findings to the whole class.*

1. Do you have a class like this at your institution?
2. What is it called?
3. What is the course description? (You can find out by looking in a college catalog.)
4. What books are required for this class? (You can find out by visiting the college bookstore.)
5. What department offers this course?
6. Which students are required to take this course? (You can find out by speaking with an advisor or by visiting the department.)

Think about the title for Reading Selection 1, Textbook Reconnaissance. Answer the following questions before you read.

1. What does the word **reconnaissance** mean? Check your dictionary and write a definition here.

   reconnaissance [ri-kon'e-sens] *noun*

   _____

   _____

2. Which field of study or professional area do people often associate with the term reconnaissance?

_____

3. Why do you think the author, Ellis, combines the idea of reconnaissance with textbooks?

_____

4. Can you predict what the tone of this selection may be?

   a. complex   **b.** straightforward   **c.** humorous   **d.** cautious

☐ Reading the Selection

Dave Ellis, author of *Becoming a Master Student*

Dave Ellis wrote the first edition of *Becoming a Master Student* more than twenty years ago. The reading selections in this chapter are from the ninth edition (©2000). In each revision, Ellis included new ideas sent to him by students and professors. Ellis also authored *Falling Awake: Creating the Life of Your Dreams* (©2002). He is an influential writer, teacher, and presenter. In this selection, Ellis describes a strategy for reading academic textbooks.

Reading Selection 1

TEXTBOOK RECONNAISSANCE

By Dave Ellis

1   Start becoming a master student this moment. Do a 15-minute "textbook reconnaissance" of this book. Here's how:

2   First, read the table of contents. Do it in three minutes or less. Next, look at every page in the book. Move quickly. Scan headlines. Look at pictures. Notice forms, charts and diagrams.

3   A textbook reconnaissance shows you where a course is going. It gives you the big picture. That's useful because brains work best when going from the general to the specific. Getting the big picture before you start makes details easier to recall and understand later on.

4   Your textbook reconnaissance will work even better if, as you scan, you look for ideas you can use. When you find one, write down the page number and a short description of it in the space below. The idea behind this technique is simple: It's easier to get excited about a course if you know it's going to be useful, interesting, or fun.

5   When you have found the five interesting ideas, stop writing and continue your survey. Remember, look at every page, and do it quickly. And here's another useful tip for the master student: Do it now.

Useful Ideas

page #	Description

Source: Ellis, D., (2000). *Becoming a Master Student*. Boston: Houghton Mifflin, p. 1.

☐ Assessing Your Learning

Demonstrating Comprehension

EXERCISE **3** **Outlining**

In outline form, list the steps needed for a fifteen-minute "Textbook Reconnaissance." Start each phrase with an action verb. The first line is done as an example.

1. *Read the table of contents.* _____

2. _____

    a. _____

    b. _____

    c. _____

    d. _____

3. _____

*Apply the Textbook Reconnaissance strategy to this book or another academic textbook you have. Your instructor will time you. **You have fifteen minutes.** Have a paper or your reading journal handy for step 3, but don't spend a lot of time writing down "ideas you can use" yet. You could jot down the page number and a quick description of a **few** ideas that interest you.*

☐ Linking Concepts

EXERCISE **4** **Reading purpose and speed**

Answer the following questions about reading purpose and speed.

1. What was your purpose when reading *La Gringuita* (in Chapter 1)?

    _____

2. What do you think the purpose for reading might be when you read Selection 3, *Muscle Reading*?

    _____

3. Which do you think should probably be read at the slowest speed?

    a. *La Gringuita*   **b.** *Textbook Reconnaissance*   **c.** *Muscle Reading*

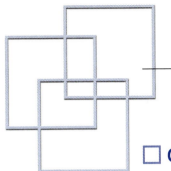

Reading Assignment 2

☐ Getting Ready to Read

EXERCISE 5 Participating in class discussion

*Students who take **study skills** or **student life** courses spend a lot of time exploring their own practices as students and clarifying academic goals. It is common to complete self-evaluation instruments and surveys. Answer the following questions about this type of exercise. Work with a partner and share your responses.*

1. Have you completed an evaluation form or survey recently?

   _____

2. If yes, what was the topic?

   _____

3. Where were you when you completed the survey?

   _____

4. About how long did it take? _____

5. Was it easy to answer all the questions? _____

6. Was it a multiple-choice format? _____

7. Why do you think multiple-choice formats are common for surveys and evaluations?

   _____

8. Who used the information learned from your responses?

   _____

EXERCISE 6   **Predicting from a title and illustration**

Look ahead to Selection 2, The Discovery Wheel. *Notice the title and illustration of a sample discovery wheel. Then answer the questions that follow.*

1. Who will complete the Discovery Wheel? _____

2. How many areas will be probed? _____

3. Which one will be the most interesting for you?

   _____

4. What do you think you will learn from this selection? _____

   _____

EXERCISE 7   **Previewing vocabulary**

*Before completing the survey, try to guess the meaning of the **bold** words.*

1. Shade each section of the Discovery Wheel to the **appropriate** level.

   a. approved   **b.** similar   **c.** highest   **d.** accurate

2. I have adequate time each day to **accomplish** what I plan.

   a. finish   **b.** assemble   **c.** further   **d.** reach

3. I apply techniques that **enhance** my memory skills.

   a. control   **b.** strengthen   **c.** change   **d.** ensure

4. I can **recall** information when I am under pressure.

   a. find   **b.** review   **c.** remember   **d.** connect

5. I am aware of my cultural **biases** and open to understanding people with different backgrounds.

   a. viewpoints   **b.** conditions   **c.** forms   **d.** knowledge

6. I am **candid** with others about who I am, what I feel, and what I want.

   a. insecure   **b.** shy   **c.** positive   **d.** truthful

☐ Reading the Selection

Read the selection and complete the survey. Carefully follow the directions for assigning points and calculating totals. As you read, keep in mind that words from the Academic Word List (AWL) in the reading selections have dotted underlines.

Reading Selection 2

THE DISCOVERY WHEEL

Sample Discovery Wheel

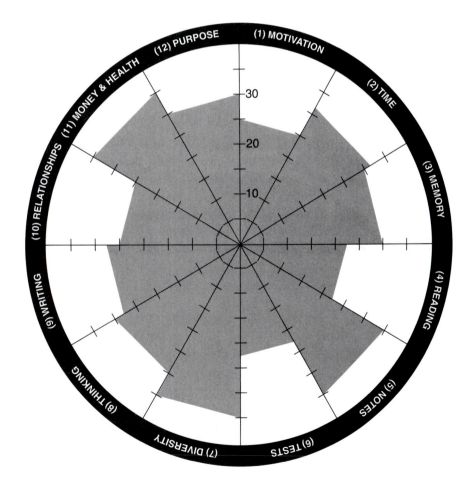

1   The Discovery Wheel is another opportunity to tell the truth to yourself about the kind of student you are and the kind of student you want to become.

2   This is not a test. There are no trick questions, and the answers will have meaning only for you.

3   Here are two suggestions to make this exercise more effective. First, think of it as a beginning of an opportunity to change. There is another Discovery Wheel at the end of this book. You will have a chance to measure your progress, so be honest about where you are now. Second, lighten up. A little laughter can make self-evaluations a lot more effective.

4   Here's how the Discovery Wheel works. By the end of this exercise, you will have filled in a circle similar to the one on this page. The Discovery Wheel circle is a picture of how you see yourself as a student. The closer the shading comes to the edge of the circle, the higher the evaluation. In the above example, the student has rated her reading skills as low and her note-taking skills as high.

5   It is dangerous, however, to think of these evaluations in terms of "higher" and "lower" if those designations reflect a negative judgment. The Discovery Wheel is not a permanent picture of who you are. It is a picture of how you view your abilities as a student today.

6   To begin this exercise, read the following statements and award yourself points for each section and shade the Discovery Wheel at the end to the appropriate level.

7   For an online version of this exercise, visit Houghton Mifflin's World Wide Web site at http://esl.college.hmco.com/students.

SURVEY		This statement is . . . true of me		1
always or almost always	often	about half the time	seldom	almost never
5 points	*4 points*	*3 points*	*2 points*	*1 point*

1. _____ I start courses highly motivated, and I stay that way.

1. _____ I periodically refine my long-term goals.

2. _____ I know what I want to get from my education.

2. _____ I regularly define short-term goals.

3. _____ I enjoy learning.

3. _____ I write a plan for each day and each week.

4. _____ I study even when distracted by activities of lower priority.

4. _____ I assign properties to what I choose to do each day.

5. _____ I am satisfied with how I progress toward achieving goals.

5. _____ I plan review time so that I don't have to cram before tests.

6. _____ I use knowledge of learning styles to support my success in school.

6. _____ I plan regular recreation time.

7. _____ I am excited about the courses I take.

7. _____ I adjust my study time to meet the demands of individual courses.

8. _____ I have a clear idea of the benefits I expect to get from my education.

8. _____ I have adequate time each day to accomplish what I plan.

_____ **Total score (1)** *Motivation*

_____ **Total score (2)** *Time*

SURVEY		This statement is . . . true of me		2
always or almost always	often	about half the time	seldom	almost never
5 points	*4 points*	*3 points*	*2 points*	*1 point*

1. _____ I am confident in my ability to remember.

1. _____ I preview and review reading assignments.

2. _____ I remember people's names.

2. _____ When reading, I underline or highlight important passages.

3. _____ At the end of a lecture, I can summarize what was presented.

3. _____ When I read, I ask questions about the material.

4. _____ I apply techniques that enhance my memory skills.

4. _____ When I read textbooks, I am alert and awake.

5. _____ I can recall information when I'm under pressure.

5. _____ I relate what I read to my life.

6. _____ I remember important information clearly and easily.

6. _____ I select a reading strategy to fit the type of material I am reading.

7. _____ I can jog my memory when I have difficulty recalling.

7. _____ I take effective notes when I read.

8. _____ I can relate new information to what I have already learned.

8. _____ When I don't understand what I am reading, I note my questions and I find answers.

_____ **Total score (3)** *Memory*

_____ **Total score (4)** *Reading*

SURVEY		This statement is . . . true of me		3
always or almost always	often	about half the time	seldom	almost never
5 points	*4 points*	*3 points*	*2 points*	*1 point*

1. _____ When I am in class, I focus my attention.

1. _____ I feel confident and calm during an exam.

2. _____ I take notes in class.

2. _____ I manage my time during exams, and I am able to complete them.

3. _____ I am aware of various method for taking notes and choose those that work best for me.

3. _____ I am able to predict test questions.

4. _____ My notes are valuable for review.

4. _____ I can examine essay questions in the light of what I know and come to new and original conclusions during a test.

5. _____ I review my class notes within twenty-four hours.

5. _____ I adapt my test-taking strategy to the kind of test I am taking.

6. _____ I distinguish important material and notice key phrases in a lecture.

6. _____ I understand what essay questions ask and can answer them completely and accurately.

7. _____ I copy material the instructor writes on the board or overhead projector.

7. _____ I start reviewing for tests at the beginning of the term and review regularly.

8. _____ I can put important concept into my own words.

8. _____ My sense of personal worth is independent of my test scores.

_____ **Total score (5)** *Notes*

_____ **Total score (6)** *Tests*

SURVEY		This statement is . . . true of me		4
always or almost always	often	about half the time	seldom	almost never
5 points	*4 points*	*3 points*	*2 points*	*1 point*

1. _____ I am aware of my culture biases and open to understanding people with different backgrounds.

1. _____ I have flashes of insight, and solutions to problems appear to me at unusual times.

2. _____ I build rewarding relationships with people from other cultures and races.

2. _____ I use brainstorming to generates solutions to a variety of problems.

3. _____ I can point out examples of discrimination and effectively respond to them.

3. _____ When I get stuck on a creative project, I use specific methods to get unstuck.

4. _____ I use school-based services to support my success.

4. _____ I see problems and decisions as opportunities for learning and personal growth.

5. _____ I use community -based resources to support my success.

5. _____ I am willing to consider different points of view and alternative solutions.

6. _____ I take specific steps to make a successful transition into higher education.

6. _____ I can state the assumptions that underlie a series of assertions.

7. _____ I am in regular contact with instructors and students who share my academic interests.

7. _____ I can detect common errors in logic.

8. _____ I effectively integrate schooling with my family and work lives.

8. _____ I approach courses in mathematics and science with confidence.

_____ **Total score (7)** *Diversity*

_____ **Total score (8)** *Thinking*

SURVEY	This statement is . . . true of me			5
always or almost always	often	about half the time	seldom	almost never
5 points	*4 points*	*3 points*	*2 points*	*1 point*

1. _____ I approach writing with confidence.

1. _____ I develop and maintain mutually supportive relationships.

2. _____ I can effectively plan and research a large writing assignment.

2. _____ I am candid with others about who I am, what I feel, and what I want.

3. _____ I create first draft without stopping to edit or criticize my writing.

3. _____ Other people tell me I am a good listener.

4. _____ I revise my writing for clarity, accuracy, and coherence.

4. _____ I communicate my upset and anger without blaming others.

5. _____ My writing affirms women and is free from sexist expressions.

5. _____ I make and keep promises that stretch me to my potential.

6. _____ When writing, I actually credit ideas and facts from other people.

6. _____ I am able to learn from various instructors with different teaching styles.

7. _____ I know ways to prepare and deliver effective speeches.

7. _____ I have the ability to make friends and create valuable relationships in a new setting.

8. _____ I am confident when I speak before others.

8. _____ I am open to being with people I don't especially like in order to learn from them.

_____ **Total score (9)** *Writing*

_____ **Total score (10)** *Relationships*

SURVEY		This statement is . . . true of me		6
always or almost always	often	about half the time	seldom	almost never
5 points	*4 points*	*3 points*	*2 points*	*1 point*

1. _____ I budget my money and am in control of my personal finances.

2. _____ I am confident that I will have enough money to complete the education I want.

3. _____ I repay my debts on time.

4. _____ My sense of personal worth is independent of my financial condition.

5. _____ I exercise regularly and eat to maintain a healthful weight.

6. _____ My emotional health supports my ability to learn.

7. _____ I notice changes in my physical condition and respond effectively.

8. _____ I am in control of any alcohol or drugs I put in my body.

_____ **Total score (11)**
Money & Health

1. _____ I see learning as a lifelong process.

2. _____ I relate school to what I plan to do for the rest of my life.

3. _____ I learn by contributing to others.

4. _____ I revise my plans as I learn, change, and grow.

5. _____ I am clear about my purpose in life.

6. _____ I know that I am responsible for my own education.

7. _____ I take responsibility for the quality of my life.

8. _____ I am willing to accept challenges even when I am not sure how to meet them.

_____ **Total score (12)**
Purpose

☐ Assessing Your Learning

Demonstrating Comprehension

EXERCISE 8 **Filling in your Discovery Wheel**

Using the total score from each category, shade in each section of the Discovery Wheel. Use different colors if you want. For example, you could use green to denote areas you want to work on. (Note: Scores of 40 indicate a completely filled in slice.)

Filling in Your Discovery Wheel

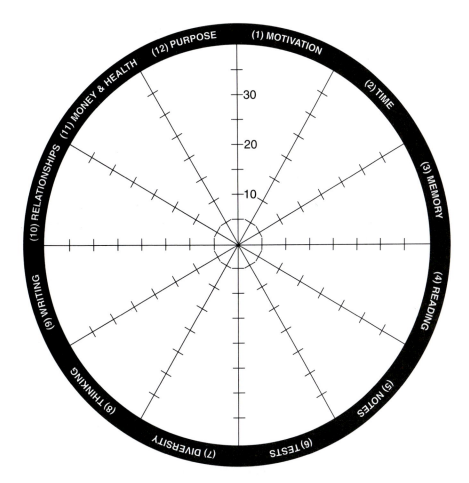

☐ **Focusing on Study Skills**

EXERCISE 9   **Writing in your reading journal**

In Becoming a Master Student, *Ellis completes his Discovery Wheel activity with the following reading journal assignment. Respond to his ideas in your own reading journal.*

DISCOVERY STATEMENT

N ow that you have completed your Discovery Wheel, spend a few minutes with it. Get a sense of its weight, shape, and balance. How would you feel if you ran your hands around it? How would it sound if it rolled down a hill? How would it look? Would it roll at all? Is it balanced? Make your observations without judging the wheel as good or bad. Simply be with the picture you have created. After you have spent a few minutes studying your Discovery Wheel, on separate paper (in your reading journal), complete the following sentences. Don't worry if you can't think of something to write. Just write whatever comes to mind. Remember, this is not a test.

1. This wheel is an accurate picture of my ability as a student because . . .

2. My self-evaluation surprises me because . . .

3. The two areas in which I am strongest are _____ and

   _____. They are related because . . .

4. The areas in which I want to improve are _____ and

   _____.

5. One thing I might do differently from now on is . . .

6. I want to concentrate on improving these areas because . . .

Source: Ellis, D., *Becoming a Master Student*, 2000, pp. 14–17.

Share something valuable you have learned with your instructor and classmates.

☐ Learning Vocabulary

EXERCISE 10   Understanding the language of surveys

Survey writers must be very careful about language choices because they are seeking accurate and honest responses. Survey items must be written in a clear and concise manner. Furthermore, the survey cannot be too long, or else respondents will become fatigued and may not finish it.

Look back at the survey you just completed. Were some items more difficult for you to understand than others because of the language? In each section, circle the number of items that may have seemed more difficult to understand—items you had to think about a little longer before assigning a number. When you finish, compare your choices with another student's. Did you find similar items to be difficult? What should you do if you are completing a survey and find an item you do not understand?

If you have the time, read the survey out loud to a partner while you review the use of language. Take turns reading every other sentence.

EXERCISE 11   Practicing with expressions in collocations

Words develop relationships with each other Some words are partnered together more frequently than others. These combinations, when considered as units, are called collocations. Reading Selection 2, the survey, provides many examples of typical word combinations.

Use each word group listed below in an original sentence. The word units are presented with their survey categories. Vary the location of the word units in your sentences so that they come in the middle or at the end. Make it personal and begin as many sentences as possible with "I." The first one is done for you as an example. (Remember that words with dotted underlines are AWL words.)

1. achieving goals (*Motivation*)

   I am committed to achieving my goals.

2. cramming before tests (*Time*)

   _____

3. to accomplish what (*Time*)

   _____

4. jog my memory (*Memory*)

   _____

5. key phrases (*Notes*)

   _____

6. important concepts (*Notes*)

   _____

7. essay questions (*Tests*)

   _____

8. cultural biases (*Diversity*)

   _____

9. flashes of insight (*Thinking*)

   _____

10. get stuck on (*Thinking*)

    _____

11. assumptions that underlie (*Thinking*)

    _____

12. lifelong process (*Purpose*)

    _____

13. accept challenges (*Purpose*)

    _____

When you finish, share examples on the blackboard.

EXERCISE 12   Understanding academic vocabulary

Listed below are some AWL words from The Discovery Wheel *commonly found in academic texts. Evaluate your knowledge of each word with the following criteria:*

Don't know at all	Recognize but don't know well	Know well	Use in my own writing

1. evaluation (¶ 3)	15. accurately (survey 6)	29. approach (survey 8)
2. appropriate (¶ 6)	16. biases (survey 7)	30. research (survey 9)
3. priority (survey 1)	17. discrimination (survey 7)	31. edit (survey 9)
4. achieving (survey 1)	18. respond to (survey 7)	32. clarity (survey 9)
5. adjust (survey 1)	19. resources (survey 7)	33. accuracy (survey 9)
6. adequate (survey 2)	20. integrate (survey 7)	34. coherence (survey 9)
7. techniques (survey 3)	21. insight (survey 8)	35. maintain (survey 10)
8. enhance (survey 3)	22. generate (survey 8)	36. mutually (survey 10)
9. recall (survey 3)	23. alternative (survey 8)	37. potential (survey 10)
10. aware of (survey 5)	24. assumptions (survey 8)	38. finances (survey 11)
11. lecture (survey 5)	25. underlie (survey 8)	39. process (survey 12)
12. concepts (survey 5)	26. series (survey 8)	40. contributing (survey 12)
13. adapt (survey 6)	27. detect (survey 8)	41. revise (survey 12)
14. strategy (survey 6)	28. logic (survey 8)	42. challenges (survey 12)

**Master
Student Tip**

You can know words on two levels: active and passive. To acquire vocabulary, you need to consciously change passive knowledge of a word to active knowledge.

EXERCISE 13 **Learning academic vocabulary**

Which words listed in Exercise 12 do you need to add to your active vocabulary? Make a commitment to use at least five words from the list today and tomorrow when you speak or write. List the five words you selected here:

_____ _____ _____ _____ _____

EXERCISE 14 **Understanding versus learning new vocabulary**

1. *Try to recall at least three of the seven strategies listed in Chapter 1 for understanding the meanings of new words.*

   looking for repeated occurrences of the word
   _____

   _____

   _____

2. *Review your strategies with your classmates. Then apply the most appropriate strategies and master the meanings of the AWL words.*
3. *Contrast **understanding** the meanings of words to **learning** words in order to acquire them as part of your active vocabulary. How are **learning** strategies different from **understanding** strategies? (Exercise 13 is an example of a learning strategy.) Write your answer here.*

   Understanding and learning words are two different things.
   _____

   _____

   _____

   _____

   _____

☐ Linking Concepts

EXERCISE 15   **Specifying benefits**

In the first part of this chapter, you tried out a study skill strategy called Textbook Reconnaissance. Then, you completed a self-evaluation survey and reflected on how you see yourself as a student. Think about the benefits of applying strategies such as Textbook Reconnaissance. How can increasing your self-awareness and learning about study skills lead to positive outcomes? In the chart that follows, list three examples of study or student-life skills you read about. Next to each skill/strategy you list, write a positive effect. An example has been provided.

Skill/Strategy	Positive effect
Example: 1. Assigning priorities	I spend more time on things that are really important and accomplish them.
2.	
3.	
4.	

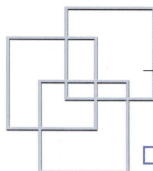

Reading Assignment 3

☐ Getting Ready to Read

EXERCISE 16 Writing in your reading journal

Ellis uses the label muscle reading for his nine-step strategy for reading academic textbooks. Do you read chapters in a textbook different from the way you read chapters in a novel? What is your reading process? Think of a chapter you have read in an academic textbook. What was the class? What was the subject of the chapter? Was this textbook chapter in English or in another language?

*Take **ten minutes** to freewrite in your reading journal. Your instructor can time you. Write about your reading process. **How** did you read that chapter? What reading strategies did you apply?*

EXERCISE 17 Participating in class discussion

*Each person should anonymously write on a piece of paper **one** thing he or she does when reading a chapter in a textbook. Pass the paper to another classmate. Read and pass again. Pass one more time. Finally, **three** volunteer students can share the most interesting reading process step they came across during the pass-and-share activity.*

☐ Reading the Selection

This time, we will not preview vocabulary. As you read, have two highlighters ready. Use one to mark important content (ideas to remember) and another to mark important words to remember and learn. Think about your content and word selection **process** as you mark.

Reading Selection 3

MUSCLE READING

How Muscle Reading Works

1   The key idea behind Muscle Reading is that your textbooks have something you want. They offer knowledge and valuable information. Sometimes the value is so buried that extracting it requires skill and energy. Muscle Reading is a three-phase technique you can use to accomplish that extraction. Each of the three phrase has three steps. To assist your recall of the nine steps, memorize these short sentences: Pry out questions. Root up answers. Recite, review, and review again.

2   Take a moment to invent images for each of those sentences. First, visualize or feel yourself prying questions out of a text. These are questions you want answered based on your brief survey of the assignment. Make a mental picture of yourself scanning the territory, spotting a question, and reaching into the text to pry it out. Hear yourself saying, "I've got it. Here's my question."

3   Then root up the answers to your questions. Get your muscles involved. Flex. Feel the ends of your fingers digging into the text to root up the answers to your questions.

4   Finally, hear your voice reciting what you have learned. Hear yourself making a speech about the material. Hear yourself singing it.

5   These sentences are an acrostic. The first letter of each word stands for one Muscle Reading process. Thus:

Pry	**Out**	**Questions.**	**Root**	**Up**	**Answers.**
R	U	U	E	N	N
E	T	E	A	D	S
V	L	S	D	E	W
I	I	T		R	E
W	N	I		L	R
	E	O		I	
		N		N	
				E	

Recite, Review, and **Review** again.

E	E	E
C	V	V
I	I	I
T	E	E
E	W	W

6   Configured another way, the three phrases and nine steps look like this:

Before you read: Pry out questions.
Step 1: Preview
Step 2: Outline
Step 3: Question
While you read: Root up answers.
Step 4: Read
Step 5: Underline
Step 6: Answer
After you read: Recite, review, and review again.
Step 7: Recite
Step 8: Review
Step 9: Review again

7   A nine-step reading strategy might seem cumbersome and unnecessary for a two-page reading assignment. It is. Keep in mind that Muscle Reading is not an all-or-nothing package. Use it appropriately. You can choose what steps to apply as you read. The main point is to preview, read, and review. The nine steps are just strategies for accomplishing those tasks.

8   Muscle Reading takes a little time to learn. At first you might feel it's slowing you down. That's natural. Mastery comes with time and practice. If you're still concerned about time, give yourself some options.

9   For example, apply the techniques on the following pages to just one article or part of a chapter.

Before You Read: Pry Out Questions

Step 1: Preview

10   Before you begin, survey the entire assignment. You did a survey of this book for Exercise 1: "Textbook reconnaissance." Research indicates that this technique, called previewing, can significantly increase your comprehension of reading material.

11   If you are starting a new book, look over the table of contents and flip through the text page by page. Even if your assignment is merely a few pages in a book, you can benefit from a brief preview of the table of contents.

12   Keep the preview short. If the entire reading assignment will take less than an hour, your preview might take five minutes. Previewing is also a way to get yourself started when an assignment looks too big to handle. It is an easy way to step into the material.

13   When previewing, look for familiar concepts, facts, or ideas. These items can help link new information to previously learned material. Look for ideas that spark your imagination or curiosity. Ask yourself how the material can relate to your long-term goals. Inspect drawings, diagrams, charts, tables, graphs, and photographs.

14   Keep an eye out for summary statements. If the assignment is long or complex, read the summary first. Many textbooks have summaries in the introductions or at the end of each chapter.

15   Read all chapter headlines, section titles, and paragraph headlines. These are often brief summaries in themselves.

16   If you expect to use a book extensively, read the preface. The author often includes a personal perspective in a preface. A picture of the person behind the words can remove barriers to understanding. Look for lists of recommended articles. If you have difficulty with a concept, sometimes another viewpoint can help you nail it down.

17   Before you begin reading, take a few moments to reflect on what you already know about this subject, even if you think you know nothing. This technique prepares your brain to accept the information that follows.

18   Finally, determine your reading strategy. Skimming might be enough for some assignments. For others, all nine steps of Muscle Reading might be appropriate. Ask yourself these questions: How will I be tested on the material? How useful will this knowledge be later? How much time can I afford to spend on this assignment?

19   To clarify your reading strategy, you might write the first letters of the Muscle Reading acrostic in a margin or at the top of your notes and check off the steps you intend to follow. Or write the Muscle Reading steps on 3" × 5" cards and use them for bookmarks.

20   You don't have to memorize what you preview to get value from this step. Previewing sets the stage for incoming information by warming up a space in you mental storage area.

Step 2: Outline

21   The amount of time you spend on this step will vary. For some assignments (fiction and poetry for example), skip it. For other assignments, a 10-second mental outline is all you need.

22   With complex material, take time to understand the structure of what you are about to read. If your textbook provides chapter outlines, spend some time studying them.

23   If a text does not provide an outline, sketch a brief one in the margin of your book or at the beginning of your notes. Then, as you read take notes and fill in your outline.

24   Section titles and paragraph headlines can serve as major and minor topics for your outline. If assigned reading does not contain section titles or headlines, you can outline the material as you read. In this case, outlining actively organizes your thoughts about the assignment.

25   Use whatever outline style works best for you. Some readers prefer your traditional Roman numeral outlines. Others prefer mind maps or notes in the Cornell format. (These methods are explained in Chapter Five.) If your text includes headings in bold or italic print, you can also outline right in the text. Assign numbers or letters to each heading, just as you would for a traditional outline.

26   Outlining can make complex information easier to understand.

Step 3: Question

27   Ask yourself what you want from an assignment before you begin reading. Your preview might suggest some questions. Imagine the author is in the room with you. What would you ask him? How can he help you get what you want from your education? Create a dialogue. Begin your active participation in the book before you start to read.

28   Write down a list of questions. Be tough. Demand your money's worth from your textbook. If you do not understand a concept, write specific questions about it. The more detailed your questions, the more powerful this technique becomes. Knowledge is born of questions.

29   If a reading assignment seems irrelevant, sit back for a minute and think about what it is you want from your time in school. Check to see if your education will be complete without this piece of the puzzle. Even if a particular assignment doesn't have personal meaning for you at the moment, it may be tied to a broader goal like getting a certain grade in class.

30   Another useful technique is to turn the chapter headings and section titles into questions. For example, if a subtitle is "Transference and Suggestion," you can ask yourself, What are transference and suggestion? How does transference relate to suggestion? Make up a quiz as if you were teaching this subject to your classmates.

31   Make the questions playful or creative. Have fun with this technique. You don't need to get an answer to every question you ask. The purpose of making up questions is to get your brain involved in the assignment. Take your unanswered questions to class, where they can be springboards for discussion.

32   Learning to ask effective questions takes practice, and you can discover rewards for developing this skill. The questions you formulate help you stay alert through complicated reading.

33   Boredom and fatigue tend to disappear when you're busy finding answers. In fact, when you find one, expect a burst of energy. It might be a small burst, if it was a small question. Or it might bring you right out of your chair if the question was important to you. If you find a series of answers in a reading assignment, you might finish the assignment feeling more energetic than when you began.

34   For some assignments, you might spend considerable time previewing, outlining, and asking questions before you start reading. The potential rewards are understanding and remembering more of what you read and saving time.

While You Read: Root Up Answers

Step 4: Read

35   At last! You have previewed the assignment, organized it in your mind, and formulated questions. Now you are ready to begin reading.

36   As you read, be conscious of where you are and what you are doing. Practice Power process #2: "Be here now." When you notice your attention wandering, gently bring it back to the present.

37   One way to stay in the here and now is to make tick marks on scrap paper whenever you notice your attention flagging.

38   You might make many tick marks at first. That's OK. The marks signify your inattentiveness, so don't be too discouraged by lots of them. Most students notice that as they pay attention to their attention, the number of tick marks decreases. If a personal problem or some other concern is interfering with your concentration, experiment with this idea. Write down the problem along with a commitment to a future course of action. Getting a problem down on paper, with a commitment to take action, can free your mind for the present task.

39   Another way to stay focused is to hold marathon reading sessions. Schedule breaks and set a reasonable goal for the entire session. Then reward yourself with an enjoyable activity for five or ten minutes every hour or two. With practice, some students find they can stay focused up to three hours without a break.

40   For difficult reading, set shorter goals. Read for a half-hour, then break. Most students find that shorter periods of reading distributed throughout the day and week can be more effective than long sessions.

41   You can use the following three technique to stay focused as you read. First, visualize the material. Form mental pictures of the concepts as they are presented. If you read that a voucher system can help control cash disbursements, picture a voucher handing out dollar bills.

42   Second, read it out loud—especially complicated material. Some of us remember better and understand more quickly when we hear an idea.

43   Third, get a "feel" for the subject. For example, let's say you are reading about a microorganism, a paramecium, in your biology text. Imagine what it would feel like to run your finger around the long, cigar-shaped body of the organism. Imagine feeling the large fold of its gullet on one side, and feel the hairy little cilia as they wiggle in your hand.

44   A final note: It's easy to fool yourself about reading. Just having an open book in your hand and moving your eyes across a page doesn't mean you are reading effectively. Reading textbooks takes energy, even if you do it sitting down. One study revealed that corporation presidents usually wear out the front of their chairs first. Approach your reading assignment like the company president. Sit up. Keep your spine straight. Use the edge of your chair. And avoid reading in bed, except for fun.

Step 5: Underline

45   Deface your books. Use them up. Have fun writing and coloring in them. Indulge yourself as you never could with your grade-school texts. Keeping textbooks clean and neat might not help you get what you want from them.

46   The purpose of making marks in a text is to create signals for reviewing. Underlining or highlighting can save lots of time when you study for tests.

47   A secondary benefit of marking is that when you read with a pen in your hand, you are involving another mode of perception, your kinesthetic sense—that is, your sense of touch and motion. Being physical with your books can help build strong neural pathways in your memory.

48   Avoid underlining or highlighting too soon. Wait until you've completed a section or concept to make sure you know what is important. Then mark up the text. Sometimes, stopping after each paragraph works best. For some assignments, you might want to read a larger section before deciding what to mark.

49   Some people prefer colored highlighters to pens for marking up a text. Pens can make underlined sections —in other words, the important parts—harder to read than the rest of book. You can still use a pen for making notes in the margins and circling important sections.

50   Underline or highlight sparingly, usually less than 10 percent of the text. If you mark up too much on a page, you defeat the purpose, which is to flag the most important material for review. Write in the margins of your texts. Write summary statements and questions. Mark passages that you don't understand. If you find a list or series of elements in a paragraph, you can circle and number them.

51   It's true that marking your textbooks can lower their resale value. The money you lose by doing it is ridiculously small compared to the value of your education. Writing in your textbooks helps you wring every ounce of value out of them.

Step 6: Answer

52   As you read, get answers to your questions and write them down. Fill in your outline. Write down new questions and note when you don't get the answers you wanted to find. Use these notes to ask questions in class, or see your instructor personally.

53   When you read, create an image of yourself as a person in search of the answers. You are a detective, watching for every clue, sitting erect in your straight-back chair, demanding that your textbook give you what you want—the answers.

After You Read: Recite, Review, & Review (Again)

Step 7: Recite

54   Talk to yourself about what you have read. Or talk to someone else. When you finish reading an assignment, make a speech about it. One classic study suggests that you can profitably devote up to 80 percent of your study time to active reciting.[1]

55   One way to get yourself to recite is to look at each underlined point. Note what you marked, then put the book down and start talking out loud. Explain as much as you can about that particular point. To make this technique more effective, do it in front of a mirror. It may seem silly, but the benefits can be enormous. You can reap them at exam time.

56   Friends are even better than mirrors. Form a group and practice teaching each other what you have read. One of the best ways to learn time is to teach it to someone else.

57   There is a secret buried in this suggestion. That secret is, have someone else do the work. Your instructors might not appreciate this suggestion, but it can be a salvation when you're pressed for time. Find a friend you trust and split up the reading assignment. Each of you can teach half the assignment to the other. (Warning: You might be far better versed in the part you read and teach. And if your friend misses an important part, you could miss it too.) Talk about your reading whenever you can.

Step 8: Review

58   Plan to do your first complete review within 24 hours of reading the material. Sound the trumpets, this is critical: A review within 24 hours moves information from your short-term memory to your long-term memory. It can save you hours later on. Review within one day. If you read it on Wednesday, review it on Thursday.

1. Gates, G. S. (1917). Recitation as a factor in memorizing. *Archives of Psychology*, 40.

59   During the review, look over your notes and clear up anything you don't understand. Recite some of the main points again.

60   At first, you might be discouraged by how much you think you forgot from the previous day. Don't worry. Notice how quickly you pick up the material the second time. One of the characteristics of memory is that even when you cannot recall something immediately, you can relearn it more easily if you have already learned it once. And relearning wears a deeper path into your memory.

61   This review can be short. You might spend as little as 15 minutes reviewing a difficult two-hour reading assignment. Investing that time now can save you hours later when studying for exams. Also remember that you can stop to review and check your comprehension at any point, even before you complete a whole reading assignment.

Step 9: Review Again

62   The final step in Muscle Reading is the weekly or monthly review. This step can be very short—perhaps only four or five minutes per assignment. Simply go over your notes. Read the highlighted parts of your text. Recite one or two of the more complicated points.

63   The purpose of these reviews is to keep the neural pathways to the information open and to make them more distinct. That way, the information can be easier to recall. You can accomplish these short reviews anytime, anywhere, if you are prepared.

64   Conduct a five-minute review while you are waiting for a bus, for your socks to dry, or for the water to boil. Three-by-five cards are a handy review tool. Write ideas, formulas, concepts, and facts on cards and carry them with you. These short review periods can be effortless and fun.

65   Sometimes longer review periods are appropriate. For example, if you found an assignment difficult, consider rereading it. Start over, as if you had never seen the material. Sometimes a second reading will provide you with surprising insights. Your previous experience acts as a platform from which you can see aspects that didn't appear during the first reading.

66   Schedule some review periods well in advance. You might set aside one hour on a Saturday or a Sunday to review several subjects. Keep your reviews short and do them frequently.

67   Finally, take some time to reflect on what you read. As you walk to and from class, in your discussions with other students, or before you go to bed at night, turn over new ideas in your mind. Take time to play with them. Develop a habit of regular review.

68   Psychologists speak of the primacy-recency effect,[2] which suggests that we most easily remember the first and last items in a presentation. Previewing and reviewing your reading is a powerful way to put this theory to work for you.

Source: Ellis, D. (2000). *Becoming a Master Student*. Boston: Houghton Mifflin, pp. 108–115.

☐ Assessing Your Learning

Demonstrating Comprehension

EXERCISE 18 Outlining

Can you remember the three main phases and nine important steps of Muscle Reading? Complete this outline. (If you need help, return to the beginning of the reading selection.)

Muscle Reading

p_ry out questions _____

      Step 1.   P_____

      Step 2.   O_____

      Step 3.   Q_____

R _____

      Step 4.   R_____

      Step 5.   U_____

      Step 6.   A_____

R_____

      Step 7.   R_____

      Step 8.   R_____

      Step 9.   R_____

2. Rosnow, R. & Robinson, E. (1967). *Experiments in Persuasion*. New York: Academic Press.

EXERCISE **19** **Learning through teaching**

When writing about step 7, "Recite," Ellis states, "One of the best ways to learn anything is to teach someone else." *Divide the class into nine teams, one for each step. Each team should teach the class about what they have read. Be prepared to help your classmates learn the section you are responsible for teaching. Include a demonstration and examples from your own experiences to illustrate the Muscle Reading step they need to **know**, **remember**, and **use**.*

☐ Focusing on Study Skills

Ellis discusses the importance of being an active and engaged reader. He indicates that writing and talking about what you have read can improve your comprehension and retention. There are two ways to give credit to the authors of materials you have read and want to refer to. You can use direct quotation, or paraphrase. To paraphrase is to restate what someone else has said in your own words. Paraphrasing is very common when you are trying to remember and learn material. In this paragraph you have just read, there are two examples of paraphrase sentence types. Can you find them?

In Exercise 20, you will practice paraphrasing some of Ellis's ideas. Listed in the box are some useful expressions to help you.

Expressions to introduce paraphrases					
Ellis	compares	. . .	Ellis	states	that . . .
	contrasts			says	
	identifies			indicates	
	describes			suggests	
	discusses			implies	
				argues	
				writes	
According to Ellis . . .					

POWER GRAMMAR

Verbs for Paraphrasing

1. The verb that presents a paraphrase is called a reporting verb. The reporting verb can be in the present or past tense. Using present tense makes the ideas feel close or immediately relevant to a current situation. Using past tense makes the ideas feel less immediate and can also affect the tense of the second verb. Compare these three:

   He indicates that talking about what you have read can improve your comprehension.

   He indicated that talking about what you have read can improve your comprehension.

   He indicated that talking about what you had read could improve your comprehension.

2. Many reporting verbs are followed by *that*. Notice that the use of *that* requires a "subject + verb" structure to follow. Which verbs in the expressions box above need to be followed by a "that + subject + verb" structure?

EXERCISE 20   Working with another's ideas

Select four important ideas you read about in the Muscle Reading selection. Paraphrase them using expressions from the box. Remember to use your own words to express Ellis's ideas. Also include a comment about each idea. (In formal writing, you would include the year that Ellis published the article in parentheses after his name. For now, because we're only referring to one work, you can skip this formality.)

Example:

1. Ellis compares reading to gardening. He talks about rooting up answers and feeling your fingers digging. This makes me think about working in a garden and feeling very connected to the subject.

2. _____

_____

_____

_____

_____

_____

3. _____

_____

_____

_____

_____

_____

4. _____

_____

_____

_____

_____

_____

5. _____

_____

_____

_____

_____

_____

When you finish, share examples on the blackboard.

☐ Assessing Your Learning at the End of a Chapter

Revisiting Chapter Objectives

Return to the first page of this chapter. Think about the chapter objectives. Put a check mark next to the ones you feel secure about. Review material in the chapter you still need to work on. When you are ready, answer the chapter review questions below.

☐ Practicing for a Chapter Test

EXERCISE 21   **Reviewing comprehension**

Check your comprehension of main concepts, or ideas, in this chapter by answering the following chapter review questions.

1. List the steps needed to conduct a textbook reconnaissance. Name a book from one of your current classes that you did a textbook reconnaissance on.
2. Complete this sentence about your Discovery Wheel survey. An area in which I want to improve is . . .
3. Is it always necessary to complete all nine steps of Muscle Reading? Explain your answer.
4. Describe a benefit from asking questions before you read.
5. Identify a strategy to use if you are feeling distracted when you read.
6. Explain the use of distributed practice with respect to reading.
7. In general, how much should you highlight on a textbook page?

EXERCISE 22   **Reviewing academic vocabulary**

Here are some academic vocabulary words that were introduced in this chapter. Confirm the words whose meanings you know. Identify the words that are not yet part of your active vocabulary. Relearn the words you need to relearn.

accurately	adapt	adjust	appreciate	approach
appropriate	aspects	assist	benefit	biases
brief	challenges	charts	clarify	classic

commitment	concentration	conduct	considerable	corporation
create	detective	devote	discrimination	distinct
distributed	edit	elements	energetic	enormous
evaluation	extracting	final	focused	format
formulate	generate	goals	highlight	image
indicates	insights	inspect	investing	involving
irrelevant	link	major	margins	mental
methods	minor	mutually	options	percent
perception	phase	physical	previously	primacy
priority	process	psychologists	remove	research
revealed	revise	schedule	series	significantly
signify	sketch	specific	strategies	structure
summary	survey	tasks	techniques	territory
texts	theory	topics	traditional	transference
vary	visualize			

WEB POWER

Go to http://esl.college.hmco.com/students to view more readings about study skills, plus exercises that will help you study the selections and the academic words in this chapter.

Studying Memory

ACADEMIC FOCUS: PSYCHOLOGY

Academic Reading Objectives

After completing this chapter, you should be able to:

✓ Check here as you master each objective.

1. Ask significant questions ☐
2. Generate and assess solutions ☐
3. Clarify understanding of issues ☐
4. Use textual clues to compare structure and style of academic materials ☐
5. Interpret charts and graphs ☐
6. Recognize and locate sources ☐

Psychology Objectives

1. Define psychology ☐
2. Explain the value of case studies ☐
3. Relate cited references to psychological studies ☐
4. Describe basic memory processes ☐
5. Identify three primary types of memory ☐
6. Contrast explicit and implicit memory ☐

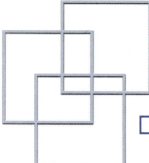

Reading Assignment 1

INTRODUCING PSYCHOLOGY

☐ Getting Ready to Read

Psychology courses are offered by many colleges under an area of social sciences. Usually, an introductory psychology course meets a general education requirement. General education courses are core courses required for all students regardless of major. The institution identifies courses believed to provide a general academic knowledge base essential for dialogue across disciplines. Sometimes students want to focus only on their majors. Broad educational experiences, though, help students understand ideas from different perspectives and think about connections more deeply. Further, it is common for freshman-level students to be uncertain about their majors and to decide to change majors. Being open to learning from textbooks and educators in a variety of disciplines can lead students to resources that can greatly affect their educational career decisions.

Getting Ready to Read Assignment 1 has three parts. First, you ask and answer some questions in class. Second, you go outside your classroom, approach at least two students you see, and ask them some questions. Third, you analyze your findings. The purpose of these tasks is for you to better understand decisions about majors and to think about how studying psychology can be beneficial.

EXERCISE 1 Participating in class discussion

Discover the following about your instructor and classmates. Think about how to phrase your questions before you ask them. Find out . . .

1. what majors your instructor has had and what influenced her or his academic decisions.
2. if some of your classmates already have university degrees and how they chose their majors.
3. if your instructor has taken a psychology course or courses and what he or she thinks about them.
4. if some of your classmates have already taken a psychology class and, if so, ask them to give an example of something practical they learned and remember.

EXERCISE **2** **Collecting data**

Consider this a mini-field study. Take about fifteen to twenty minutes to go out to an area where students congregate. Work with a partner for added confidence if you prefer. Follow these steps:

A. Observe the books the students have with them.

B. Politely get the attention of a student whose book titles you observe lead you to believe he or she is taking advanced courses.

C. Explain your situation, and if the student agrees to be interviewed, ask the following questions:
   1. What is your major?
   2. Did you ever change majors? If yes, what was your first major?
   3. Did you take a psychology class at this college? If yes, which one, and what do you remember about reading the psychology textbook?

D. Repeat these questions with at least one more person.

EXERCISE **3** **Tabulating and analyzing findings**

Return to your own classroom to share and discuss your findings with the whole class. Start by listing this information on the board:

   1. How many people were interviewed?
   2. How many changed their majors?
   3. Which majors were popular?
   4. Continue with additional questions/categories.

What conclusions can you draw?

If you have time, write a summary report together with your partner. Include descriptive information and implications.

Bernstein, D. A.,
Clark-Stewart, A.,
Penner, L. A., Roy, E. J.,
& Wickens, C. D.
(2000).
Psychology (5th ed.)
Boston:
Houghton Mifflin.

> **Muscle
> Reading
> Reminder**
>
> *Phase One:*
> **Preview**
> **Outline**
> **Question**

☐ Reading Strategy

Phase One of Muscle Reading includes three steps: Preview, Outline, and Question. Apply these three steps to the passages in this chapter. Do you remember each step?

Previewing, Outlining, and Questioning

To **preview**, look for familiar concepts, facts, or ideas that catch your interest and are related to your goals. Look at visual elements and read section titles and summary statements. Determine your reading strategy. How will you use what you learn from your reading? How will you be tested on the material? How much time do you need?

To **outline**, mentally note the section titles.

To **question**, write down actual questions about the possible content. You could transform section titles into question structures if other ideas do not come right to your mind.

Phase One of Muscle Reading prepares your mind for reading efficiently and learning. Remember to take these steps <u>before</u> reading the sections on the next pages. Spend a few extra minutes on the front end, preparing to read, and your experience will be much richer. You will have set the stage for learning.

One always has time enough, if one will apply it well.

Johann Wolfgang Van Goethe

☐ Reading the Selection

The reading selections in this chapter come from a college-level introductory psychology textbook. Reading Selection 1 comes from Chapter 1, an introduction. Subsequent reading selections come from a later chapter on memory. Two reminders: (1) Words with a dotted underline are AWL words, commonly found in academic texts across disciplines, and (2) it is helpful to underline in two colors—one for important content and another for useful new words to learn.

Reading Selection 1

CHAPTER 1: "INTRODUCING PSYCHOLOGY"

Muscle Reading Reminder

Phase Two:
Read
Underline
Answer

1   On the afternoon of July 24, 1998, the United States Capitol Building was already crowded with tourists as new arrivals lined up to go through a security check point at the public entrance. Russell Eugene Weston, Jr., was in line too, but he wasn't there to tour the building. Because he knew that the metal detector at the check point would be set off by the .38 caliber pistol he carried, he tried to walk around it. When the Capitol police officer Jacob Chestnut attempted to stop him, Weston drew his weapon and shot the officer in the head, killing him. Though hit by bullets fired by other police officers, Weston managed to run down a hallway and burst into the offices of Congressman Tom Delay, where another Capitol guard, special agent John Gibson, rose to challenge him. After an exchange of gunfire, Gibson, too, lay dead and Weston was gravely wounded. As investigators tried to find out what prompted Weston's deadly attack, it emerged that he had been diagnosed in 1996 as a paranoid schizophrenic[1] and placed in a mental hospital. This was after years of odd behavior, which included Weston's claims that both the Kennedy family and President Clinton were his close friends and that he was being spied on[2] by the government through his neighbors' TV satellite dishes. Weston was later released from the hospital because his doctors believed he was not a threat to himself or others if he took his prescribed antipsychotic medication.

2   How could the hospital staff's judgment and decisions about Weston have been so wrong? Do all mental patients pose a similar threat to society? If not, how can we tell which of them are dangerous and which are not? Are mental disorders such as

---

1. **par•a•noi•a** (păr´ə-noi´ə) *n.* A psychotic disorder characterized by delusions of persecution or grandeur. **par•a•noi•ac** (-noi´ak´, -noi´ĭk) *n.* –**par•a•noid** *adj.* & *n.*
   schiz•o•phre•ni•a (skĭt´sə-frē´nē-ə, -frĕn´ē-ə) *n.* A severe mental disorder in which a person loses touch with reality and withdraws from other people. –**schiz´o•phren´ic** (-frĕn´ĭk) *adj.* & *n.*
2. **spy** (spī) *v.* To observe secretly with hostile intent; To investigate intensively.

schizophrenia caused by faulty genes,[3] imbalances in brain chemicals, bad childhood experiences, or all of these factors? Can people like Weston be cured by drugs or psychotherapy? Will those who witnessed Weston's murderous attack be able to accurately recall what they saw and provide useful testimony at a trial? How will the witnesses' own lives be affected? Will they ever recover from their traumatic experience? Finally, why do newspaper and television accounts of this and other similar incidents so strongly affect millions of people who are thousands of miles away from the scene of the tragedy?

3   Psychologists study questions like these because **psychology** is the science that seeks to understand behavior and mental processes, and to apply that understanding in the service of human welfare. They have not yet provided final answers; but as you will see in later chapters, psychologists' research in areas such as judgment and decision-making, psychological disorders, memory, stress and coping, and social cognition has yielded important clues and valuable theories about why people think, feel, and behave as they do. That research tells part of the story of psychology, but there is much more. We wrote this book to give you a better understanding of what psychology is, what psychologists study, where and how they work, what they have—and have not— discovered so far, and how their discoveries are being put to practical use. In this chapter we present an overview of psychology as it exists today, and as it developed. Then we describe the unity and diversity of contemporary psychology, including the differing approaches to understanding psychological phenomena, and the many sub fields in which psychologists work.

Source: Bernstein, D. A., Clark-Stewart, A., Penner, L. A., Roy, E. J., & Wickens, C. D. (2000). *Psychology* (5th ed.)(p. 3) Boston: Houghton Mifflin Company.

---

3. **gene** (jēn) *n.* A segment of DNA, located at a particular point on a chromosome, that determines hereditary characteristics.

☐ Assessing Your Learning

Demonstrating Comprehension

EXERCISE 4   Checking comprehension

Check your understanding of the selection by answering the following questions:

1. Paragraph 1 begins with an anecdote about Weston. Who was he, and why did his story introduce this selection from the beginning of the psychology textbook?
2. Paragraph 2 consists of a stream of questions. Can you answer some of these questions?
3. Paragraph 3 has two main purposes. Identify the two purposes.
4. Identify and define the principle concept discussed in paragraph 3.
5. Although the continuation of Chapter 1 is not included here, as an effective reader, you could anticipate the contents of Chapter 1. Based on the information given in paragraph 3, what would you expect to read about? Fill in the blanks below to show the main topics the content will include.

The World of Psychology: An Overview

_____

_____

Unity and Diversity in Psychology

_____

_____

☐ Focusing on Psychology

Readings in psychology and other social sciences blend writing styles that include scientific and narrative. Often, narrative features include case studies or case examples of individuals or groups who exhibit traits, qualities, characteristics, or behaviors a social scientist wants to illustrate. As a reader, it is important to think about how the writing styles used in social science literature help make concepts accessible. Much of what you read about comes from familiar experiences that have been researched and analyzed by field experts.

EXERCISE 5 **Comparing texts**

Check your observations by answering the following questions:

1. Which paragraph from Reading Selection 1 exhibits a narrative style? _____

2. Which paragraph exhibits a scientific style? _____

3. Identify differences in grammar between the two paragraphs.

   _____

   _____

   _____

4. Identify differences in tone between the two paragraphs.

   _____

   _____

   _____

5. Explain how Weston's story helps you learn about psychology.

   _____

   _____

   _____

POWER GRAMMAR

Verb Tenses and Writing Styles

Taking time to analyze patterns in verb tenses as you read can aid your comprehension. In academic texts, past tense forms are used for discussing past events, observations, experiment results, case studies, descriptions of past work, and conclusions. This is called narrative style. To bring a present or more immediate focus to texts, with reports, discussions, and generalizations, writers use present, present perfect, and future forms including modals. This is called expository style. It is writing to give information or an explanation of difficult material.

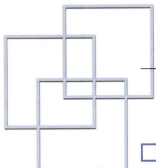

Reading Assignment 2

THE NATURE OF MEMORY

☐ Getting Ready to Read

Reading Selection 2 comes from Chapter 7 in *Psychology* (Bernstein et al., 2000). Chapter 7, titled "Memory," is thirty-five pages long. It includes six theoretical sections and three supporting sections. Here we will read the first section only, "The Nature of Memory." As the chapter is introduced, the authors include an outline.

Read the chapter outline on the next page and then answer the questions that follow.

STRATEGY

Reading Chapter Outlines

Taking the time to read a chapter outline before you read a textbook chapter puts you in the driver's seat. Looking at a map before you take a trip helps you to make navigation decisions as you travel. Chapter outlines are like maps. Reading them carefully lets you know what lies ahead.

Chapter 7: Memory

OUTLINE

EXERCISE 6   **Using a textbook's chapter outline**

Answer the following questions:

1. Without looking back at the outline, how much do you remember about what you might be reading? How many sections are there? What is the first one about? What is the last one about? Can you remember something about the middle sections? What do your answers to these questions mean?

2. Now look back carefully at the headings for Section 1, "The Nature of Memory." Write two questions you could ask yourself about each part of Section 1 before you read.

Example:

- Basic Memory Processes:

  How many memory processes are there?

  Is there an order to memory processes?

- Types of Memory: _____

  _____

- Explicit and Implicit Memory: _____

  _____

- Focus on Research Methods: Measuring Explicit Versus

  Implicit Memory: _____

  _____

- Models of Memory: _____

  _____

3. Which chapter section listed in the outline sounds most interesting to you? Why? How is that section relevant to your interests at this time in your life?

4. Explain how working with an outline before you read can help you remember more and learn more.

EXERCISE **7**   **Reading question strategy**

*As you read Selection 2, keep in mind Phase Two of Muscle Reading: **Read**, **Underline**, and **Answer**. Form mental answers to the questions you wrote in Exercise 6. Refine and ask more questions to answer as you read. Use true question structures to maintain a Q-A dialogue in English in your mind. Think about the kinds of questions your instructor might ask you about concepts and content.*

Reading Selection 2

CHAPTER 7: MEMORY

1   Several years ago an air traffic controller at Los Angeles International Airport cleared a US Airways flight to land on runway 24L. A couple of minutes later, the US Airways pilot radioed the control tower that he was on approach for 24L, but the controller did not reply because she was preoccupied by a confusing exchange with another pilot. After finishing that conversation the controller told a Sky West commuter pilot to taxi onto runway 24L for takeoff, completely forgetting about the US Airways flight that was about to land on the same runway. The US Airways jet hit the commuter plane, killing thirty-four people. The controller's forgetting was so complete that she assumed the fireball from the crash was an exploding bomb. How could the controller's memory have failed her at such a special time?

2   Memory is full of paradoxes. It is common, for example, for people to remember the name of their first grade teacher, but not the name of someone they just met a minute ago. And consider Rajan Mahadevan. He once set a world's record by reciting from memory the first 31,811 places for pi (the ratio of the circumference of a circle to its diameter), but on repeated visits to the psychology building at the University of Minnesota, he had trouble recalling the location of the nearest restroom (Biederman et al., 1992). Like perception, memory is selective. Whereas people retain a great deal of information, they also lose a great deal (Bjork & Vanhuele, 1992).

3   Memory plays a critical role in your life. Without memory, you would not know how to shut off your alarm clock, take a shower, get dressed, or recognize objects. You would be unable to communicate with other people because you would not remember what words mean, or even what you had just said. You would be unaware of your own likes and dislikes, and you would have no idea who you are in any meaningful sense (Kihlstrom, 1993). In this chapter we describe what is known about both memory and forgetting. First, we discuss what memory is—the different kinds of memory, and the different ways we remember things. Then we examine how new memories are acquired and later recalled, and why they are sometimes forgotten. We continue with a discussion of the biological bases of memory, and we conclude with some practical advice for improving memory and study skills.

Drawing on Memories: The human memory system allows people to encode, store, and retrieve a lifetime of experiences. Without it, you would have no sense of who you are.

The Nature of Memory

4   Mathematician John Griffith estimated that, in an average lifetime, a person will have stored roughly five hundred times as much information as can be found in all of the volumes of the *Encyclopedia Britannica* (Hunt, 1982). The impressive capacity of human memory depends on the operation of a complex mental system (Schacter, 1999).

Basic Memory Processes

5   We know a psychologist who sometimes drives to work and sometimes walks. On one occasion, he drove, forgot that he had driven, and walked home. When he failed to find his car in its normal spot the next morning, he reported the car stolen. The police soon called to say that "some college kids" had probably stolen the car because it was found on campus (next to the psychology building!). What went wrong? There are several possibilities, because memory depends on three basic processes—encoding, storage, and retrieval (see Figure 7.1).

6   First, information must be put into memory, a step that requires **encoding**. Just as incoming sensory information must be coded so that it can be communicated to the brain, information to be remembered must be put in a form that the memory system can accept and use. In the memory system, sensory information is put into various *memory codes*, which are mental representations of physical stimuli. Imagine that you see a billboard[1] that reads "Huey's Going Out of Business Sale," and you want to remember it so you can take advantage of the sale later. If you encode the sounds of the words as if they had been spoken, you are using **acoustic encoding**, and the information is represented in your memory as a sequence of sounds. If you encode the image of the letters as they were arranged on the sign, you are using **visual encoding**, and the information is represented in your memory as a picture. Finally, if you encode the fact that you saw an ad for Huey's you are using **semantic encoding**, and the information is represented in your memory by its general meaning. The type of encoding used can influence what is remembered. For example, semantic encoding might allow you to remember that a car was parked in your neighbors' driveway just before their house was robbed. If there was little or no encoding, you might not be able to remember the make, model, or color of the car.

1. **bill·board** (bĭl′bôrd′, -bōrd′) *n.* A large upright board used to display advertisements in public places and alongside highways.

7   The second basic memory process is **storage**, which refers to the maintenance of information over time, often over a very long time. When you find it possible to use a pogo stick[2] or to recall a vacation from many years ago, you are depending on the storage capacity of your memory.

8   The third process, **retrieval**, occurs when you locate information stored in memory and bring it to consciousness. Retrieving stored information such as your address or telephone number is usually so fast and effortless that it seems automatic. Only when you try to retrieve other kinds of information—such as the answer to a quiz question that you know but cannot quite recall—do you become aware of the searching process. Retrieval processes include both recall and recognition. To *recall* information, as on an essay test, you have to retrieve it from memory without much help. *Recognition* is retrieval aided by clues, such as alternatives given in a multiple-choice test item. Accordingly, recognition tends to be easier than recall.

Figure 7.1

Basic Memory Processes

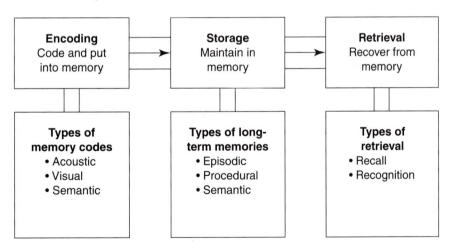

Remembering something requires first that the items be encoded—put in a form that can be placed in memory. It must then be stored and, finally, retrieved, or recovered. If any of these processes fails, forgetting will occur.

2. **po•go stick** (pō′gō stĭk) *n.* A stick with handles, a spring, and footrests used to propel oneself along the ground by hopping.

Types of Memory

9   When was the last time you made a credit card purchase? What part of speech is used to modify a noun? How do you keep your balance when you are skiing? To answer these questions you must use your memory. However, each may require a different type of memory (Brewer & Pani, 1984). To answer the first question, you must remember a particular event in your life; to answer the second one, you must recall a piece of general knowledge that is unlikely to be tied to a specific event. And the answer to the final question is difficult to put into words but appears in the form of your remembered actions when you get up on skis. How many types of memory are there? No one is sure, but most research suggests that there are at least three basic types. Each is named for the kind of information it handles (Reed, 1992).

10   Memory of a specific event that happened while you were present—that is, during an "episode" in your life—is called **episodic memory**. Examples are what you had for dinner yesterday, what you did last summer, or where you were last Friday night. Generalized knowledge of the world that does not involve a specific event is called **semantic memory**. For instance, you can answer a question like "Are wrenches pets or tools?" without remembering any specific event in which you learned that wrenches are tools. As a general rule, people convey episodic memories by saying, "I remember when …," whereas they convey semantic memories by saying, "I know that …" (Tulving, 1982). Finally, memory of how to do things, such as skiing without falling (and riding a bike, reading a map, tying a shoelace) is called **procedural memory**. Often procedural memory consists of a complicated sequence of movements that cannot be described adequately in words. For example, a gymnast might find it impossible to describe the exact motions in a particular routine.

11   Many activities require all three types of memory. Consider the game of tennis. Knowing the official rules, or how many sets are needed to win a match involves semantic memory. Remembering which side served last requires episodic memory. Knowing how to lob or volley involves procedural memory.

Linkages

Learning by Doing

Procedural memories involve skills that can usually be learned only through repetition. This is why parents not only tell children how to tie a shoe but also show them the steps and let them practice. Factors that enhance skill learning are described in Chapter 6.

Explicit and Implicit Memory

12   Memory can be categorized in terms of its effects on thoughts and behaviors. For example, you make use of **explicit memory** when you deliberately try to remember something and are consciously aware of doing so (Masson & MacLeod, 1992). Let's say that someone asks you about your last vacation; as you attempt to remember where you went, you would be using explicit memory to recall this episode from your past. Similarly, if you have to answer a question on an examination, you would be using explicit memory to retrieve the information needed to give the correct answer. In contrast, implicit memory is the unintentional recollection and influence of prior experiences (Nelson, 1999). For example, while watching a movie about a long car trip, you might begin to feel tense because you subconsciously recall the time you had engine trouble on such a trip. But you are not aware that it is this memory that is making you tense. Implicit memory operates automatically and without conscious effort. As another example, perhaps you've found yourself disliking someone you just met, but didn't know why. One explanation is that implicit memory may have been at work. Specifically, you may have reacted in this way because the person bears a resemblance to someone from your past who treated you badly. In such instances, people are usually unable to recall the person from the past and, indeed, are unaware of any connection between the two individuals (Lewicki, 1985). Episodic, semantic, and procedural memories can be explicit or implicit, but procedural memory usually operates implicitly. This is why, for example, you can skillfully ride a bike even though you cannot explicitly remember all of the procedures necessary to do so.

13   It is not surprising that experience affects how people behave. What is surprising is that they are often unaware that their actions

have been influenced by previous events. Because some influential events cannot be recalled even when people try to do so, implicit memory has been said to involve "retention without remembering" (Roediger, 1990).

Making Implicit Memories: By the time they reach adulthood, these children may have no explicit memory of the interaction they had in early childhood with friends from differing ethnic groups, but research suggests that their implicit memories of such experiences could have an unconscious effect on their attitudes toward judgments about members of those groups.

Focus on Research Methods:
Measuring Explicit Versus Implicit Memory

14   In Canada, Endel Tulving and his colleagues undertook a series of experiments to map the differences between explicit and implicit memory (Tulving, Schacter, & Stark, 1982).

■ **What was the researcher's question?**

15   Tulving knew he could measure explicit memory by giving a recognition test in which participants simply said which words on a list they remembered seeing on a previous list. The question was, How would it be possible to measure implicit memory?

■ How did the researcher answer the question?

16   First, Tulving asked the participants in his experiment to study a long list of words—the "study list." An hour later, they took a recognition test involving explicit memory—saying which words on a new list had been on the original study list. Then, to test their implicit memory, Tulving asked them to perform a "fragment completion" task (Warrington & Weiskrantz, 1970). In this task, participants were shown a "test list" of word fragments such as *d-l—iu-*, and asked to complete the word (in this case *delirium*). On the basis of *priming* studies such as those described in Chapter 9, Tulving assumed that memory from a previous exposure to the correct word would improve the participants' ability to complete the fragment, even if they were unable to consciously recall having seen the word before. A week later, all participants took a second test of their explicit memory (recognition) and implicit memory (fragment completion) of the study list. Some of the words on this second test list had been on the original study list, but none had been used in the first set of memory tests. The independent variable in this experiment, then, was the amount of time that elapsed since the participants read the study list (one hour versus one week), and the dependent variable was performance on each of the two types of memory tests, explicit and implicit.

■ What did the researcher find?

17   As shown in Figure 7.2, explicit memory for the study list decreased dramatically over time, but implicit memory was virtually unchanged. Results from several other experiments also show that the passage of time affects one type of memory but not the other (Komatsu & Naito, 1992; Mitchell, 1991). For example, it appears that the aging process has fewer negative effects on implicit memory than explicit memory (Light, 1991).

■ What do the results mean?

18   The work of Tulving and others supports the idea of disassociation, or independence between explicit and implicit memory, suggesting that the two may operate on different principles (Gabrieli et al., 1995). Indeed, some researchers believe that explicit and implicit memory may involve the activity of distinct neural systems in the brain (Squire, 1987; Tulving & Schacter, 1990).

■ **What do we still need to know?**

19   Psychologists are now studying the role of implicit memory (and disassociations between explicit and implicit memory) in such important psychological phenomena as amnesia (Schacter, Church, & Treadwell, 1994; Tulving, 1993), depression (Elliot & Greene, 1992), problem solving (Jacoby, Marriot, & Collins, 1990), prejudice and stereotyping (Fiske, 1998), the development of self-concept in childhood (Nelson, 1993), and even the power of ads to associate brand names with good feelings (Duke & Carlson, 1993). The results of these studies shed new light on implicit memory and how it operates in the real world.

20   While some researchers claim that implicit memory and explicit memory involve different structures in the brain (Schacter, 1992; Squire, 1987; Tulving & Schacter, 1990), others argue that the two types of memory entail different cognitive processes (Nelson, McKinney, & Bennett, in press; Roediger, Guynn, & Jones, 1995). Indeed, some social psychologists are trying to determine whether consciously held attitudes are independent of *implicit social cognitions*—past experiences that unconsciously influence a person's judgments about a group of people (Greenwald & Banaji, 1995). A case in point would be a person whose explicit thoughts about members of some ethnic group are positive, but whose implicit thoughts are negative. Early work on implicit memory for stereotypes seemed to indicate that explicit and implicit stereotypes are indeed independent (Devine, 1989), but more recent research suggests that they are to some extent related (Lepore & Brown, 1997). Further research is needed to determine what mechanisms are responsible for implicit versus explicit memory and how they are related to one another (Nelson et al., in press).

Figure 7.1

Measures of Explicit and Implicit Memory

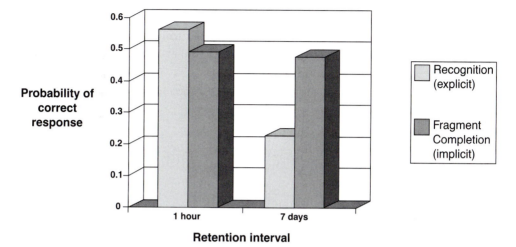

This experiment showed that the passage of time greatly affected people's recognition (explicit memory) of a word list but left fragment completion (implicit memory) essentially in tact. Results such as these suggest that explicit and implicit memory may be different memory.

Source: Bernstein, D. A., Clark-Stewart, A., Penner, L. A., Roy, E. J., & Wickens, C. D. (2000). Psychology (5th ed.) (pp. 214–218). Boston: Houghton Mifflin Company.

Summary

The Nature of Memory

21   Human memory depends on a complex mental system.

Basic Memory Processes

22   There are three basic memory processes. *Encoding* transforms stimulus information into some type of mental representation. Encoding can be *acoustic* (by sound), *visual* (by appearance), or *semantic* (by meaning). *Storage* maintains information in the memory system over time. *Retrieval* is the process of gaining access to previously stored information.

Types of Memory

23   Most psychologists agree that there are at least three types of memory. *Episodic memory* contains information about specific events in a person's life. *Semantic memory* contains generalized knowledge about the world. *Procedural memory* contains information about how to do various things.

Explicit and Implicit Memory

24   Most research on memory has concerned *explicit memory*, the processes through which people deliberately try to remember something. Recently, psychologists have also begun to examine *implicit memory*, which refers to unintentional recollection and influence of prior experiences.

Source: Bernstein, D. A., Clark-Stewart, A., Penner, L. A., Roy, E. J., & Wickens, C. D. (2000). *Psychology* (5th ed.) (p. 246). Boston: Houghton Mifflin Company.

<table>
<tr><td>

**Muscle
Reading
Reminder**

Phase Three:
**Recite
Review
Review
Again**

</td></tr>
</table>

☐ Assessing Your Learning

Demonstrating Comprehension

**Master
Student Tip**

Authors include visual elements in textbooks to help readers see connections among ideas. In this chapter, you have seen illustrations, photographs, and a chart and graph. You have already learned that previewing visual elements before you read results in more effective reading. Reviewing with the visual elements in a chapter is an effective way to deepen your understanding of what you read and to help you remember important concepts.

EXERCISE 8 **Explaining charts and graphs**

Work with a partner. Each one should prepare to explain one of the charts below to the other. Think before you speak. Mentally rehearse your explanation before you tell your partner. Explain the theories about memory in complete sentences.

Student A: Explain Figure 7.1.

Figure 7.1

Basic Memory Processes

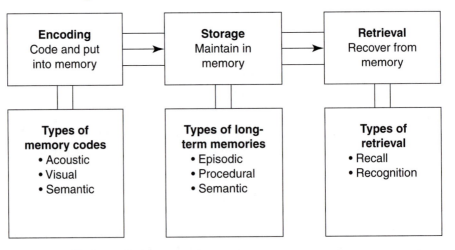

Remembering something requires first that the items be encoded—put in a form that can be placed in memory. It must then be stored and, finally, retrieved, or recovered. If any of these processes fails, forgetting will occur.

Student B: Explain Figure 7.2.

Figure 7.2

Measures of Explicit and Implicit Memory

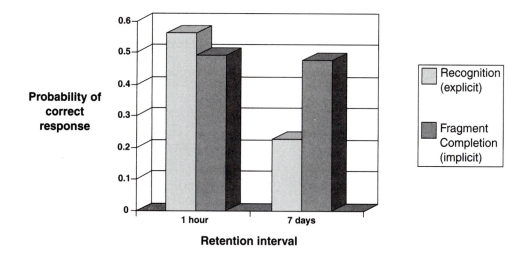

This experiment showed that the passage of time greatly affected people's recognition (explicit memory) of a word list but left fragment completion (implicit memory) essentially in tact. Results such as these suggest that explicit and implicit memory may be different memory.

Tulving, Schacter, & Stark, 1982

EXERCISE **9** **Using a chapter outline to learn and review**

*Before reading Selection 2, you previewed the chapter by looking at the
authors' outline, and you wrote down some questions. Were your questions
answered as you read? Use the outline section below and work with your
partner again to talk through what you learned about memory. If you need
help putting your ideas into complete sentences, look back at the Summary
section at the end of Reading Selection 2. Reread the summary statements
and try to memorize them.*

Chapter 7: Memory

OUTLINE

The Nature of Memory

Basic Memory Processes
Types of Memory
Explicit and Implicit Memory
Focus on Research Methods: Measuring Explicit Versus
Implicit Memory

Student A: Explain Basic Memory Processes.
Student B: Explain Types of Memory.
Student A: Explain Explicit and Implicit Memory.
Student B: Explain Measuring Explicit Versus Implicit Memory.

Memorizing a definition or explanation is only a first step in the
learning process. A valuable technique for learning in a strategic way is to
purposefully associate concepts with meaningful examples. To illustrate,
when the authors discussed the concept of encoding, they used the story
of a billboard with an ad, "Huey's Going Out of Business Sale." Their
example helped you understand acoustic, visual, and semantic encoding. I
still remember when I first learned about encoding and memory. My
instructor suggested a practical application related to parking lots. He said
that when you leave your car, you should look at the number or letter of
the parking area, and also say it out loud. In this way you encode the
information in multiple ways and you are more likely to remember where
you parked. Try it next time you park!

EXERCISE 10 **Using examples to enhance learning**

Brainstorm with your classmates to come up with relevant examples for each concept below. Think about how identifying an example enhances your learning.

1. acoustic encoding *Saying a parking spot number out loud.*

2. visual encoding _____

3. semantic encoding _____

4. storage _____

5. retrieval _____

6. recall _____

7. recognition _____

8. episodic memory _____

9. semantic memory _____

10. procedural memory _____

11. explicit memory _____

12. implicit memory _____

EXERCISE 11 **Associating examples with concepts**

Each student can write one example on a sheet of paper. The examples are passed in, and then read aloud. As each example is read, the class can guess which concept it illustrates. The example "author" should be quiet when her/his example is read.

> *Saying a parking spot number out-loud*

Class response: *acoustic encoding*

☐ Learning Vocabulary

EXERCISE 12   Noticing context to enhance understanding

This exercise includes sentence excerpts from Reading Selection 2. Each sentence contains a vocabulary item that may be new to you. A careful look at the context will provide you with clues for understanding the new word. After reading each sentence, highlight or underline the sentence parts that help you understand the meaning of the unfamiliar vocabulary item. Then explain it in your own words. The first one is done for you as an example.

1. (¶ 2) Memory is full of paradoxes. It is common, for example, for people to remember the name of their first grade teacher, but not the name of someone they just met a minute ago.

   A paradox is something surprising—like why we remember one person's name when we don't remember another person's name.

2. (¶ 2) Like perception, memory is selective. Whereas people retain a great deal of information, they also lose a great deal.

   _____

   _____

3. (¶ 3) Then we examine how new memories are acquired and later recalled, and why they are sometimes forgotten.

   _____

   _____

4. (¶ 4) Mathematician John Griffith estimated that, in an average lifetime, a person will have stored roughly five hundred times as much information as can be found in all of the volumes of the *Encyclopedia Britannica*.

   _____

   _____

5. (¶ 6) In the memory system, sensory information is put into various *memory codes*, which are mental representations of physical stimuli.

   _____

   _____

6. (¶ 6) If you encode the sounds of words as if they had been spoken, you are using acoustic encoding, and the information is represented in your memory as a sequence of sounds.

_____

_____

7. (¶ 6) If you encode the image of the letters as they were arranged on the sign, you are using visual encoding, and the information is represented in your memory as a picture.

_____

_____

8. (¶ 6) Finally, if you encode the fact that you saw an ad for Huey's you are using semantic encoding, and the information is represented in your memory by its general meaning.

_____

_____

9. (¶ 7) The second basic memory process is storage, which refers to the maintenance of information over time, often over a very long time.

_____

_____

10. (¶ 8) The third process, retrieval, occurs when you locate information stored in memory and bring it to consciousness.

_____

_____

11. (¶ 8) Retrieval processes include both recall and recognition. To _recall_ information, as on an essay test, you have to retrieve it from memory without much help. _Recognition_ is retrieval aided by clues, such as alternatives given in a multiple-choice test item. Accordingly, recognition tends to be easier than recall.

_____

_____

EXERCISE 13 Selecting new vocabulary to learn

Return to Reading Selection 2. Begin with paragraph 9. Look for words that are new to you and are important to learn. As you select the words or expressions, identify parts of the text surrounding the new words that can help you understand the meaning of the new words. Make a personal vocabulary list for this chapter. Discriminate active and passive vocabulary choices.

EXERCISE 14 Reviewing academic vocabulary

Listed below are some AWL words from the reading selections. Evaluate your knowledge of each word with the following criteria:

Don't know at all	Recognize but don't know well	Know well	Use in my own writing

Go back to the paragraphs indicated in the table below to see a context for words you want to add to your active vocabulary. Then, try a new strategy for learning these words. Visit the Houghton Mifflin website http://esl.college.hmco.com/students for help in making flash cards.

Reading Selection 1, Chapter 1: Introducing Psychology			
1. detector (¶ 1)	5. chemicals (¶ 2)	9. seeks (¶ 3)	13. contemporary (¶ 3)
2. emerged (¶ 1)	6. factors (¶ 2)	10. processes (¶ 3)	14. phenomena (¶ 3)
3. odd (¶ 1)	7. affected (¶ 2)	11. welfare (¶ 3)	
4. released (¶ 1)	8. recover (¶ 2)	12. diversity (¶ 3)	

Reading Selection 2, The Nature of Memory

1. assumed (¶ 1)	13. capacity (¶ 7)	25. enhance (¶ 11)	37. ethnic (¶ 13)
2. grade (¶ 2)	14. occurs (¶ 8)	26. categorized (¶ 12)	38. attitudes (¶ 13)
3. ratio (¶ 2)	15. automatic (¶ 8)	27. explicit (¶ 12)	39. colleagues (¶ 14)
4. whereas (¶ 2)	16. aided (¶ 8)	28. contrast (¶ 12)	40. undertook (¶ 14)
5. role (¶ 3)	17. alternatives (¶ 8)	29. implicit (¶ 12)	41. series (¶ 14)
6. unaware (¶ 3)	18. purchase (¶ 9)	30. prior (¶ 12)	42. participant (¶ 15)
7. acquired (¶ 3)	19. modify (¶ 9)	31. tense (¶ 12)	43. variable (¶ 16)
8. estimated (¶ 4)	20. involve (¶ 10)	32. reacted (¶ 12)	44. dramatically (¶ 17)
9. physical (¶ 6)	21. instance (¶ 10)	33. affects (¶ 13)	45. depression (¶ 19)
10. stimuli (¶ 6)	22. procedural (¶ 10)	34. retention (¶ 13)	46. stereotypes (¶ 20)
11. sequence (¶ 6)	23. consists (¶ 10)	35. adulthood (¶ 13)	47. mechanism (¶ 20)
12. maintenance (¶ 7)	24. adequately (¶ 10)	36. interaction (¶ 13)	

Identifying new words to learn from a word list can be helpful, but words are not used in isolation. When we communicate, many different word combinations are possible. Some word combinations, though, are more probable than others; that is, some combinations occur more frequently than others and feel more natural together for users of the language. The arrangement of how words "co-occur" or "co-locate" is called collocation. For example, the word *detector* in paragraph 1 is frequently put together with the word *metal*. In English, you could commonly hear people say: "metal detector," but they wouldn't usually say "gun detector" even though a metal detector could be used to locate the presence of a gun.

EXERCISE 15   **Working with academic words in collocations**

In this exercise, common collocations are provided to practice with nouns from the academic words in the list above. Fill in each blank with the best choice. The first one has been done for you as an example. Choose from the nouns listed in the box.

alternative	factors	ratio
attitude	instances	stereotypes
chemicals	mechanism	stimuli
depression	participant	variable
detector	phenomena	welfare

	Common expressions before	Nouns
1	to look for, propose, seek, or suggest (a/an)	*alternative*
2	the right, an open, a flexible, a positive, or a negative	
3	to recover from, be affected by, or suffer from	
4	a natural, mysterious, odd, or psychological	
5	an independent or dependent	
6	a simple, useful, complicated, or a defense	
7	an active, eager, reluctant, (un)willing	
8	a metal, or a smoke	
9	social, public, economic, individual, or human	
10	environmental or physical	
11	in similar, in certain, in some	
12	harsh, noxious, or toxic	

> Whenever you encounter new words, think about which words commonly collocate with your new words. Understanding word associations can help you learn, remember, and use new words.

☐ Focusing on Psychology

Cited References and Research Themes

As you read Selection 2, you probably noticed references from the works of many psychology researchers. When psychology students and instructors discuss theories or consider research, they recognize the importance of knowing about experiments and studies that support the theories. If a theory is well researched, they can have greater confidence in accepting it as credible.

Paragraph 2 on page 98 has two references cited. This paragraph is repeated below to help you see the connection between the sources and the studies or theoretical concepts for which the researchers are cited.

2   Memory is full of paradoxes. It is common, for example, for people to remember the name of their first grade teacher, but not the name of someone they just met a minute ago. And consider Rajan Mahadevan. He once set a world's record by reciting from memory the first 31,811 places for pi (the ratio of the circumference of a circle to its diameter), but on repeated visits to the psychology building at the University of Minnesota, he had trouble recalling the location of the nearest restroom (Biederman et al., 1992). Like perception, memory is selective. Whereas people retain a great deal of information, they also lose a great deal (Bjork & Vanhuele, 1992).

The expression *et al.* is Latin for "and others." Checking the references section at the end of the psychology textbook, one finds:

> Biederman, I., Cooper, E. E., Fox, P. W., & Mahadevan, R. S. (1992). Unexceptional spatial memory in an exceptional memorist. *Journal of Experimental Psychology: Learning, Memory, and Cognition, 18,* 654–657.

This reference indicates that four researchers contributed to the article about their research on this paradox of memory: Biederman, Cooper, Fox, and Mahadevan. What was their research about? They observed paradoxes in Mahadevan's memory abilities. They contrasted his ability to remember the first 31,811 places for pi, with his inability to remember how to get to the nearest restroom. What does this prove?

_____

_____

The second cited source is Bjork & Vanhuele, 1992. This study is about the selective nature of memory. Even though we have not read the study or looked up the title in the references section, we can tell it supports the finding that people retain some information in their memories and lose other information.

Here is another example, from paragraph 3:

---

3   Memory plays a critical role in your life. Without memory, you would not know how to shut off your alarm clock, take a shower, get dressed, or recognize objects. You would be unable to communicate with other people because you would not remember what words mean, or even what you had just said. You would be unaware of your own likes and dislikes, and you would have no idea who you are in any meaningful sense (Kihlstrom, 1993).

With what general idea about memory is Kihlstrom associated?

_____

_____

EXERCISE 16   Matching cited sources and research themes

Listed in the box are cited sources from Selection 2. The paragraph where the citation is located follows the source for your reference. Match each cited source with the correct theory, study, or ideas associated with the researcher(s). You will need to reread the paragraphs indicated in order to do this exercise. Note that some letters will be selected more than once.

Matching Chart			
Cited sources	**Paragraph number**		**Associated research theme**
1. Kihlstrom, 1993	(¶ 3)	D	**A.** Connections between resemblances & implicit memories
2. Brewer & Pani, 1984	(¶ 9)		**B.** Explicit memory
3. Reed, 1992	(¶ 9)		**C.** Implicit memory
4. Tulving, 1982	(¶ 10)		**D.** Memory and identity
5. Masson & MacLeod, 1992	(¶ 12)		**E.** Semantic vs. episodic memory
6. Nelson, 1999	(¶ 12)		**F.** Types of memory
7. Lewicki, 1985	(¶ 12)		
8. Roediger, 1990	(¶ 13)		

EXERCISE 17   Expressing research themes of cited sources

*Return to the **Focus on Research** section, paragraphs 14 to 20. Notice how many sources are cited in this part of the chapter. Explain the connections between the cited references to research themes.*

Example:

Tulving, Schacter, & Stark contrasted explicit and implicit memory.

☐ Assessing Your Learning at the End of a Chapter

Revisiting Chapter Objectives

Return to the first page of this chapter. Think about the chapter objectives. Put a check mark next to the ones you feel secure about. Review material in the chapter you still need to work on. When you are ready, complete the chapter review items below.

☐ Practicing for a Chapter Test

EXERCISE 18 **Reviewing comprehension**

Check your comprehension of main concepts, or ideas, in this chapter by responding to the following chapter review items.

1. Write a list of survey questions you could ask students at your college about a study area of interest to you.

2. What did you learn about students and their majors from the mini-field study you conducted at the beginning of this chapter? Identify and compare two resources at your college that can help students in making and evaluating decisions about their majors and career goals.

3. Contrast narrative and scientific text styles.

4. Define psychology.

5. Describe three basic memory processes.

6. Contrast three primary types of memory.

7. Contrast explicit and implicit memory.

8. The graph below comes from a later section in the psychology chapter. Although you have not read this section, use the information provided to comment on primacy and recency effect and memory.

Figure 7.9

A Serial Position Curve

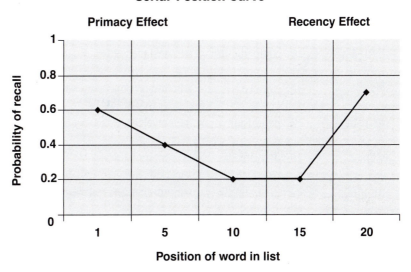

The probability of recalling an item is plotted here as a function of its serial position in a list of items. Generally, the first several items and the last several items are most likely to be recalled.

Academic Vocabulary

Here are some academic vocabulary words you learned in this chapter. Put a check mark next to words you know the meaning of. Identify words you need more practice with. Look for these words whenever you read. Use them when you speak and write. For extra practice, identify the part of speech and one related word form for each word listed.

Example:

Acquired is a verb. Two related forms are acquire and acquires.

1. acquired	13. colleagues	25. explicit	37. phenomena	49. seeks
2. adequately	14. conclude	26. facto	38. physical	50. selective
3. adulthood	15. consists	27. implicit	39. prior	51. sequence
4. affected	16. contemporary	28. instance	40. procedural	52. similar
5. aided	17. contrast	29. interaction	41. processes	53. stereotypes
6. alternatives	18. depression	30. involve	42. purchase	54. stimuli
7. assumed	19. detector	31. maintenance	43. ratio	55. tense
8. attitudes	20. dramatically	32. mechanism	44. reacted	56. unaware
9. aware	21. emerged	33. modify	45. recover	57. undertook
10. capacity	22. enhance	34. occurs	46. released	58. variable
11. categorized	23. estimated	35. odd	47. retention	59. welfare
12. chemicals	24. ethnic	36. participant	48. role	60. whereas

WEB POWER

Go to http://esl.college.hmco.com/students to view
more readings and activities for learning about
psychology and the nature of memory.

Chapter 4

Leaving Footprints: Nature's Memory

ACADEMIC FOCUS: ENVIRONMENTAL SCIENCE

Academic Reading Objectives

After completing this chapter, you should be able to:

✓ Check here as you master each objective.

1. Identify changes in purpose or tone ☐
2. Relate personal-experience knowledge to readings ☐
3. Distinguish important information to include in process diagrams or charts ☐
4. Articulate cause-effect relationships ☐
5. Apply knowledge gained by connecting ideas from one reading selection to another ☐
6. Apply new strategies for improving vocabulary ☐

Environmental Science Objectives

1. Define environmental science and give examples of work done by environmental scientists ☐
2. Explain environmental sustainability ☐
3. Discuss controversial environmental issues ☐
4. Analyze governmental roles ☐
5. Assess environmental problems and generated solutions ☐
6. Identify the steps in the scientific method ☐

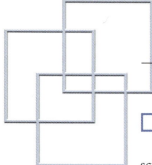

Reading Assignment 1

ENVIRONMENTAL SCIENCE

☐ Getting Ready to Read

The first sentence of the reading selection describes environmental science this way:

> How humans can best live within the Earth's environment is the theme of what is loosely called environmental science, the interdisciplinary study of humanity's relationship with other organisms and the non-living physical environment.

The reading then lists several sciences and academic disciplines that contribute to environmental science. In Exercise 1, you test your knowledge of these different areas.

EXERCISE 1 Understanding science disciplines

The left column in the box is a list of disciplines that contribute to environmental science. How many of these do you know already? Work with a partner and try to match the discipline with its description. When you finish, compare your list with those of your classmates.

Matching chart	
Discipline	**The science or study of …**
1. agriculture	__5__ human populations
2. biology	_____ growing food and farming
3. chemistry	_____ morals, values, and behavior
4. cultural anthropology	_____ how matter is structured
5. demography	_____ the production, distribution, and consumption of goods and services
6. ecology	_____ life and living organisms
7. economics	_____ Earth's features, climates, and peoples
8. engineering	_____ human relationships in society
9. ethics	_____ the design of machines, roads, waterways, & bridges
10. geography	_____ matter and energy
11. geology	_____ relationships between organisms and environments
12. law	_____ human behavior specific to a country, or people
13. natural resources of	_____ control & supervision of parts management the natural environment such as water, forests, & agriculture
14. physics	_____ Earth's structure and history
15. politics	_____ rules of conduct and justice systems
16. sociology	_____ the structure of government

EXERCISE 2   **Participating in class discussion**

Before you read Selection 1, discuss the following questions with a partner and the rest of your classmates.

1. Which of the disciplines in Exercise 1 are new to you?
2. Were you surprised that environmental science includes disciplines like law, ethics, and politics? Why or Why not?
3. Make a list of things you think environmental scientists do.

☐ Reading for a Purpose

Does the natural world have a memory? The record of Earth's memory is around us every day, in a tree stump or a polluted lake or the footprints we leave behind when we walk on the beach. Environmental scientists study the results of human interaction with Earth and try to restore the natural balance. As you read Selection 1, think about how Earth's memory affects you in your everyday life.

The word **sustain** means to support or strengthen somebody or something so that it can stay alive or keep going. For example, you are sustained by food. One main concern of environmental scientists is "environmental sustainability." You will read Selection 1 to find out what environmental sustainability is. After you read, be prepared to write a definition of environmental sustainability in your own words.

☐ Reading the Selection

The reading selections in this chapter are from a textbook written for college students. Reading Selection 1 comes from Chapter 1, an introductory chapter. The subsequent reading selections are from later chapters about controversial environmental issues and a pollution control project. Two reminders: (1) Words with a dotted underline are AWL words, commonly found in academic texts across disciplines; and (2) It is helpful to underline in two colors—one for important content and another for useful new words to learn.

Reading Selection 1

OUR CHANGING ENVIRONMENT

Environmental Science

1 How humans can best live within the Earth's environment is the theme of what is loosely called environmental science, the interdisciplinary study of humanity's relationship with other organisms[1] and the non-living physical environment. Environmental science is interdisciplinary because it uses and combines information from many disciplines, such as biology (particularly ecology), geography, chemistry, geology, physics, economics, sociology (particularly demography, the study of populations), cultural anthropology, natural resources management, agriculture, engineering, law, politics, and ethics.

2 Environmental science encompasses[2] many complex and interconnected problems involving human population, Earth's natural resources, and environment pollution. Pollution is any alteration of air, water, or soil that harms the health, survival, or activities of humans and other living organisms.

Environmental Sustainability

3 One of the most important and most frequently used terms in environmental science is environmental sustainability. Broadly speaking, environmental sustainability is the ability of the environment to function indefinitely without going into a decline from the stresses imposed by human society on natural systems (such as soil, water, and air) that maintain life. When the environment is used sustainably, humanity's present needs are met without endangering the welfare of future generations. Environmental sustainability applies at many levels, including community, regional, national, and global levels.

1. **or•gan•ism** (ôr′gə-nĭz′əm) *n.* A living thing, such as a plant or animal.
2. **en•com•pass** (ĕn-kŭm′pəs) *v.* To include; surround.

4   Many experts in environmental science think that human society is
not operating sustainably because of the following human behaviors:
1. We are using non-renewable resources such as fossil fuels[3] as
    if they were present in unlimited supplies.
2. We are using renewable resources such as fresh water faster
    than they can be replenished[4] naturally.
3. We are polluting the environment with toxins as if the
    capacity of the environment to absorb[5] them were limitless.
4. Our population continues to grow despite the Earth's finite
    ability to support us.

5   If left unchecked, these activities may reach the point of
environmental catastrophe,[6] threatening the life-support systems of
the Earth to the extent that recovery is impossible.

6   At first glance, the issues may seem simple. Why don't we just
stop the over-consumption, population growth, and pollution?
These solutions are more complex than they may initially seem, in
part because of various interactions among ecological, social,
cultural, and economic factors. Our inadequate understanding of
how the complex, dynamic environment "works" and how different
human choice affect the environment is a major reason that
problems of environmental sustainability are difficult to resolve.
Because of the effects of many interactions between the
environment and humans are unknown or difficult to predict, we
generally do not know if corrective actions should be taken
before—or after—our scientific understanding is complete.

7   The key challenge, then, is to meet immediate human needs
while protecting the environment for the long term. We try to
present a balanced evaluation of the many causes of environmental
problems. We also provide the scientific foundation to evaluate
these problems, and we suggest various courses of action based on
our current understanding of the environment.

Raven, P. H., & Berg, L. R. (2001). *Environment* (3rd ed.)(pp. 5–6). Hoboken, NJ:
John Wiley & Sons.

3. **fos•sil fu•el** (fŏs′əl fyo͞o′ əl) *n.* Material left of or by a plant or animal that lived
    long ago that burns, such as natural gas, petroleum, and coal.
4. **re•plen•ish** (rĭ-plĕn′ĭsh) *tr.v.* To restore a supply of something.
5. **ab•sorb** (əb-sôrb′) *v.* To soak up or take in.
6. **ca•tas•tro•phe** (kə-tăs′trə-fē) *n.* A great, often sudden, disaster.

☐ Assessing Your Learning

Demonstrating Comprehension

EXERCISE 3 Checking comprehension

Check your understanding of Selection 1 by answering the following questions. First try to answer the questions 1–3 without going back to the selection. Then go back to the selection to see what information you forgot. Add information to your answers. Respond to questions 4–5 based on your own experience.

1. In your own words, write the meaning of "environmental sustainability."

2. What are some human actions that threaten environmental sustainability?

3. Why are environmental problems difficult to solve?

4. Can you think of an environmental problem that is a concern in the area where you live now?

5. Can you think of an environmental problem that was a concern in an area where you lived before?

EXERCISE 4 Recognizing an author's purpose

The purpose or reason why an author writes a text can vary. The author might write a text to give information, or to convince the reader to change his or her mind or behavior, or simply to entertain the reader. In Selection 1, the authors have more than one purpose.

Review the selection. Complete the chart on the next page by identifying the authors' purpose for each paragraph, and then explain what words in the paragraph are clues to the authors' purpose. The first and last have been done for you as examples.

Paragraph	Authors' purpose (inform or persuade)	Why did you choose this purpose?
¶ 1	Inform	They define words and give examples.
¶ 2		
¶ 3		
¶ 4		
¶ 5		
¶ 6		
¶ 7	Provide an overview	They identify three broad goals.

EXERCISE 5   **Recognizing a change in tone**

In Reading Selection 1, the authors' tone also changes. Contrast paragraph 6 with paragraphs 1 and 2. How are they different? What words are clues to the tone of each paragraph?

_____

_____

☐ Focusing on Science

In science textbooks, it is important to know the exact meaning of concept words. Science textbooks often use direct context clues so that the exact definition of a word is clear. Sometimes the other words in a sentence will tell exactly what the word means, and other times you can understand the meaning from examples in the sentence.

EXERCISE 6   Learning science vocabulary

*Read the sentences below. Underline or highlight the words that help you understand the meaning of the **bold** words. Write D in front of the sentence if the clue is a definition. Write E in front of the sentence if the clue is an example. The first one has been done for you as an example.*

1.   __D__   How humans can best live within the Earth's environment is the theme of what is loosely called **environmental science** . . .

2.   _____   Environmental science is **interdisciplinary** because it uses and combines information from many disciplines.

3.   _____   **Pollution** is any alteration of air, water, or soil that harms the health, survival, or activities of humans and other living organisms.

4.   _____   Broadly speaking, **environmental sustainability** is the ability of the environment to function indefinitely without going into a decline from the stresses imposed by human society on natural systems (such as soil, water, and air) that maintain life.

5.   _____   We are using **non-renewable** resources such as fossil fuels as if they were present in unlimited supplies.

6.   _____   We are using **renewable** resources such as fresh water faster than they can be replenished naturally.

☐ Learning Vocabulary

STRATEGY

Reading Strategy

The base form of a word is called the root word or headword. Word families can be built from each headword by adding affixes to the word. A prefix comes *before* the headword, and a suffix comes *at the end of* a headword. Usually, one form of a word is more common and familiar than other forms. Knowing different word forms can enrich your vocabulary.

EXERCISE **7**   **Studying a common prefix**

For this exercise, you will work with the common prefix, inter-.

1. Find these words in the text and explain the meaning of each word.

   interdisciplinary (¶ 1) _____

   _____

   interconnected (¶ 2) _____

   _____

   interactions (¶ 6) _____

   _____

2. Identify the headword for each word.

   interdisciplinary (¶ 1) _____

   interconnected (¶ 2) _____

   interactions (¶ 6) _____

3. Write a collocation for each word.

   (¶ 1) _Environmental science is interdisciplinary._____

   interconnected (¶ 2) _____

   _____

   interactions (¶ 6) _____

   _____

4. List three other words that begin with *inter-*.

   _____

   _____

   _____

EXERCISE 8   Studying common suffixes

For this exercise, you will work with three common suffixes.

1. Find five words in paragraph 1 that end with the suffix *-ology*.

    _____

    _____

    _____

    _____

    _____

2. What does *-ology* mean?

    _____

3. Find four words in paragraph 1 that end with the suffix *-ics*.

    _____

    _____

    _____

    _____

4. What does *-ics* mean? _____

5. Find three words in paragraph 6 that end with the suffix *-ic*.

    _____

    _____

    _____

6. What does *-ic* mean? _____

EXERCISE 9 Reviewing academic vocabulary

Listed below are some AWL words from the reading selections. Evaluate your knowledge of each word. Review the paragraphs indicated to see the words in context again. Decide which ones you want to add to your active vocabulary

Reading Selection 1, Our Changing Environment			
1. physical (¶ 1)	**7.** indefinitely (¶ 3)	**13.** finite (¶ 4)	**19.** inadequate (¶ 6)
2. resources (¶ 1)	**8.** decline (¶ 3)	**14.** issues (¶ 6)	**20.** dynamic (¶ 6)
3. ethics (¶ 1)	**9.** imposed (¶ 3)	**15.** consumption (¶ 6)	**21.** resolve (¶ 6)
4. survival (¶ 2)	**10.** generations (¶ 3)	**16.** initially (¶ 6)	**22.** challenge (¶ 7)
5. sustainability (¶ 3)	**11.** regional (¶ 3)	**17.** interactions (¶ 6)	**23.** foundation (¶ 7)
6. function (¶ 3)	**12.** global (¶ 3)	**18.** factors (¶ 6)	

Select five AWL words you want to learn well. Create a graphic organizer for each word with the following parts:

- Example sentence or phrase
- Words commonly found with that word (collocations)
- Related word forms
- Synonyms of the word

Use a dictionary to find the information you need. Here is an example of how to make a graphic organizer for a word:

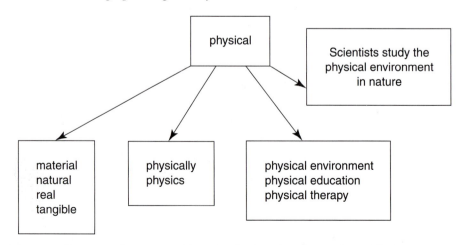

☐ Questions for Discussion

EXERCISE 10 **Thinking about behaviors**

Paragraph 6 of Selection 1 asks, "Why don't we just stop the over-consumption, population growth, and pollution?" Work with a group of three or four other students. Discuss this question. In the chart below, list reasons why it is difficult to stop these human behaviors. Then make a list of what you might do in your own lives to make changes.

	Overconsumption	Population growth	Pollution
Why is it difficult to stop these behaviors?			
What can you change in your lives?			

☐ Linking Concepts

STRATEGY

Reading Actively

One way to improve your reading comprehension is to be an active reader. Active readers try to make connections between the reading text and what they already know, their prior knowledge. This process helps them understand and remember what they have read.

EXERCISE **11** **Relating personal knowledge to reading**

Paragraph 4 in Selection 1, includes a list of ways that human society is not operating sustainably. Make connections between the text and what you already know by completing this chart with two of your own examples to illustrate each point. After you finish, compare your answers with your classmates' answers.

Ways we are not operating sustainably	Examples
1. We are using non-renewable resources such as fossil fuels as if they were present in unlimited supplies.	1. In the United States, people use cars rather than public transportation; this wastes gas. 2.
2. We are using renewable resources such as fresh water faster than they can be replenished naturally.	1. 2.
3. We are polluting the environment with toxins as if the capacity of the environment to absorb them were limitless.	1. 2.
4. Our population continues to grow despite Earth's finite ability to support us.	1. 2.

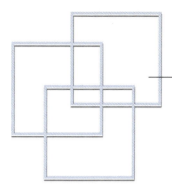

Reading Assignment 2

OLD-GROWTH FORESTS OF THE PACIFIC NORTHWEST

☐ Getting Ready to Read

EXERCISE 12 **Participating in class discussion**

Look at the photographs above. They show traditional and modern logging. Discuss the following questions.

1. What is logging, and what do loggers do?
2. What products come from logging?
3. What happens to the land after logging occurs?
4. What might be a point of conflict between environmentalists and loggers?

☐ Reading for a Purpose

EXERCISE **13** **Listing details**

*Prepare separate paper to keep next to you as you read this selection. As
you read, make a list of things the loggers wanted or were concerned about,
and do the same for the environmentalists. This listing of details will help
you better understand both sides of a controversial issue.*

Loggers	Environmentalists
jobs	forest habitat

Old-growth forests
are found along the
Pacific coast of the
United States from
Alaska to Northern
California.

Reading Selection 2

OLD-GROWTH FORESTS OF THE PACIFIC NORTHWEST

1   Although legislative approaches have generally been effective in
dealing with environmental problems, some issues are so
contentious that they are difficult to resolve. One such controversy
escalated during the late 1980's and 1990's in western Oregon,
Washington, and northern California and continues today. The media
portrayed this issue as a drama that pitted people's livelihoods[1]
against the environment. At stake were thousands of jobs and the
future of large tracts of old-growth (virgin) coniferous[2] forest, along
with the existence of organisms that depend on the forest. One of
these forest animals, the northern spotted owl, came to symbolize the

1. **live•li•hood** (līv′lē-hŏŏd′) *n.* Ways of earning money to live.
2. **co•nif•er•ous** (kō-nĭf′ər-əs) *adj.* Having needles and pine cones, chiefly
   evergreen.

confrontation because of its dependence on mature forest for habitat.[3] These birds are species that usually need large areas of intact forest to supply them with food such as flying squirrels and red tree voles (a mouse-like animal). The northern spotted owl is currently listed as a threatened species under the Endangered Species Act.[4]

The Environmental Significance of Old-Growth Forests

2   Old-growth forests, by definition, have never been logged. They are very different from forests that were logged and have re-grown. For one thing, many of the redwoods and sequoias in old-growth forests are ancient—some as old as 2000 years. Many trees have attained immense sizes. Some Douglas firs, for example are 91 m (300 ft) tall and 4.9 m (16 ft) in diameter. Old-growth forests usually contain trees of the same age and size.

3   Because most of the forests in the United States have been logged at one time or another, the amount of old-growth forest represents a small fraction of the total forested area in the United States. This fraction is decreasing because old-growth forests in the United States are found only in the Pacific Northwest and Alaska.

4   Biologists regard the remaining old-growth forest of Douglas fir, coastal redwoods, sequoias, and spruce in the Pacific Northwest as living laboratories. These forests demonstrate the complexity of a natural ecosystem[5] that has not been extensively altered by humans. When one of the ancient trees dies, for example, it eventually crashes to the ground, felling other trees in its path. This provides an open area in the forest canopy.[6] Sunlight penetrates the ground floor, and plants grow in profusion,

3. **hab·i·tat** (hăb´ĭ-tăt´) *n.* The area or natural environment in which an animal or a plant normally lives or grows.
4. **En·dan·gered Spe·cies Act** 1973 law that requires the government to protect a plant or an animal whose population is so low that it is in danger of becoming extinct.
5. **e·co·sys·tem** (ĕ´kō-sĭs´təm) *n.* The community of a certain area that includes the plants, animals, microorganisms, and physical environment.
6. **can·o·py** (kăn´ə-pē) *n.* The uppermost layer in a forest, formed by the upper branches of the trees.

providing food for many forest animals. The fallen tree also provides habitat for many organisms. Voles, for example, live in crevices[7] provided by the rotting log. Voles are an essential part of the forest because they feed on certain fungi. Undigested fungal spores[8] are spread throughout the forest in vole droppings.[9] These fungi form associations with tree roots and provide the trees with mineral nutrients released from the fallen tree as it decays.

Old-growth forest

5   To environmentalists, the old-growth forests are a national treasure to be protected and cherished. These stable forest ecosystems provide the primary biological habitats for many species, including the northern spotted owl and 40 other endangered or threatened species. Provisions of the Endangered Species Act require the government to protect the habitat of endangered species so that their numbers can increase. To enforce this law, in 1991 a court ordered the suspension of logging in about 1.2 million hectares of federal forest where the owl lives.

The Commercial Significance of Old-Growth Forests

Northern spotted owl

6   The timber[10] industry bitterly opposed the 1991 moratorium,[11] stating that thousands of jobs would be lost if the northern spotted owl habitat were to be set aside. Many rural communities in the Pacific Northwest did not have diversified economies; timber was their main source of revenue. Thus, a major confrontation over the future of the old-growth forest ensued between the timber industry and environmentalists. Strong feelings were expressed on both sides—witness the bumper sticker reading: "Save a logger, kill an owl."

7. **crev•ic** (krĕv′ĭs) *n.* Narrow cracks or openings.
8. **fun•gal spores** (fŭng′gəl spôrz) *n.* Small, usually single-celled reproductive bodies of a fungus (e.g., mushroom).
9. **drop•pings** (drŏp′ingz) *n.* The waste matter from the bowels of animals.
10. **tim•ber** (tĭm′bər) *n.* The wood from trees before it has been processed into building materials.
11. **mor•a•to•ri•um** (môr′ə-tôr′ē-əm) *n.* A suspension or ban of some activity, preventing an action from taking place for a period of time.

Complexities of the Controversy that Were Seldom Portrayed by the Media

7   The situation was more complex than simply jobs versus the owl, however. The timber industry was already declining in terms of its ability to support people in the Pacific Northwest. During the decade between 1977 and 1987, logging in Oregon's national forests increased by over 15%, whereas employment dropped by 15%—an estimated 12,000 jobs—during the same period. The main cause of this decline was automation of the timber industry. In addition, the timber industry in that region had not been operating sustainably—that is, they removed trees faster than the forest could regenerate.[12] If the industry continued to log at their 1980's rates, most of the remaining old-growth forests would have disappeared within 20 years.

8   Timber is not as important to the economy of the Pacific Northwest as it used to be, a change that began long before the northern spotted owl controversy. States in the Pacific Northwest diversified, and by the late 1980's, the timber industry's share of the economy in Oregon and Washington was less than 4%. Although some had predicted economic disaster in 1991 when logging was blocked in the old-growth forest, Oregon's unemployment rate in 1994 was the lowest in 25 years. Oregon attracted several high-technology companies, which produced more jobs than had been lost from logging. (Interestingly, a 1994 analysis by the Institute for Southern Studies concluded that states that protect their natural resources and have good environmental records have the best long-term prospects for economic development. An important factor in Oregon's economic growth is its quality of life, which in turn, is a result of its forests and other natural resources.)

The Political Solution to the Controversy

9   In 1993, President Clinton convened a much-publicized timber summit in Portland, Oregon, with members from all sides of the issue. The 1994 Northwest Forest Plan that arose from this summit represented a compromise[13] between environmental and timber interests. A federal judge approved the plan in December 1994.

12. **re•gen•er•ate** (rĭ-jĕn′ ə-rāt′) *v.* To grow again, re-create.
13. **com•pro•mise** (kŏm′prə-mīz) *n.* A settlement of an argument in which each side gives up some of what it wants.

10   Thanks to a healthy infusion of federal aid to the area, some timber workers were retrained for other kinds of careers. State programs, such as the "Jobs for the Environment" project funded by the state of Washington, also helped reduce unemployment. Hundreds of former loggers were employed by "Jobs for the Environment" and similar programs to restore watersheds[14] and salmon habitat in the forests they used to harvest.

11   As a result of the Northwest Forest Plan, logging was resumed on federal forests of Washington, Oregon, and northern California. However, only about one fifth of the logging that occurred during the 1980's was permitted. The plan, along with previous congressional and administrative action, reserved about 75% of federal timber lands to safeguard watersheds and provide protection for the northern spotted owl and other species, including salmon and other fishes.

12   As happens with many compromises, neither environmentalists nor timber-cutting interests were happy with the Northwest Forest Plan. Some environmentalists did not think the plan was scientifically sound and worried that it took too many risks with conservation values. Timber-cutting interests challenged the legality of the plan and tried to revoke[15] or revise the laws that restricted logging. They proposed turning over a significant area of federal timberlands to local counties, where timber interests have more political clout.[16] They also asked Congress to pass legislation allowing a greater harvest of timber because of the economic hardship.

13   Responding to powerful timber interests, a controversial bill that permitted salvage logging[17] in national forests was signed into law in 1995. The law allowed loggers to cut dead trees and trees weakened by insects, disease, or fire, as well as "associated trees," healthy trees considered to be in danger of catching a disease. The law, which expired at the end of 1996, allowed loggers access to parts of the forest that had been declared off-limits by the Northwest Forest Plan as well as other national forest areas not normally open to logging. It also exempted timber companies from complying with provisions of the Clean Water Act and Endangered Species Act.

14. **wa•ter•shed** (wô′tər-shĕd′) *n.* Mountains or other high places whose water drains into a river, river system, or other body of water.
15. **re•voke** (rĭ-vōk′) *v.* To make something void by reversing, recalling, or withdrawing; cancel.
16. **po•lit•i•cal clout** (pə-lĭt′ĭ-kəl-klout) *n.* The power and influence of a government or politician.
17. **sal•vage log•ging** (săl′vĭj lô′gĭng) *n.* Logging the damaged trees.

14   Forestry scientists and environmentalists opposed the salvage logging law because dead and diseased trees have important ecological roles in forests. Taxpayer advocates, such as the National Taxpayers Union, opposed the law because it costs taxpayers money. The U.S. Forest Service annually spends millions of dollars more to harvest trees in national forests than it earns from the timber sales. In 1994, for example, the federal government spent $100 million to build and maintain roads through national forests; timber companies haul lumber on these roads. Taxpayer advocates[18] consider road construction in national forests a subsidy to the timber industry because it did not pay for any of the road construction or repair costs. In 1999 a federal judge ruled the U.S. Forest Service and Bureau of Land Management, the two government agencies overseeing logging of old-growth forests on federal land, had not adequately carried out the provisions of the 1994 Northwest Forest Plan. Specifically, the Northwest Forest Plan had required that the federal agencies complete extensive surveys of 77 local endangered and threatened species before granting the timber industry permission to log. The judge agreed with the 13 environmental groups that brought the suit against the federal agencies that the agencies had failed to complete the surveys. This ruling triggered a new round of bitter legal battles between timber interests and environmentalists in the Pacific Northwest.

An Economic Case for Preserving Old-Growth Forests

15   According to environmental economists, the old-growth forests that remain should not be logged because a cost-benefit analysis indicated the resulting loss to society is too great. Not only do taxpayers subsidize the timber industry, but the financial benefits associated with preserving these forests (such as protection of species and increased recreation) also outweigh the cost of preservation (such as loss of logging jobs and an increased price of wood). There are so few intact old-growth forests that the cost of losing even a single stand[19] is unacceptably high. The public is therefore willing to pay a great deal to preserve any remaining old-growth forests.

Raven, P. H., & Berg, L. R. (2001). *Environment* (3rd ed.)(pp. 54–57). Hoboken, NJ: John Wiley & Sons.

18. **tax•pay•er ad•vo•cate** (tăks′pā′ər ăd′və-kāt) *n.* Someone who supports or works for taxpayers.
19. **stand** (stănd) *n.* A group or growth of tall plants or trees.

☐ Assessing Your Learning

Demonstrating Comprehension

EXERCISE 14   **Answering multiple-choice questions**

Check your understanding of Reading Selection 2 by choosing the best answer for the following items. First try to answer the questions without going back to the selection. Then go back to the text to find any additional information you need.

1. What were the two sides of the controversy?
   a. Legislatures against loggers
   b. Washington and Oregon against California
   c. Loggers' jobs against forest preservation
   d. Northern spotted owl against the Endangered Species Act

2. The difference between old-growth forests and other forests is that old-growth forests
   a. are bigger and more common.
   b. have sequoias and Douglas firs.
   c. were logged and replenished.
   d. have never been logged.

3. Voles are important because they
   a. are eaten by owls.
   b. spread fungal spores in the forest.
   c. live in rotting logs.
   d. only live in old-growth forests.

4. Why do environmentalists want to protect old-growth forests?
   a. Many threatened species will become extinct if they lose their habitats.
   b. They want the court-ordered suspension of logging.
   c. The owl lives in federal forest land.
   d. Northern spotted owls are the most important animals in the forest.

5. Why are old-growth forests important to the timber industry?
   a. These forests could be a source of revenue and jobs.
   b. The old-growth trees are of higher quality than those in other forests.
   c. These forests are a source of major confrontation.
   d. People care about what happens to the northern spotted owl.

6. We can infer that even if those in the timber industry had been allowed to cut down the trees in old-growth forests, many loggers would still have lost their jobs.
   a. True   b. False

7. Which of the following was part of the compromise that was reached in 1994?
   a. Loggers were retrained for other careers.
   b. Permitted logging was reduced to one-fifth of what it had been in the 1980s.
   c. About 75 percent of federal forests were protected from logging.
   d. All of the above

8. Salvage logging was seen as a good thing by Congress, loggers, and forestry scientists.
   a. True   b. False

9. According to some taxpayer advocates, how does the government subsidize the timber industry?
   a. It gives money to the loggers who cut the most trees.
   b. It builds and maintains roads that loggers use to remove the timber.
   c. It contributes funding for the costs of the court cases.
   d. All of the above

10. According to Reading Selection 2, there are more economic benefits to preserving old-growth forest than there are logging old-growth forests.
    a. True   b. False

☐ Focusing on Science

Reading Selection 2 mentions several kinds of animals and plants. Although you can understand the main idea of the reading selection without knowing the specific type of plant or animal, in science it is important to be exact. The best way to learn the names of plants and animals is to see the living organisms in the wild. However, that is not always possible. Photographs on the Internet or in textbooks can help you learn about things you cannot experience in person.

EXERCISE 15   Studying plants and animals

Here is a list of specific plants and animals mentioned in Selection 2. Work with a partner. Use the Internet with a search engine like Google, or use a science book or encyclopedia. Find a photograph of each of the following plants or animals. In your own words, write a description of the each animal or plant.

1. redwood <u>These are some of the world's tallest trees. They</u>
   <u>can live to be 2000 years old and grow to over 300 feet tall.</u>
   <u>They are found on the California coast.</u>

2. sequoia _____
   _____
   _____

3. Douglas fir _____
   _____
   _____

4. spruce _____
   _____
   _____

5. coniferous trees _____
   _____
   _____

6. fungi _____

_____

_____

7. red tree vole _____

_____

_____

8. flying squirrel _____

_____

_____

9. northern spotted owl _____

_____

_____

10. salmon _____

_____

_____

S T R A T E G Y

Diagramming a Process

Many times science textbooks have descriptions of complex processes. It is easier to understand and remember these processes if you make a diagram of the process.

Red tree voles are small, mouse-like rodents.

EXERCISE 16 **Making a process diagram**

Near the end of paragraph 4 of Selection 2, there is an explanation of how red voles help the trees they live in. Make a process diagram showing how voles make essential contributions to the forest ecosystem. You might start your diagram like this:

Voles live in crevices of fallen trees. ⟶

EXERCISE 17 **Recognizing changes in purpose or tone**

Reread paragraph 15, thinking about purpose and tone, and then answer these questions:

1. How is the authors' purpose in paragraph 15 different from the purpose in paragraph 14?

_____

_____

_____

_____

2. In paragraph 15, the authors use expressions that intensify: "too," "not only . . . but" "so few," "a great deal." How does the use of these expressions affect tone?

_____

_____

☐ Learning Vocabulary

EXERCISE 18 **Reviewing academic vocabulary**

Listed below are some AWL words from Reading Selection 2. Evaluate your knowledge of each word. Review the paragraphs indicated to see the words in context again. Decide which ones you want to add to your active vocabulary.

Reading selection 2, old-growth forest of the Pacific Northwest			
1. controversy (¶ 1)	**12.** primary (¶ 5)	**23.** project (¶ 10)	**34.** access (¶ 13)
2. media (¶ 1)	**13.** enforce (¶ 5)	**24.** funded (¶ 10)	**35.** roles (¶ 14)
3. drama (¶ 1)	**14.** suspension (¶ 5)	**25.** restore (¶ 10)	**36.** advocates (¶ 14)
4. symbolize (¶ 1)	**15.** federal (¶ 5)	**26.** occurred (¶ 11)	**37.** annually (¶14)
5. mature (¶ 1)	**16.** diversified (¶ 6)	**27.** previous (¶ 11)	**38.** construction (¶ 14)
6. species (¶ 1)	**17.** source (¶ 6)	**28.** administrative (¶11)	**39.** subsidy (¶ 14)
7. significance (¶ 2)	**18.** revenue (¶ 6)	**29.** legality (¶ 12)	**40.** specifically (¶ 14)
8. attained (¶ 2)	**19.** automation (¶ 7)	**30.** restricted (¶ 12)	**41.** granting (¶14)
9. altered (¶ 4)	**20.** analysis (¶ 8)	**31.** legislation (¶ 12)	**42.** triggered (¶ 14)
10. eventually (¶ 4)	**21.** prospects (¶ 8)	**32.** responding (¶ 13)	**43.** indicated (¶ 15)
11. stable (¶ 5)	**22.** convened (¶ 9)	**33.** controversial (¶ 13)	

The following activity will help you study these vocabulary words with your classmates.

1. Work with a partner. Each pair is responsible for an equal number of different words on the list (depending on class size).
2. Together, write definitions for each word your pair is responsible for. Write only the definition, without identifying the word. You could write the definitions on note cards or on separate slips of paper. Make sure each definition fits the meaning of the word as it is used in context. You can write definitions in your own words, or check a dictionary for help. Both you and your partner must agree to the wording of the definition.
3. Pass your definitions in to your instructor or a lead student.
4. Then listen as definitions are read aloud and look at your word list to identify which word matches the definition.
5. Afterward, discuss which definitions were clear and which could be improved. Suggest how the definitions could be improved.

☐ Linking Concepts

EXERCISE 19 Relating ideas from two texts

One way to remember what you have read is to think about new concepts you have learned and link them to other concepts or ideas in a reading text. By answering the following questions, you will be linking concepts you learned in Selection 1 to concepts you learned in Selection 2.

1. Which discipline listed in paragraph 1 of the Selection 1 were reflected in the controversy of logging old-growth forests?
2. Were the loggers using the resources of the forest sustainably? What facts support your answer?
3. Which of the four problems listed in paragraph 4 of Selection 2 is related to this reading? Explain why you chose that problem.
4. Are old-growth forests renewable or non-renewable resources? Explain your answer.

EXERCISE 20   **Solving problems**

Reading Selection 2 illustrates how government and lawmakers can be involved in environmental problems. Can government regulate the environment?

Described below are four environmental problems that may require regulation. Divide the class into four teams, and select one problem per team. Each team will act as lawmakers trying to solve an environmental problem. Team members must try to come up with a solution to the problem and then present the problem and solution to the whole class.

1. You are from a country that just made a major change in government. The previous government was more concerned with economic development than with care of the environment. The power plants built during this time severely polluted the air. Many of the children in your country have diseases such as asthma and emphysema because of this pollution. You need to improve the quality of the air, but you don't have a lot of money to improve the power plants. Also, the people are very poor and not able to pay high prices for electricity.

2. You are the manager of a large national wildlife park. Your problem is a sudden great increase in the deer population in the park. The deer are eating so much that they are destroying a rare kind of tree that grows in the park. You discover that the increase in the number of deer is a result of a decrease in the number of wolves—a natural predator of the deer. Because wolves also kill their farm animals, the people who live on farms just outside the park have been shooting the wolves that come on their farms.

3. Coffee plants need shade to grow, so most coffee farms have big trees around them to provide the shade. A scientist developed a coffee plant that does not need shade. This means the farmers can cut down the big trees and plant more coffee plants. With more coffee plants, the farmers can make more money. However, the big shady trees were the winter home of many of the most beautiful songbirds. Since the shade trees were cut down, the population of songbirds has decreased very quickly. Some songbird species are becoming threatened.

4. You are from a poor country where the typical family has eight children. The country's population is growing quickly. There are already shortages of food and clean water. You are afraid that many of the children will die of starvation or disease because of the shortages. The people in your country are very religious, and it is against their religion to practice birth control.

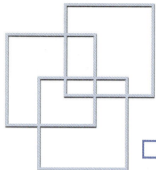

Reading Assignment 3

ENVIRONMENTALISTS AT WORK—CASE IN POINT: LAKE WASHINGTON

☐ Getting Ready to Read

EXERCISE 21 Studying changes and consequences

Reading Selection 3 is about how an increased number of people moving to the Seattle area caused an environmental problem. Before you read, think about the problems that high population density can cause in the following areas. Write down ideas about causes and effects.

1. Air pollution _____

   _____

2. Water pollution _____

   _____

3. Garbage disposal _____

   _____

EXERCISE 22 Reading strategy for a longer passage

Phase One of Muscle Reading includes three steps: Preview, Outline, and Question. Apply these three steps to Reading Selection 3. Do you remember each step?

To **preview**, look for familiar concepts, facts, or ideas that catch your interest and are related to your goals. Look at visual elements and captions, and read section titles. Determine your reading strategy. How will you use what you learn from your reading? How will you be tested on the material? How much time do you need for this long passage?

To **outline**, mentally note the section titles and think about organization.

To **question**, write down actual questions about the possible content—things you don't know or questions you hope the text will answer. You could transform section titles into question structures if other ideas do not come right to your mind.

Many textbooks, like Reading Selection 3, have questions at the end. Read the questions before you read the text. The questions usually focus on what is important in the text. In longer text, you can read efficiently by scanning the text, looking for the answers to the questions.

Reading Selection 3

ENVIRONMENTALISTS AT WORK—CASE IN POINT: LAKE WASHINGTON

<table>
<tr><td>

Muscle Reading Reminder

Phase Two:
Read
Underline
Answer

</td><td>

1   J ust as generals study old battles in order to learn how battlefield decisions are made, we can study an environmental battle that was successfully waged in the 1950's to learn how environmental problems are solved. The battle was fought over the pollution of Lake Washington, a large, (86 km^2 or 33.2 mi^2), deep freshwater lake forming the eastern boundary of the city of Seattle. During the first part of the 20th century, the Seattle metropolitan area expanded eastward toward the lake from the shores of Puget Sound, an inlet of the Pacific Ocean. As this expansion occurred, Lake Washington came under increasingly intense environmental pressures. Recreational use of the lake expanded greatly, and so did its use for waste disposal. Sewage[1] arrangements in particular had a major impact on the lake.

</td></tr>
</table>

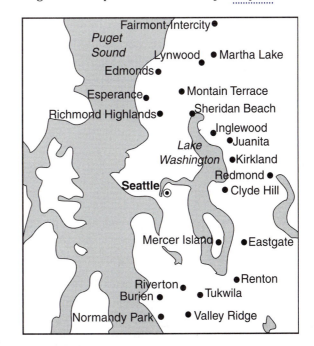

1. **sew•age** (sōō´ĭj) *n.* Liquid and solid waste from toilets that is carried away in sewers or drains.

Birth of an Environmental Problem

2   Like many U.S. cities, Seattle is surrounded by suburbs, each with individual municipal governments. These suburbs expanded rapidly in the 1940's, generating an enormous waste disposal problem. Between 1941 and 1954, ten suburban sewage treatment plants began operating at points around the lake, with a combined daily discharge of 75.7 million ltr (20 million gal) into Lake Washington. Each plant treated the raw sewage to break down the organic[2] material within it and released the effluent—that is, treated sewage—into the lake. By the mid-1950's, a great deal of treated sewage had been poured into the lake. Try multiplying 75.7 million ltr per day by 365 days per year by 5 to 10 years: Enough effluent was dumped to give about 25 to 50 ltr (6.5 to 13 gal) of it to every man, woman, and child living today.

Oscillatoria

3   Gabriel Comita and George Anderson, doctoral students at the University of Washington in Seattle, were the first to note the effects of this discharge on the lake. Their studies of the lake's microscopic organisms in 1950 indicated that large masses of oscillatoria, a filamentous[3] cyanobacterium, or blue-green alga,[4] were growing in the lake. The abundance[5] of these long strings of photosynthetic bacterial[6] cells in Lake Washington was unexpected. The growth of such large numbers of cyanobacteria requires a plentiful supply of nutrients, and deepwater lakes such as Lake Washington do not usually have enough dissolved nutrients to support cyanobacterial growth. Deepwater lakes are particularly poor in the essential nutrient phosphorus.[7] The amount of filamentous cyanobacteria in Lake Washington's waters hinted that the lake was somehow changing, becoming richer in dissolved nutrients such as phosphorus.

2. **or•gan•ic** (ôr-găn´ĭk) *adj.* Relating to living things.
3. **fil•a•men•tous** (fĭl´ə-měn´təs) *adj.* Consisting of a thin, thread-like substance.
4. **al•ga** (ăl´gə) *n.* A water plant with a simple structure.
5. **a•bun•dance** (ə-bŭn´dəns) *adj.* A great amount or quantity.
6. **bac•te•ri•al** (băk tîr´ē-əl) *adj.* Relating to any of a large group of very small one-celled organisms, some of which cause disease.
7. **phos•pho•rus** (fŏs´fər-əs) *n.* A yellowish chemical that is an essential part of living cells and that can be used in making fertilizers.

Sounding the Alarm

4   In July 1955, a technical report by the Washington Pollution
Control Commission sounded one of the first public alarms. Citing
the work of Comita and Anderson, it concluded that the treated
sewage effluent that was being released into the lake's waters was
raising the lake's levels of dissolved nutrients to the point of
serious pollution. Whereas primary treatment, followed by
chlorination,[8] was ridding it of bacteria, it was not eliminating many
chemicals, particularly phosphorus, a major component of
detergents. In essence, the treated sewage was fertilizing the lake
by enriching it with dissolved nutrients.

5   The process of nutrient enrichment of freshwater lakes is well
understood by ecologists, who call it eutrophication. Eutrophication is
undesirable because, as Comita and Anderson had already begun to
observe, high nutrient levels contribute to the growth of filamentous
cyanobacteria. These photosynthetic organisms need only three
things in order to grow: light for photosynthesis,[9] which they get from
the sun; carbon atoms, which they get from carbon dioxide dissolved
in water; and nutrients such as nitrogen and phosphorus, which were
provided by the treated sewage. Without the nutrients, cyanobacteria
cannot grow; supply the nutrients, and soon mats of cyanobacteria
form a green scum[10] on the surface of the water, and the water begins
to stink from the odor of rotting organic matter.

6   Then the serious problem begins: the deep-water bacteria that
decompose the masses of dead cyanobacteria multiply explosively,
consuming vast quantities of oxygen in the process, until the lake's
deeper waters become so depleted that they can no longer support
other organisms that require oxygen to live. Fish can no longer
extract enough oxygen through their gills, and neither can the
myriad[11] of tiny invertebrates[12] that populate freshwater lakes.

8. **chlo•ri•na•tion** (klôr′ə-nā′shən) *n.* The addition of chlorine.
9. **pho•to•syn•the•sis** (fō′tō-sĭn′thĭ-sĭs) *n.* The chemical process by which plants
    use light to change water and carbon dioxide into food.
10. **scum** (skŭm) *n.* A filmy layer of impure matter that forms on the surface of a
    liquid or a body of water.
11. **myr•i•ad** (mĭr′ē-əd) *n.* A very large, indefinite number.
12. **in•ver•te•brate** (ĭn-vûr′tə-brĭt) *n.* Animal, such as insects or worms, without a
    backbone.

7   On July 11, 1955, the local newspaper mentioned the Pollution Control Commission's technical report in an article entitled, "Lake's Play Use Periled by Pollution." The article did not grab the public's attention, but a month later, something else did: the annual Gold Cup Yacht[13] Races, when spectators saw magnificent sailboats slicing cleanly though green scum and smelled the odor of rotting cyanobacteria. These detractions to what had been a popular summer holiday raised protest among spectators and lakeshore residents.

Collecting clumps of cyanobacteria in Lake Washington during the 1950s

8   On the day of the yacht race, Anderson collected a water sample from the lake that contained a filamentous cyanobacterium that neither Anderson nor earlier investigators had ever encountered in large numbers in the lake: *Oscillatoria rubescens*. The presence of this cyanobacterium proved to be a vital clue. When Anderson's professor at the University of Washington, W.T. Edmondson, reviewed the literature on eutrophication, he came across the name *Oscillatoria rubescens* again and again in the lists of organisms found in polluted lakes.

13. **yacht** (yät) *n.* Expensive sailing or motor-driven boat used for pleasure cruises or racing.

9   To Edmondson, the abundance of oscillatoria in Lake Washington was a clear warning. On October 13, 1955, the *University of Washington Daily* ran a story, "Edmondson Announces Pollution May Ruin Lake," in which Edmondson announced the likely meaning of the large masses of oscillatoria. From this point on, the scientific case was clear: the eutrophication of Lake Washington was demonstrably at an advanced stage, and unless it was reversed, it would soon destroy the water quality of the lake.

Scientific Assessment

10   Scientific assessment of an environmental problem verifies that a problem exists and builds a sound set of observations on which to base a solution. Lake Washington's microscopic life had been the subject of a detailed study in 1933. Thus, when the telltale[14] signs of pollution first appeared in 1950, Edmondson's student quickly detected changes from the previous study. Without the earlier study's careful analyses of the many microorganisms living in the lake, understanding the changes that were occurring would have been delayed or possibly missed entirely.

W. T. Edmonson on Lake Washington

14. **tell·tale** (tĕl′tāl′) *adj.* Serving to indicate or reveal.

11   Edmondson examined and compared the earlier study of the lake and <u>confirmed</u> that there had indeed been a great increase in dissolved nutrient in the lake's water. Surmising[15] that the added nutrients were the result of sewage treatment discharge into the lake by suburban communities, Edmondson formed the <u>hypothesis</u> that treated sewage was introducing so many nutrients into the lake that its waters were beginning to support the growth of photosynthetic cyanobacteria.

12   Edmondson's hypothesis made a clear prediction: the continued addition of phosphates[16] and other nutrients to the lake would change its surface into a stinking mat of rotting cyanobacteria, unfit for swimming or drinking, and the beauty of the lake would be only a memory. Bolstering[17] his prediction was the fact the lakes near other cities, such as Madison, Wisconsin, had deteriorated after receiving discharges of treated sewage.

Making a Model

13   Edmondson constructed a graphical model of the lake, which predicted that the decline could be reversed: if the pollution were stopped, the lake would clean itself at a predictable rate, reverting to its previous, unpolluted state within five years. In freshwater lakes, iron <u>reacts</u> with phosphorus to form an insoluble complex that sinks to the bottom of the lake and is buried in the sediments.[18] Thus, if additional phosphorus was not introduced into the lake from sewage effluent, the lake would slowly recover. In April 1956, Edmondson outlined three steps that would be necessary in any serious attempt to save the lake:
1. <u>comprehensive</u> regional planning by the many suburbs that ringed the lake;
2. complete <u>elimination</u> of sewage discharge into the lake; and,
3. <u>research</u> to <u>identify</u> the key nutrients that were causing the cyanobacteria to grow.

His proposals received <u>widespread</u> publicity in the Seattle area, and the stage was set to bring scientists and civic leaders together.

15. **sur•mis•ing** (sər-mīz′ing) *v.* Concluding or guessing something on little evidence.
16. **phos•phate** (fŏs′fāt′) *n.* Phosphorus-containing compound, often used in fertilizers and detergents.
17. **bol•ster•ing** (bōl′stər-ing) *v.* Strengthening; supporting.
18. **sed•i•ment** (sĕd′ ə-mənt) *n.* Tiny pieces of solid matter, such as dirt, that fall to

Risk Analysis

14 It is one thing to suggest that the addition of treated sewage to Lake Washington stop, and quite another to devise an acceptable alternative. Further treatment of sewage can remove some nutrients, but it may not be practical to remove all of them. The alternative is to dump the sewage somewhere else—but where? In this case, officials decided to discharge the treated sewage into Puget Sound. In their plan, a ring of sewers to be built around the lake would collect sewage treatment discharges, treat them further, and then transport them to be discharged at great depth into Puget Sound.

15 Why go to all the trouble and expense of treating the discharges further, if you are just going to dump them? And why bother discharging them deep under water? It is important that the solution to one problem not produce another. The plans to further treat the discharge and release it at great depth were formulated in an attempt to minimize the environmental impact of diverting Lake Washington's discharge into Puget Sound. It was assumed that sewage effluent would have less of an impact on the greater quantity of water in Puget Sound than on the much smaller amount of water in Lake Washington. Also, nutrient chemistry in marine waste is different from that in fresh water. Puget Sound is naturally rich in nutrients, and phosphate does not control cyanobacterial growth there as it does in Lake Washington. The growth of photosynthetic bacteria and algae in Puget Sound is largely limited by tides, which mix the water and transport the tiny organisms into deeper water, where they cannot get enough light to grow rapidly.

16 Practically any course of action that can be taken to address an environmental problem has its own impacts on the environment, which must be assessed when evaluating potential solutions. Environmental impact analyses often involve studies by geographers, chemists, and engineers as well as ecologists and other biologists. Furthermore, the decision whether to implement a plan to restore or protect the environment is almost always affected by social, political, and economic concerns. Any proposal is inevitably and rightly constrained by existing laws and by the citizens who will be affected by the decision.

The Evergreen Floating Bridge across Lake Washington

Public Education

17   Despite the technical bulletin published by the Washington Pollution Control Commission in 1955, local sanitation authorities were not convinced that urgent action was necessary. Public action requires further education, and it was at this stage the scientists played a key role. Edmondson and other scientists wrote articles for the general public that contained concise[19] explanations of what nutrient enrichment is and what problems it causes. The general public's awareness of the problem increased as local newspapers published these articles.

18   In December 1956, Edmondson wrote a letter in an effort to alert a committee established by the mayor of Seattle to examine regional problems affecting Seattle and its suburbs. Edmondson explained that even well-treated sewage would soon destroy the lake, and that Lake Washington was already showing signs of deterioration. He received an encouraging response and prepared for the committee a nine-page report of his scientific findings. After presenting his data showing that the mass of cyanobacteria varied

19. **con•cise** (kən-sīs´) *adj.* Said in a few words.

in strict proportion to the amounts of nutrients being added to the lake, Edmondson posed a series of questions: "How has Lake Washington changed?" "What will happen if nothing is done to halt nutrient accumulation?" "Why not poison the cyanobacteria and then continue to discharge the effluent?" He then answered the questions and outlined two alternative courses of public action—do nothing, or stop adding nutrients to the lake—and made a clear prediction about the consequences of each.

Political Action

19   Edmondson's report was widely circulated among local governments, but implementing its proposals presented serious political problems because there was no governmental mechanism that would permit the many local suburbs to act together on regional matters such as sewage disposal. On September 9, 1958, voters approved a public referendum[20] to create a regional government to deal with the sewage disposal problem.

20   At the time it was passed, the Lake Washington plan was the most ambitious and most expensive pollution control project in the United States. Every household in the area had to pay $2 a month in additional taxes for construction of a massive trunk sewer to ring the lake, collect all the effluent, treat it, and discharge it into Puget Sound.

Building a new sewer trunk line around Lake Washington

20. **ref•er•en•dum** (rĕf´ə-rĕn´dəm) *n.* A direct vote by the people on an issue rather than on a candidate.

21   Groundbreaking ceremonies for the new project were held in July 1961. As Edmondson had predicted, the lake had deteriorated further. In 1963, the first of the waste treatment plants around the lake began to divert its effluent into the new trunk sewer. One by one, the others diverted theirs until the last effluent was diverted in 1968. The lake's deterioration stopped by 1964, and then its condition began to improve.

Follow-Through

22   By carefully analyzing what was happening in the lake, Edmondson could predict that the lake would recover fully. Some environmental scientists disagreed with him, arguing that dissolved phosphorus, the key nutrient regulating cyanobacterial growth, would not dissipate for decades, if ever. A lot depended on assumptions about the chemical makeup of the sediment at the bottom of the lake. Edmondson's hypothesis was correct. Water returned to normal within a few years. Oscillatoria persisted until 1970, but eventually it disappeared. By 1975 the lake was back to normal.

23   Every environmental intervention is an experiment, and continued monitoring is necessary because environmental scientists work with imperfect tools. There is a great deal we do not know, and every added bit of information increases our ability to deal with future problems. The unanticipated always lurks just beneath the surface of any experiment carried out in nature. It was not anticipated, for example, that the quality of the water would continue to get better. By 1980, the lake was cleaner than at any time in recent memory. Before the recovery, the presence of filamentous cyanobacteria such as oscillatoria had limited the population of a microscopic organism called daphnia because cyanobacterial filaments clog daphnia's feeding apparatus. The disappearance of oscillatoria and other filamentous cyanobacteria allowed the lake's daphnia population to flourish[21] and become dominate among the many kinds of invertebrates that lived there. Because daphnia are very efficient eaters of nonfilamentous algae, levels of these algae fell, too, so that the water became even clearer.

---

21. **flour·ish** (flûr′ĭsh) *v.* To grow or develop well or in great amounts.

Working Together

24   The reversal of the pollution of Lake Washington is a particularly clear example of how environmental science can work to identify, address, and help solve environmental problems. Many environmental problems facing us today are far more complex than Lake Washington's, however, and public attitudes are often different. Lake Washington's pollution problem was solved only because the many small towns involved in the problem cooperated in seeking a solution.

25   Today, confrontations over an environmental problem frequently make it difficult to reach an agreement. Even scientists disagree among themselves and call for additional research to help them arrive at a consensus. In such an atmosphere, politicians often compromise by adopting a "wait-and-see" approach.

26   Such delays are really a form of negative action because the consequences of many environmental problems are so serious that they must be acted on before a scientific consensus is reached. The need for additional scientific studies should not prevent us from taking action on such serious regional and global issues as stratospheric ozone depletion and global climate warming. We need to recognize the uncertainty inherent in environmental problems, consider a variety of possible approaches, weigh the cost, benefits, and probable outcomes of each, and set in motion a policy that is flexible enough to allow us to modify it as additional information becomes available. In the final analysis, then, environmental scientists identify a problem and often suggest a solution, but implementation depends on a political decision that is influenced by social and economic agendas as well as scientific evidence.

Raven, P. H., & Berg, L. R. (2001). *Environment* (3rd ed.) (pp. 31–36). Hoboken, NJ: John Wiley & Sons.

Muscle Reading Reminder

Phase Three:
Recite
Review
Review Again

☐ Assessing Your Learning

Demonstrating Comprehension

EXERCISE 23   **Reading to find answers**

Reread the passage, looking for the answers to the following questions. Highlight the answers in Selection 3 and write the number of each question by the highlighted answer. The first one has been explained for you as an example.

1. Why do environmentalists study the environmental battle over Lake Washington?

   to learn how an environmental problem was solved and to think

   about finding solutions to new problems using similar methods.

   This answer is found in paragraph 1.

2. What caused Lake Washington's environmental problem?
3. Who first discovered that there was an environmental problem?
4. How was treated sewage affecting the lake?
5. What is eutrophication?
6. How does eutrophication affect fish and invertebrates?
7. How did the public first become aware of the pollution problem in Lake Washington?
8. How did the 1933 study help Edmondson's scientific assessment?
9. What was Edmondson's hypothesis?
10. What was Edmondson's solution to the problem?
11. Why was it better to dump the treated sewage in Puget Sound than in Lake Washington?
12. What do environmentalists have to think about when they develop a course of action to solve an environmental problem?
13. How did Edmondson convince people that urgent action was necessary?
14. What changes did local governments have to make to solve the problem?
15. Did the lake recover exactly as Edmondson predicted? Explain.

EXERCISE 24   **Making a process diagram**

Make a diagram showing the steps in the process of eutrophication. (See paragraphs 5 and 6.) You can use the diagram you made about the red tree vole after Reading Selection 2 as a model. You might start your diagram like this:

1. Treated Sewage Effluent + Light + Carbon + Nutrients (nitrogen & phosphorous)

☐ Learning Vocabulary

As noted in earlier chapters, words that frequently occur together are called **collocations**. For example the word *impact* in paragraph 1 is frequently put together with the word *major*. So, in English you could commonly hear people say "It had a major impact," but they wouldn't usually say "It had a main impact." Even though the words *major* and *main* have similar meanings, they are not always used with the same words. Here are some other words that go with *impact*:

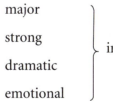

major
strong
dramatic
emotional

impact

STRATEGY

When you learn collocations, you can learn English more quickly because you not only know the word but you also know other words that go with it. Look for collocations whenever you read. This will help you learn vocabulary more quickly and easily.

EXERCISE **25** **Working with collocations**

Match each word or expression with its collocation.

A.

1. important _____

2. outside _____

3. strong _____   **a.** clue (¶ 8)

4. telltale _____   **b.** pressure (¶ 1)

5. under _____

6. vital _____

7. intense _____

B.

1. to advance _____

2. because of _____

3. to reach _____

4. to suffer _____

5. to form _____   **a.** the consequences (¶ 26)

6. to face _____   **b.** a hypothesis (¶ 11)

7. to propose _____

8. to confirm _____

9. to formulate_____

10. to accept _____

EXERCISE 26   **Working with idiomatic expressions**

Some groups of words in English have a specific meaning when they are combined in a certain way. These are called idiomatic phrases. The idiomatic phrases below come from the Selection 3. Match each phrase with its meaning.

_____ "ran a story" (¶ 9)

_____ "ringed the lake" (¶ 13)

_____ "course of action" (¶ 16)

_____ "at this stage" (¶ 17)

_____ "lurks just beneath the
                  surface" (¶ 23)

_____ "wait and see" (¶ 25)

_____ "set in motion" (¶ 26)

1. started

2. went around the lake

3. distribute a newspaper
       article

4. don't take action

5. certain point in a
       process

6. plan for the future

7. close by, but not in sight

☐ Focusing on Science

EXERCISE 27   **Identifying cause-and-effect relationships**

Scientists often try to discover the reason why something happens; they look for the cause. Some words that signal a cause-and-effect relationship are "because of," "as a result of," and "therefore." Can you identify causes and effects?

As a whole class, build a chart that shows some of the cause-and-effect relationships in Selection 3. Here is an example:

Causes	Effects
Population in the Seattle metropolitan area expanded	■ Recreational use of the lake ■ Waste disposal in the lake expanded.

EXERCISE 28   **Identifying process steps in a scientific study**

The main purpose of this passage is to illustrate the steps environmentalists use to solve environmental problems successfully. The authors give us a particular example to illustrate a general process. The steps can then be applied to other problems. Can you identify the steps in the process? This chart shows the general process for solving an environmental problem.

Finish the chart by adding bulleted lists with some of the specific events that occurred as the Lake Washington problem was assessed and solved. The first one has been done for you as an example.

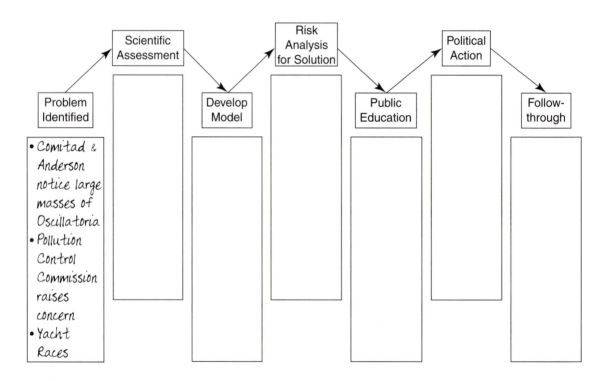

The process that scientists use to answer questions or solve problems is called the scientific method. Here are the basic steps in the scientific method:

1. Ask a question or identify a problem.
2. Develop a hypothesis, or educated guess, to explain the problem.
3. Design an experiment to test the hypothesis and collect data.
4. Analyze or interpret the data.
5. Share the new knowledge.

EXERCISE 29   **Following the scientific method**

How did the environmentalist use the scientific method for the problem of Lake Washington?

Complete the chart below with specific details from Selection 3 that give examples of how the scientific method was applied to this situation.

1. Problem	Lake Washington becomes polluted and is covered with clumps of cyanobacteria.
2. Hypothesis (¶ 13)	
3. Experiment (¶ 14)	
4. Analysis (¶ 22–23)	
5. Share knowledge (¶ 24)	

☐ Linking Concepts

EXERCISE 30   Relating ideas from three texts

Answer these questions to link concepts you learned in Reading Selections 1 and 2 to those you learned in Reading Selection 3.

1. Compare Reading Selection 2 with Reading Selection 3. How are the problems (over-logging and water pollution) similar? How are they different?

2. What role did government play in each environmental problem?

3. Which discipline listed in paragraph 1 of Reading Selection 1 were reflected in the problem of Lake Washington?

4. Was Lake Washington being used sustainably? What facts support your answer?

5. Which of the four problems listed in paragraph 4 of Reading Selection 1 is related to Reading Selection 3? Explain why you chose that problem.

6. Is Lake Washington a renewable or non-renewable resource? Explain your answer.

☐ Assessing Your Learning at the End of a Chapter

Revisiting Chapter Objectives

Return to the first page of this chapter. Think about the chapter objectives. Put a check mark next to the ones you feel secure about. Review material in the chapter you still need to work on. When you are ready, answer the chapter review questions on the next page.

☐ Practicing for a Chapter Test

EXERCISE 31   **Reviewing comprehension**

Check your comprehension of main concepts, or ideas, in this chapter by answering the following chapter review questions.

1. The authors' purpose in the three reading selections is mostly informative, but sometimes persuasive. Give an example of persuasive purpose.
2. Why is over-consumption difficult to stop? Give a personal-experience example.
3. Describe the process of eutrophication.
4. Explain what environmental scientists do.
5. In your own words, define environmental sustainability. Explain how this term applies to the cases of old-growth forests and Lake Washington.
6. Describe the controversy caused by logging old-growth forests.
7. Agree or disagree with this statement: Government can solve environmental problems.
8. Explain how the environmental problems of Lake Washington were solved.
9. Describe how the scientific method was applied to the problem of Lake Washington.

☐ Academic Vocabulary

Here are some academic vocabulary words that were introduced in this chapter. Confirm the words that you know the meaning of. Identify the words that are not yet part of your active vocabulary. Relearn the words that you need to relearn.

access	administrative	advocates	altered	analysis
assessment	attained	authorities	automation	available
commission	component	comprehensive	confirmed	consensus
consequences	constrained	construction	consumption	controversial
controversy	convened	convinced	cooperated	data
disposal	diversified	drama	dynamic	elimination
encountered	enforce	established	ethics	eventually
evidence	expanded	finite	flexible	foundation
function	funded	furthermore	generating	generations
global	granting	hypothesis	imposed	inadequate
indefinitely	indicated	inevitably	inherent	initially
institute	intense	interactions	intervention	issues
legality	legislation	mature	media	minimize
outcomes	persisted	policy	potential	previous
primary	proportion	prospects	published	reacts
regional	residents	resolve	resources	responding
restore	restricted	reversed	source	species
specifically	stable	subsidy	suburbs	survival
suspension	sustainability	symbolize	tiny	transport
trigger	unanticipated	vital	widespread	

Here is a way you could study the words you need to practice more. Make an audiotape of the words you want to remember. First say the word, then pause, and then say the definition of the word. The pause will allow you time to respond before you get the correct answer. While you're walking or driving to work or waiting at the bus stop, listen to your tape of the words you want to remember.

EXERCISE 32 Noticing word parts

Eleven of the AWL words in the list above include -tion. List each of these words on separate paper. All the words with -tion are noun forms. Next to each noun, write the base verb form. This form is the headword for the word family.

1. <u>automation</u>   <u>automate</u>

WEB POWER

Go to http://esl.college.hmco.com/students to view more environmental science readings, plus exercises that will help you study the selections and the academic words in this chapter.

Seeing the Big Picture

ACADEMIC FOCUS: ECONOMICS ▶
MACROECONOMICS

Academic Reading Objectives

After completing this chapter, you should be able to:

✓ Check here as you master each objective.

1. Adjust reading strategies based on textual demands ☐
2. Interpret graphs ☐
3. Identify assumptions supporting statements of theory ☐
4. Extrapolate and manipulate facts and examples to solve sample problems ☐
5. Explain and justify opinions in response to a reading ☐

Economics Objectives

1. Define gross domestic product (GDP) ☐
2. Contrast economic growth and economic fluctuations ☐
3. Identify periods of recession and periods of recovery and expansion on a graph ☐
4. Explain the relationship between recessions and unemployment, inflation, and interest rates ☐
5. Discuss the economic impact of 9/11 ☐

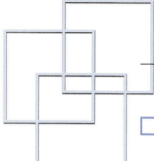

Reading Assignment 1

☐ Getting Ready to Read

Economists view the world from a monetary perspective. They consider relationships among factors that are linked to the exchange of money for goods or services (including labor). They observe patterns and trends in order to make predictions about market logic, and they recommend actions to government officials who can make fiscal and monetary policy decisions.

Reading passages in textbooks about economics is different from other types of reading you have done so far (literature, study skills, psychology, and science) in this book. Economic thought focuses on logical relationships that are often represented with mathematical formulas and graphs. You may need to read and reread text about economic theory several times before you grasp the logical sense of it. Understanding and learning economic theory also involve working with problem-solving exercises and plotting graphs. Learning the basics of economic theory can benefit you as an individual, as well as a member of society.

EXERCISE 1 Developing economic background knowledge

Aspects of economic theory are present in our lives on a daily basis. As a whole class, make a list on the board of sample economic decisions you and your classmates have made recently—things you decided to do, or not do, because of money.

Economic Decisions List:

• brought lunch from home instead of eating out

What conclusions can you draw? How did your economic decisions affect you and others? Who benefited financially from your decisions, and who did not?

EXERCISE 2 **Thinking about economics**

■ *If you have access to a television in your classroom, turn it on and flip through channels looking for any segments with economic news, commentary, or dialogue.* What conclusions can you draw? What economic issues are people interested in, and how are people affected by economic concerns? *(If a television is not available, try this as a homework assignment.)*

■ *Purchase a newspaper or visit a news website and scan articles in the business/money section.* What conclusions can you draw?

■ *As you work with this chapter, keep your eyes open for a news article of interest to you. You will later be given an assignment with the article. You could check our website at http://college.hmco.com/economics/taylor/ economics/4e/students/index.html for sample current articles.*

EXERCISE 3 **Previewing concepts**

In this chapter, several key terms are defined. Before you read, try to explain your own ideas about each concept listed in the chart below; base your explanations on your general knowledge of what the concepts might mean. Work with a partner to say what you think out loud. Keep in mind that you will learn more about these concepts when you read the selections.

Key terms		
macroeconomics	recession microeconomics	Gross Domestic Product depression
economic expansion economic fluctuations	scarce resources unemployment inflation interest rates	trend line per capita the Civil War Congress the Federal Reserve

☐ Reading the Selection

The following reading passages were selected from the textbook *Economics*, written by a noted economist and teacher, John Taylor. Taylor presents modern economic theory for college students who are new to the field. He writes in a clear manner and uses graphs and real-life examples to help students understand the basic determinants of economic growth (labor, capital, and technology) and economic fluctuations (inflation, output, and employment). The passages focus on factors that influence periods of economic expansion, recession, and fluctuations that can occur even during periods of steady growth. (To learn more, visit a useful site associated with this textbook: http://college.hmco.com/economics/students/). Reading Selection 1 introduces the concept of **macroeconomics**.

Taylor, J. (2004). *Economics* (4th ed.). Boston: Houghton Mifflin Company.

Reading Selection 1

MACROECONOMICS: THE BIG PICTURE

Introduction

1   An economic expansion is a period of continuous economic growth without a significant economic downturn. In 2001, the longest economic expansion in American history came to an end. The record-breaking expansion had begun in 1991; throughout the decade, unemployment was low and falling, as is often the case in an expansion, and spending by consumers and investors was very robust.

2   An economic downturn that ends an expansion is known as a recession. During 2001, unemployment increased, as it often does in a recession, and spending by consumers and business firms fell. While the tragic events of September 11 contributed substantially to the economy's going into recession, all indications were that the economic slowdown had begun almost six months earlier. Once the signs of recession were evident, the President, members of Congress, and the Federal Reserve[1] expressed their concern and moved quickly to implement policies that they claimed would help the economy return to a period of expansion.

3   Recent economic data seem to indicate that the slowdown was short-lived: the longest economic expansion on record seems to have been followed by one of the shortest recessions on record. Why was the expansion so long? What caused the economy to go into recession? Why was the recession so short-lived? Did the policy responses put in place in 2001 help the economy out of the recession? These are the types of questions that the study of macroeconomics helps us answer.

4   Macroeconomics is the study of the *whole market economy*. Like other parts of economics, macroeconomics uses the central idea that people make purposeful decisions with scarce resources. However, instead of focusing on the workings of one market— whether the market for peanuts or the market for bicycles— macroeconomics focuses on the economy as a whole. Macroeconomics looks at the big picture: Economic growth,

---

1. *Federal Reserve* = A U.S. banking system that consists of twelve federal reserve banks, each one serving member banks within its own district.

recessions, unemployment, and inflation are among its subject matter. You should accordingly put on your "big picture glasses" when you study macroeconomics.

5   Macroeconomics is important to you and your future. For example, you will have a much better chance of finding a desirable job after you graduate from college during a period of economic expansion than during a period of recession. Strong economic growth can help alleviate poverty, free up resources to clean up the environment, and lead to a brighter future for your generation. By studying macroeconomics, you can better understand the changes that are taking place in the economy, better understand the role of good economic policies in driving economic growth and reducing unemployment, and become a more informed and educated citizen.

6   This chapter summarizes the overall workings of the economy, highlighting key facts to remember. It also provides a brief preview of the macroeconomic theory designed to explain these facts. The theory will be developed in later chapters.

Source: Taylor, J. (2004). *Economics* (4th ed.). Boston: Houghton Mifflin Company, pp. 24–25.

☐ Assessing Your Learning

Demonstrating Comprehension

EXERCISE 4 Defining concepts

The author defines each concept below in this introductory passage. Return to the selection, find these four terms, and highlight their definitions.

1. economic expansion
2. recession
3. Federal Reserve
4. macroeconomics

EXERCISE 5   **Elaborating with examples**

With key concepts, authors often provide examples to help readers understand. Answer these questions about examples from Reading Selection 1. (Note: Key concepts are in bold.)

1. When did the most recent **economic expansion** in the United States begin? _____

   When did it end? _____

2. Identify two factors associated with this period of **economic expansion**. _____

   _____

3. When did the most recent U.S. **recession** begin? _____

4. Identify two factors associated with this period of **recession**.

   _____

   _____

5. What did the president, Congress, and the **Federal Reserve** do in response to the **recession**?

   _____

   _____

6. State the central economic theory that informs the study of **macroeconomics** and microeconomics.

   _____

   _____

7. Provide your own example of making a purposeful decision with **scarce resources**.

   _____

   _____

8. Explain the main focus of **macroeconomics**.

_____

_____

9. Identify three ways studying **macroeconomics** can help you.

_____

_____

STRATEGY

Assumptions Supporting Statements of Theory

When you read passages about economics, it is important to think through stated theories by considering ideas that are tied to the theories. There are ideas behind theories, and there are policy decisions that follow from theories. Consider the following definitions.

the · o · ry (thē′ ə-rē) *n., pl.* **the · o · ries**	A statement or set of statements designed to explain an event or group of events.
as · sump · tion (ə-sŭmp′shən) *n.*	An idea or statement accepted as true without proof; a supposition.
in · fer · ence (in′-fər-əns) *n.*	The act of arriving at an opinion or idea based on factual knowledge or evidence.

Theories, assumptions, and inferences are related because, in each case, we are working from observations. On a daily basis, we make inferences based on assumptions. Knowing that an assumption is supported by a theory can lend confidence to decision making. To make these idea connections takes practice. We often come to conclusions or make inferences about situations we are part of or observe. We give meaning to situations through interpretations. Our interpretations are based on assumptions.

Source: Definitions from *The American Heritage English as a Second Language Dictionary.* (1998). Boston: Houghton Mifflin Company.

EXERCISE 6 Identifying assumptions supporting theory

In this exercise, you are given a situation related to a theory. Suggest what someone might infer (rightly or wrongly) about the situation. Then guess a general assumption behind the inference. This is a good exercise to work with a partner on. Answers will vary!

Theory	Situation	Possible inference	Assumption
In periods of expansion, employment levels are high.	A man has been working with the same company for several years.	He feels job security.	People who stay with the same job for a long time feel secure.
In periods of expansion, consumers and investors spend more money.	A woman made a lot of money on the stock market.		
In periods of recession, unemployment increases.	A student decided to take classes this semester because he could not find a new job after being laid off.		
In periods of recession, consumer spending falls.	A storeowner has a lot of merchandise that is not selling.		
People make purposeful decisions with scarce resources.	Although a customer would like to have a new TV, she decides to postpone making the purchase.		

☐ Learning Vocabulary

When a word recurs frequently in a passage or section, a reader should consider that word a valuable one to work with and know well. Sometimes the word recurs in the same form; sometimes the word appears in related forms—members of the same word family. For example, let's start with the title:

Macroeconomics: The Big Picture

What is the most "valuable" word in this title? _____

If you answered *economics*, you are right.

EXERCISE 7 Identifying valuable words to learn

Return to Reading Selection 1 and circle the word **economic** *or a form of* **economic** *every time you see it. How many occurrences did you find?*

_____

EXERCISE 8 Learning valuable words

As noted in earlier chapters, words belong to word families. Economy *is a headword. Complete the table below about different members of this word family. Which word do you think is the most frequently occurring member?*

_____

Word form	Part of speech	Meaning or sample phrase
economy	*noun*	*The economy fluctuates.*
economics		
economies		
economical		
economically		
economist		
macroeconomics		

EXERCISE 9 Working with collocations

Surrounding each form of the word **economic** *you circled are particular common word combinations or collocations. For this exercise, start with the word* **economic** *and complete the table below to list all the possible collocations you find in Reading Selection 1.*

Collocations with the word *economic*				
1.	an		economic	*expansion*
2.		*continuous*	economic	*growth*
3.	*a*	*significant*	economic	*downturn*
4.			economic	
5.			economic	
6.			economic	
7.			economic	
8.			economic	
9.			economic	
10.			economic	
11.			economic	
12.			economic	

What conclusions can you draw? Return to the passage and make similar collocation tables on separate paper for other members of the **economy** *word family.*

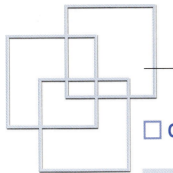

Reading Assignment 2

☐ Getting Ready to Read

EXERCISE 10 Preparing to learn main concepts

Answer these questions.

1. Reading Selection 2 is titled "Real GDP over Time." What do you

    think is the most important word in the title? _____

    If you said *GDP*, you're right. Having a firm understanding of GDP
    is crucial to your understanding this chapter.

2. Answer the following question to relate GDP to your own setting.
    Explain your response by adding reasons to support your opinion.

    How is the economy doing? _____

    _____

    _____

    _____

3. GDP is a measure of how the economy is doing. On the basis of your
    ideas above on the current state of the economy, is the GDP for this

    period high or low? _____

4. *GDP* stands for "gross domestic product." It is a measure of
    production over a specific period of time. Production includes goods
    and services. When there is growth in the production of goods and
    services, the economy is seen as good. Before reading Selection 2, turn
    to the first paragraph and read the definition of GDP. Write the
    definition here. You need to memorize this.

    _____

    _____

    _____

EXERCISE **11** **Applying a reading strategy**

*Phase One of Muscle Reading includes three steps: Preview, Outline, and
Question. Apply these steps to the readings in this chapter.*

To **preview**, skim over the passages, looking for main ideas, new
concepts, familiar concepts, facts, or ideas that catch your interest. Look at
the graphs and table. Determine your reading strategy. How will you use
what you learn from your reading? How will you be tested on this
material? How much time do you need?

To **outline**, mentally note the section titles. It could be helpful to
write out the section titles on separate paper before reading for this
chapter. Leave space to add notes and show relationships among ideas.

To **question**, write down actual questions about content. You could
transform section titles into question structures if other ideas do not come
right to your mind.

EXERCISE **12** **Previewing graphs and tables**

*This chapter includes many graphs. Spend time looking at them carefully
before you read each passage. Read the captions. Provide yourself with a
visual mental framework to get an idea of what to focus on while you read
the passages. Adjust your reading speed and eye movements to work with
graphs. Connect ideas in the passages with the graphs. The graphs illustrate
events across time, reflecting economic theories.*

☐ Reading for a Purpose

You are reading this selection in order to understand key theories of
microeconomics. You will learn the theories, understand them through
examples from various times and places, analyze graphs and tables that
illustrate the theories, and predict possible occurrences or trends based on
your new knowledge of how the economy works. As you read, highlight
important definitions and supporting points that help you understand and
learn. Remember to seek a balance in your highlighting—don't overdo it.

Muscle
Reading
Reminder

Phase Two:
Read
Underline
Answer

Reading Selection 2

REAL GDP OVER TIME

1   Gross domestic product (GDP) is the economic variable of most interest to macroeconomists. GDP is the total value of all goods and services produced in the economy during a specified period of time, usually a year or a quarter. The total value of goods and services can change either because the quantities of goods and services are changing or because their prices are changing. As a result, economists often prefer to use **real gross domestic product**[1] **(real GDP)** as the measure of production; the adjective *real* means that we adjust the measure of production to account for changes in prices over time. Real GDP, also called *output* or *production*, is the most comprehensive measure of how well the economy is doing.

2   Figure 17.1 shows the changes in real GDP in recent years in the United States. When you look at real GDP over time, as in Figure 17.1, you notice two simultaneous patterns emerging. Over the long term, increases in real GDP demonstrate an upward trend, which economists call long-term **economic growth**.[2] In the short term, there are **economic fluctuations**[3]—more transient increases or decreases in real GDP. These short-term fluctuations in real GDP are also called *business cycles*. The difference between the long-term economic growth trend and the economic fluctuations can be better seen by drawing a relatively smooth line between the observations on real GDP. Such a smooth trend line is shown in Figure 17.1. Sometimes real GDP fluctuates above the trend line, and sometimes it fluctuates below the trend line. In this section we look more closely at these two patterns: economic growth and economic fluctuations.

1. *real gross domestic product (real GDP)* = A measure of the value of all goods and services newly produced in a country during some period of time, adjusted for changes in prices over time.
2. *economic growth* = An upward trend in real GDP, reflecting expansion in the economy over time.
3. *economic fluctuations* = Swings in real GDP that lead to deviations of the economy from its long-term growth trend.

Economic Growth: The Relentless Uphill Climb

3   The large increase in real GDP shown in Figure 17.1 means that people in the United States now produce a much greater amount of goods and services each year than they did 30 years ago. Improvements in the economic well-being of individuals in any society cannot occur without such an increase in real GDP. To get a better measure of how individuals benefit from increases in real GDP, we consider average production per person, or *real GDP per capita*. Real GDP per capita is real GDP divided by the number of people in the economy. It is the total production of all food, clothes, cars, houses, CDs, concerts, education, computers, etc., per person. When real GDP per capita is increasing, then the well-being—or the standard of living—of individuals in the economy, at least on average, is improving.

Figure 17.1   Economic Growth and Fluctuations

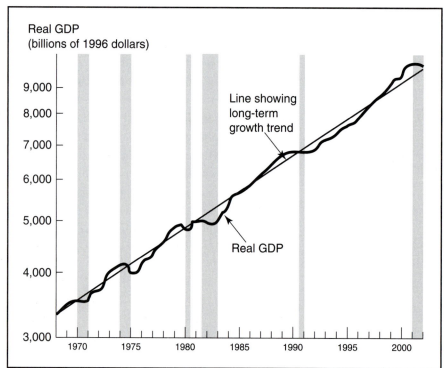

Real GDP has grown by more than $5 trillion during the last 30 years. The trend in growth is shown by the black line. At the same time, the economy has fluctuated up and down as it has grown, with six recessions—marked by the vertical shaded bars—and five subsequent expansions since 1970.

4   How much economic growth has there been during the last
30 years in the United States? The annual *economic growth
rate*—the percentage increase in real GDP each year—provides a
good measure. On the average, for the last 30 years, the annual
economic growth rate has been about 3 percent. This may not
sound like much, but it means that real GDP has nearly tripled. The
increase in production in the United States over the past 30 years is
larger than what Japan and Germany together now produce. It is as
if all the production of Japan and Germany—what is made by all the
workers, machines, and technology in these countries—were
annexed to the U.S. economy, as illustrated in Figure 17.2.

Figure 17.2   Visualizing Economic Growth

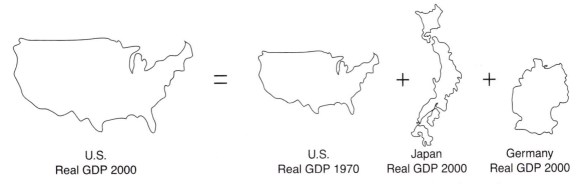

| U.S. | U.S. | Japan | Germany |
| Real GDP 2000 | Real GDP 1970 | Real GDP 2000 | Real GDP 2000 |

Over the last 30 years, production in the U.S. economy has increased by more than the total current
production of the Japanese and German economies combined. It is as if the United States had annexed
Germany and Japan.

5   How much has real GDP *per capita* increased during this
period? Because the U.S. population increased by about 100 million
people during this period, the increase in real GDP per capita has
been less dramatic than the increase in real GDP, but it is impressive
nonetheless. The annual growth rate of real GDP per capita is the
percentage increase in real GDP per capita each year. It has averaged
about 1.7 percent per year. Again, this might not sound like much,
but it has meant that real GDP per capita doubled from about
$10,000 per person in the 1950's to about $20,000 per person in the
1990's. That extra $10,000 per person represents increased
opportunities for travel, VCRs, housing, washing machines, aerobics
classes, health care, antipollution devices for cars, and so on.

6   Over long spans of time, small differences in economic growth—even less than 1 percent per year—can transform societies. For example, economic growth in the southern states was only a fraction of a percent greater than in the North in the 100 years after the Civil War. Yet this enabled the South to rise from a real income per capita about half that of the North after the Civil War to one about the same as that of the North today. Economic growth is the reason that Italy has caught up with and even surpassed the United Kingdom in real GDP per capita; 100 years ago, Italy had a real GDP per capita about half that of the United Kingdom. Economic growth is also key to improvements in the less-developed countries in Africa, Asia, and Latin America. Because economic growth has been lagging in many of these countries, their real GDP per capita is considerably less than that of the United States.

Economic Fluctuations: Temporary Setbacks and Recoveries

7   Clearly, real GDP grows over time, but every now and then real GDP stops growing, falls, and then starts increasing rapidly again. These ups and downs in the economy—that is, economic fluctuations or business cycles—can be seen in Figure 17.1.

8   One of these business cycles, the one in the early 1990's, is blown up for closer examination in Figure 17.3. No two business cycles are alike. Certain phases are common to all business cycles, however. These common phases are shown in the diagram in the margin. When real GDP falls, economists say that there is a **recession**;[4] a rule of thumb says that the fall in real GDP must last for a half year or more before the decline is considered a recession. The highest point before the start of a recession is called the **peak**.[5] The lowest point at the end of a recession is called the **trough**,[6] a term that may cause you to imagine water accumulating at the bottom of one of the dips.

9   The period between recessions—from the trough to the next peak—is called an **expansion**,[7] as shown for a typical fluctuation in the margin. The early part of an expansion is usually called a **recovery**[8] because the economy is just recovering from the recession.

Business cycle phases

4. *recession* = A decline in real GDP that lasts for at least six months.
5. *peak* = The highest point in real GDP before a recession.
6. *trough* = is the lowest point of real GDP at the end of a recession.
7. *expansion* = The period between the trough of a recession and the next peak, consisting of a general rise in output and employment.
8. *recovery* = The early part of an economic expansion, immediately after the trough of the recession.

10   The peaks and troughs of the six recessions since the late 1960's are shown by vertical bars in Figure 17.1. The shaded areas represent the recessions. The area between the shaded bars shows the expansions. The dates of all peaks and troughs back to 1920 are shown in Table 17.1. The average length of each business cycle from peak to peak is five years, but it is clear from Table 17.1 that business cycles are not regularly occurring ups and downs, like sunup and sundown. Recessions occur irregularly. There were only 12 months between the back-to-back recessions of the early 1980's, while 58 months of uninterrupted growth occurred between the 1973–1975 recession and the 1980 recession. The recession phases of business cycles also vary in duration and depth. The 1980 recession, for example, was not nearly as long or as deep as the 1973–1975 recession.

11   The 1990–1991 recession was one of the shortest recessions in U.S. history, and it was followed by the longest expansion in U.S. history. Before that recession, almost uninterrupted economic growth had occurred for most of the 1980's—from the trough of the previous recession in November 1982 to a peak in July 1990.

Figure 17.3   The Phases of Business Cycles

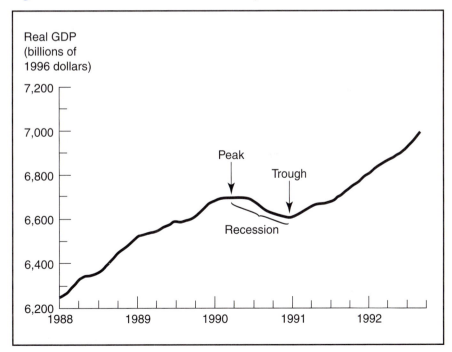

Although no two business cycles are alike, they have common features, including the *peak, recession,* and *trough,* shown here for 1990–1991.

12   Economists debate whether economic policies were responsible for the expansions of the 1980's and 1990's. We will examine these debates in later chapters. Another debate is the cause of the recession that began in 1990. The first month of the recession occurred just after Iraq invaded Kuwait, causing a disruption in the oil fields and a jump in world oil prices. Some argue that this jump in oil prices was a factor in the recession.

13   **A Recession's Aftermath.** The economy usually takes several years to return to normal after a recession. Thus, a period of bad economic times always follows a recession while the economy recovers. Remember that economists define recessions as periods in which real GDP is declining, not as periods in which real GDP is down. Despite the technical definition, many people still associate the word *recession* with bad economic times. For example, although the 1990–1991 recession ended in March 1991, most people felt that the bad economic times extended well into 1992, and they were right. But, technically speaking, the recession was over in March 1991 when GDP began to grow again—well before the effects of an improving economy were felt by most people.

14   **Recessions versus Depressions.** Recessions have been observed for as long as economists have tracked the economy. Some past recessions lasted so long and were so deep that they are called *depressions*. There is no formal definition of a depression. A depression is a huge recession.

15   Fortunately, we have not experienced a depression in the United States for a long time. Figure 17.4 shows the history of real GDP for about 100 years. The most noticeable decline in real GDP occurred in the 1929–1933 recession. Real GDP fell by 32.6 percent in this period. This decline in real GDP was so large that it was given its own designation by economists and historians—the *Great Depression*. The recessions of recent years have had much smaller declines.

Figure 17.4   Growth and Fluctuations Throughout the Twentieth Century

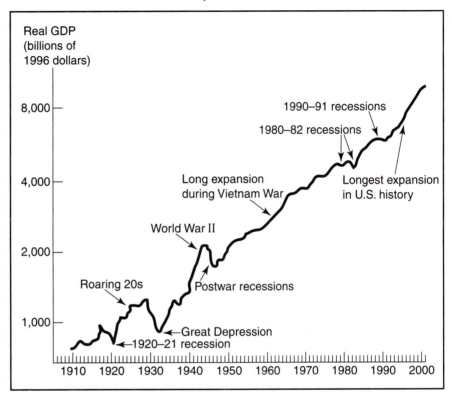

Economic growth has continued, but the size of economic fluctuations has diminished remarkably. Recent ups and downs are minuscule in comparison with the Great Depression.

16   Table 17.1 shows how much real GDP fell in each of the fifteen recessions since the 1920's. The 1920–1921 recession and the 1937–1938 recession were big enough to be classified as depressions, but both are small compared to the Great Depression. Real GDP also declined substantially after World War II, when war production declined.

Table 17.1 Comparison of Recessions

Recession Peak — Trough	Duration of Recession (months from peak to trough)	Decline in Real GDP (percent from peak to trough)	Duration of Next Expansion (months from trough to peak)
Jan 1920–Jul 1921	18	8.7	22
May 1923–Jul 1924	14	4.1	27
Oct 1926–Nov 1927	13	2.0	21
Aug 1929–Mar 1933	43	32.6	50
May 1937–Jun 1938	13	18.2	80
Feb 1945–Oct 1945	8	11.0	37
Nov 1948–Oct 1949	11	1.5	45
Jul 1953–May 1954	10	3.2	39
Aug 1957–Apr 1958	8	3.3	24
Apr 1960–Feb 1961	10	1.2	106
Dec 1969–Nov 1970	11	1.0	36
Nov 1973–Mar 1975	16	4.9	58
Jan 1980–Jul 1980	6	2.5	12
Jul 1981–Nov 1982	16	3.0	92
Jul 1990–Mar 1991	8	1.4	120
Mar 2001–	13*		

*As of April 2002.

Source: National Bureau of Economic Research

17   Clearly, recent recessions have not been even remotely comparable in severity to the Great Depression or the other huge recessions of the 1920's and 1930's. The 1990–1991 recession, for example, had only one-twentieth the decline in real GDP that occurred during the Great Depression. But because any recession rivets attention on people's hardship and suffering, there is always a tendency to view a current recession as worse than all previous recessions. Some commentators reporting on the 1990–1991 recession wondered whether it should be compared with the Great Depression. For example, in September 1992, Louis Uchitelle of the *New York Times* wrote, "Technically, the recession is over, but spiritually, it continues ... The question is, what to call these hard times. What has been happening in America since 1989 seems momentous enough to enter history as a major economic event of the 20th century."*

<table>
<tr><td>

**Muscle
Reading
Reminder**

Phase Three:
**Recite
Review
Review Again**

</td><td>

Review

- Economic growth and economic fluctuations occur simultaneously.
- Economic growth provides lasting improvements in the well-being of people. But recessions interrupt this growth.
- The Great Depression of the 1930's was a much larger downturn than recent recessions. It was about twenty times more severe than the 1990–1991 recession when measured by the decline in real GDP.

</td></tr>
</table>

Source: Taylor, J. (2004). *Economics* (4th ed.). Boston: Houghton Mifflin Company. pp. 25–31.

*Louis Uchitelle, "Even Words Fail in This Economy," *New York Times*, September 8, 1992, p. C2.

☐ Assessing Your Learning

Demonstrating Comprehension

EXERCISE 13   Defining concepts

In Reading Selection 2, each key concept listed below was defined. Return to the selection and find these ten terms. Have you highlighted their definitions? Work on memorizing these definitions. It may help to write them down many times or put them on index cards to carry with you. When you are ready, turn to a classmate and orally test each other until you truly have the definitions memorized.

1. real GDP
2. economic growth
3. economic fluctuations
4. business cycles
5. recession
6. peak
7. trough
8. expansion
9. recovery
10. depression

EXERCISE 14   Elaborating with examples

With key concepts, authors often provide examples to help readers understand. Fill in the blanks to complete these sentences with examples from different periods.

1. For the past thirty years in the United States, the real GDP has

   averaged a growth rate of about _____ percent each year.

   This indicates that people are producing _____ each year

   and that the standard of living is _____.

2. Real GDP can be averaged *per* _____. This is the total

   production of all _____ per person.

   A formula to represent this is _____ / _____.

3. For the past thirty years in the United States, the real GDP *per capita* has averaged about _____% per year.

4. In the United States, the real GDP *per capita* was about

   $_____ per person in the 1950s and about

   $_____ per person in the 1990s.

5. In the late 1800s, after the Civil War, people's incomes in the _____ were low, but 100 years later economic growth has enabled the _____ to catch up with the _____ .

6. According to the author, less developed countries in _____ _____ could benefit from an increase in real GDP per capita. Over long time periods, even a fractional difference can transform societies.

7. In the United States from 1973 to 1975, there was a long _____ . Then 58 months of growth occurred between _____ and _____ . In the early 1980s, there were two back-to-back _____ . One of the shortest U.S. recessions occurred in _____ . The longest expansion in U.S. history lasted from _____ to _____ .

8. Provide your own example of a period when real GDP starts to show recovery from a recession while people still believe they are in bad economic times.

   _____

   _____

9. Provide an example of a period of economic depression.

   _____

   _____

S T R A T E G Y

Interpreting Graphs and Tables

Selection 2, about GDP, contains four figures and one table. The figures are labeled 17.1, 17.2, 17.3, and 17.4. The table is labeled 17.1. The number 17 indicates that they come from Chapter 17 in Taylor's textbook. When you study economics, you will need to interpret graphs and sometimes produce graphs. For the next exercise, we work with interpretation. What are the graphs illustrating? To begin, practice explaining this basic figure.

First, it is important to find the part in the reading that can help you explain it. In the example below, paragraphs 8 and 9 include the information you need to interpret the model graph on the left. Notice that the first and second sentences do not really help you understand. The explanation for this model graph begins with the third sentence.

Diagram

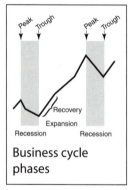

Business cycle phases

8   One of these business cycles, the one in the early 1990's, is blown up for closer examination in Figure 17.3. No two business cycles are alike. Certain phases are common to all business cycles, however. These common phases are shown in the diagram in the margin. When real GDP falls, economists say that there is a recession; a rule of thumb says that the fall in real GDP must last for a half year or more before the decline is considered a recession. The highest point before the start of a recession is called the peak. The lowest point at the end of a recession is called the trough, a term that may cause you to imagine water accumulating at the bottom of one of the dips.

9   The period between recessions—from the trough to the next peak—is called an expansion, as shown for a typical fluctuation in the margin. The early part of an expansion is usually called a recovery because the economy is just recovering from the recession.

EXERCISE 15 Interpreting graphs

A. *Look carefully at the model graph, and reread paragraphs 8 and 9. Explain the graph by filling in the blanks for this sample explanation to get the idea.*

This graph shows us common _____ in a business _____ . The blue _____ illustrates ups and _____ . The line goes up and reaches a _____ . Then the line goes down again to a _____ . As the line goes up after the _____ , the first part is considered a _____ because the economy is just recovering from a _____ . The period between _____ is called an _____ . For a decline to be called a _____ , it must last for 18 months. Expansions can last for _____ or short periods of time.

B. *Work with a partner to prepare to explain the figures from Reading Selection 1 in a similar way. Take turns. Student A could explain Figures 17.1 and 17.3. Student B could explain Figures 17.2 and 17.4. You could work together to explain table 17.1. Before you talk with each other, take time to mentally prepare your interpretation of the graphs. Find the sentences about each figure in the reading selection by scanning for the figure number in the passage. Then use the sentences from the passage to help you develop your interpretation. When you explain the graph, do not read from the book, but use your own words as you point to the features on the graphs while you are explaining.*

Memorize your explanation before you speak to your partner.

☐ Focusing on Economics

EXERCISE 16 **Checking comprehension**

On separate paper, answer the following questions in short-answer form. Imagine they are part of a test in an economics class. Write in complete sentences.

1. What is the difference between economic growth and economic fluctuations?
2. Why do bad economic times continue after recessions end?
3. How many recessions have there been since the Great Depression?
4. How do the 1990–1991 and the 2001 recessions compare?

EXERCISE 17 **Solving problems**

The graph below shows a business cycle that occurred in the United States in the 1970s. Label the peak, recession, trough, and recovery phases of this business cycle.

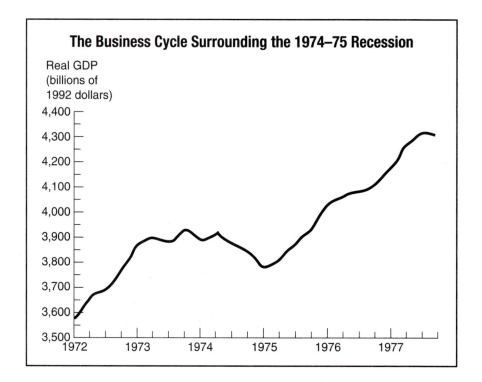

The Business Cycle Surrounding the 1974–75 Recession

Real GDP
(billions of
1992 dollars)

Reading Assignment 3

REAL GDP OVER TIME

☐ Getting Ready to Read

ACTIVITY 18 **Planning your reading strategy**

Selection 3 is similar in style to Selection 2. Prepare for reading this selection by using similar strategies. What is your plan? How will you get ready to read this selection? How do you think you might be tested on this selection?

_____

_____

_____

_____

_____

_____

_____

Reading Selection 3

UNEMPLOYMENT, INFLATION, AND INTEREST RATES

18   As real GDP changes over time, so do other economic variables, such as unemployment, inflation, and interest rates. Looking at these other economic variables gives us a better understanding of the human story behind the changes in real GDP. They also provide additional information about the economy's performance—just as a person's pulse rate or cholesterol level gives information different from the body temperature. No one variable is sufficient.

Unemployment During Recessions

19   There are fluctuations in unemployment just as there are fluctuations in real GDP. The **unemployment rate**[1] is the number

1. *unemployment rate* = The percentage of the labor force that is unemployed.

of unemployed people as a percentage of the labor force; the labor force consists of those who are either working or looking for work. Every time the economy goes into a recession, the unemployment rate rises because people are laid off and new jobs are difficult to find. The individual stories behind the unemployment numbers frequently represent frustration and distress.

20   Figure 17.5 shows what happens to the unemployment rate as the economy goes through recessions and recoveries. The increase in the unemployment rate during a recession is eventually followed by a decline in unemployment during the recovery. Note, for example, how unemployment rose during the recessions of 1969–1970 and 1973–1975. Around the time of the 1990–1991 recession, the unemployment rate rose from 5.2 percent to 7.7 percent.

Figure 17.5   The Unemployment Rate

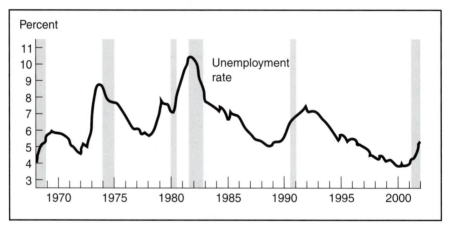

The number of unemployed workers as a percentage of the labor force—the unemployment rate—increases during recessions because people are laid off and it is difficult to find work. Sometimes the unemployment rate continues to increase for a while after the recession is over, as in 1971 and 1991. But eventually unemployment declines during the economic recovery.

21   Figure 17.6 shows how high the unemployment rate got during the Great Depression. It rose to over 25 percent; one in four workers was out of work. Fortunately, recent increases in unemployment during recessions have been much smaller. The unemployment rate reached 10.4 percent in the early 1980's, the highest level since World War II.

Figure 17.6 Unemployment During the Great Depression

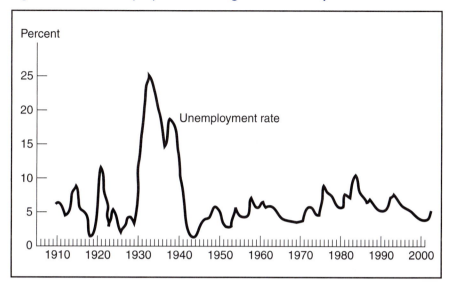

The increase in unemployment in the United States during the Great Depression was huge compared with the increases in unemployment during more mild downturns in the economy. More than one in four workers were unemployed during the Great Depression.

22   Even though the most recent recession pales in comparison to the Great Depression, it still caused a lot of pain and hardship across the country. Figure 17.7 illustrates how rapidly unemployment rose, even in what most economists described as a mild recession. In the 12 months from the end of 2000 to the end of 2001, the unemployment rate increased by almost 2 percentage points. To put this number in more human terms, the number of unemployed workers across the country increased by about 2.5 million.

Figure 17.7 **The Rapid Rise in Unemployment in 2001**

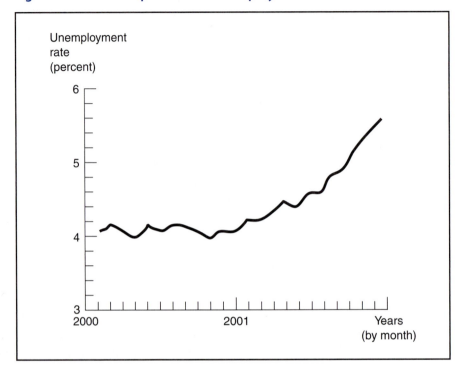

When the economy moves from expansion into recession, unemployment can climb very rapidly over a period of a few months, as we saw at the end of the long expansion in 2001.

Inflation

23   Just as output and unemployment have fluctuated over time, so has inflation. The inflation rate is the percentage increase in the average price of all goods and services from one year to the next. Figure 17.8 shows the **inflation rate** for the same 30-year period we have focused on in our examination of real GDP and unemployment. Clearly, a low and stable inflation rate has not been a feature of the United States during this period. There are several useful facts to note about the behavior of inflation.

Figure 17.8 The Ups and Downs in Inflation

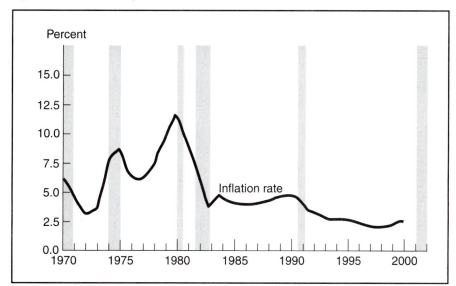

Inflation has increased before each recession and then declined during and immediately after each recession. In addition, a longer-term upward trend in inflation began in the mid-1960's and, after several ups and downs, reached a peak in 1980. In 1981–1983, America had a disinflation—a decline in the rate of inflation.

24   First, inflation is closely correlated with the ups and downs in real GDP and employment: inflation increased prior to every recession in the last 30 years and then subsided during and after every recession. We will want to explore whether this close correlation between the ups and downs in inflation and the ups and downs in the economy helps explain economic fluctuations.

25   Second, there are longer-term trends in inflation. For example, inflation rose from a low point in the mid-1960's to a high point of double-digit inflation in 1980. This period of persistently high inflation from the mid-1960's until 1980 is called the *Great Inflation*. The Great Inflation ended in the early 1980's, when the inflation rate declined substantially. Such a decline in inflation is called *disinflation*. (When inflation is negative and the average price level falls, economists call it *deflation*).

26   Third, judging by history, there is no reason to expect the inflation rate to be zero, even on average. The inflation rate has averaged around 2 or 3 percent in the 1990's in the United States.

27   Why does inflation increase before recessions? Why does inflation fall during and after recessions? What caused the Great Inflation? Why is inflation not equal to zero even in more normal times, when the economy is neither in recession nor in boom? What can economic policy do to keep inflation low and stable? These are some of the questions and policy issues about inflation addressed by macroeconomics.

Interest Rates

28   The **interest rate** is the amount that lenders charge when they lend money, expressed as a percentage of the amount loaned. For example, if you borrow $100 for a year from a friend and the interest rate on the loan is 6 percent, then at the end of the year you must pay your friend back $6 in interest in addition to the $100 you borrowed. The interest rate is another key economic variable that is related to the growth and change in real GDP over time.

29   **Different Types of Interest Rates and Their Behavior.** There are many different interest rates in the economy: the *mortgage interest rate* is the rate on loans to buy a house; the *savings deposit interest rate* is the rate people get on their savings deposits at banks; the *Treasury bill rate* is the interest rate the government pays when it borrows money from people for a year or less; the *federal funds rate* is the interest rate banks charge each other on very short-term loans. Interest rates influence people's economic behavior. When interest rates rise, for example, it is more expensive to borrow funds to buy a house or a car, so many people postpone such purchases.

30   Figure 17.9 shows the behavior of a typical interest rate, the federal funds rate, during the last 30 years. First, note how closely the ups and downs in the interest rate are correlated with the ups and downs in the economy. Interest rates rise before each recession and then decline during and after each recession. Second, note that, as with the inflation rate, there are longer-term trends in the interest rate. The interest rate rose from the mid-1960's until the 1980's. Each fluctuation in interest rates during this period brought forth a higher peak in interest rates. Then, in the 1980's, the interest rate began a downward trend; each peak was lower than the previous peak. By the early 1990's, interest rates had returned to the levels of the early 1970's.

Figure 17.9   The Ups and Downs in Interest Rates

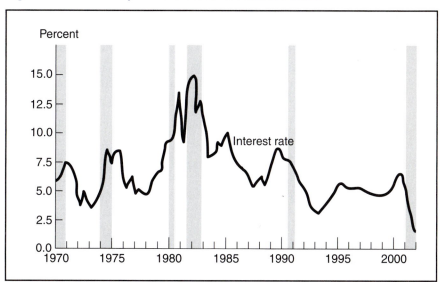

Interest rates generally rise just before a recession and then decline during and just after the recession. There was also a longer-term trend upward in interest rates in the 1970's and a downward trend in the 1980's and 1990's. (The interest rate shown here is the federal funds interest rate.)

31   **The Concept of the Real Interest Rate.** As we will see, the trends and fluctuations in interest rates are intimately connected with the trends and fluctuations in inflation and real GDP. In fact, the long-term rise in interest rates in the 1960's and 1970's was partly due to the rise in the rate of inflation. When inflation rises, people who lend money will be paid back in funds that are worth less because the average price of goods rises more quickly. To compensate for this decline in the value of funds, lenders require a higher interest rate. For example, if the inflation rate is 20 percent and you lend someone $100 for a year at 6 percent, then you get back $106 at the end of the year. However, the *average* price of the goods you can buy with your $106 is now 20 percent higher. Thus, your 6 percent gain in interest has been offset by a 20 percent loss. It is as if you receive *negative* 14 percent interest: 6 percent interest less 20 percent inflation. The difference between the stated interest rate and the inflation rate is thus a better measure of the real interest rate. Economists define the **real interest rate** as the interest rate less the inflation rate people expect. The term **nominal interest rate** is used to refer to the interest rate on a

loan, making no adjustment for inflation. For example, the real interest rate is 2 percent if the nominal interest rate is 5 percent and inflation is expected to be 3 percent (5 − 3 = 2). To keep the real interest rate from changing by a large amount as inflation rises, the nominal interest rate has to increase with inflation. Thus, the concept of the real interest rate helps us understand why inflation and interest rates have moved together. We will make much more use of the real interest rate in later chapters.

Review

- The unemployment rate rises during recessions and falls during recoveries.
- Inflation and interest rates rise prior to recessions and then fall during and just after recessions.
- There was a long-term increase in interest rates and inflation in the 1970's. Interest rates and inflation were lower in the 1990's.

Source: From Taylor, J. (2004). *Economics* (4th ed.). Boston: Houghton Mifflin Company, pp. 31–36.

☐ Assessing Your Learning

Demonstrating Comprehension

EXERCISE 19 **Recalling and verbalizing key concepts**

Reading Selection 3 included a discussion of economic variables that are part of any description of the economy's performance. For this exercise, a definition or explanation of the variable is provided, and you need to name the variable.

1. The number of unemployed people as a percentage of the labor force is called the _____.

2. The percentage increase in the average price of all goods and services from one year to the next is called the _____.

3. The amount that lenders charge when they lend money expressed as a percentage of the amount loaned is called the _____.

ACTIVITY 20 **Analyzing graphs**

Look back at Figures 17.5, 17.6, 17.7, 17.8, and 17.9 to answer these questions.

Figure 17.5

1. When was the unemployment rate the highest? _____

2. How high was it? _____

3. When did it begin climbing? _____

4. What does the colored bar represent? _____

Figure 17.6

5. How high was the unemployment rate during the Great Depression?

   _____

6. When did it drop? _____

7. What other world event was occurring when it dropped?

   _____

Figure 17.7

8. What was the unemployment rate in January 2000? _____

9. What was the unemployment rate in January 2002? _____

10. What event occurred on September 11, 2001? _____

    _____

11. Did the unemployment rate start rising before or after September 11,

    2001? _____

Figure 17.8

12. When did the inflation rate reach a peak? _____

13. When did the United States experience disinflation? _____

14. What was the general inflation rate in the 1990s? _____

Figure 17.9

15. How high was the interest rate between 1981 and 1982?

_____

16. Prior to 1981, was the general interest rate trend increasing or

decreasing? _____

17. After 1982, was the general interest rate trend increasing or

decreasing? _____

☐ Linking Concepts

ACTIVITY **21**   **Connecting economic theories with real-life**

According to Taylor, "Looking at these other economic variables gives us a better understanding of the human story behind the changes in real GDP. They also provide additional information about the economy's performance."

For each of the three key variables listed below, think of a personal human story. Share the story with your classmates in a small group. Then, each group should decide on one story to share with the whole class.

1. _Unemployment._ Do you know someone who has experienced an employment loss related to a period of recession? Describe the circumstances.
2. _Inflation._ Do you know about any other countries that have experienced high rates of inflation? When? Give examples of things that became difficult to buy because of inflation.
3. _Interest Rates._ Are you currently paying interest on a loan, or do you know someone who is? What is the interest rate? What is the loan for? Are you currently earning interest on a savings account, or do you know someone who is? What is the rate?

☐ Learning Vocabulary

ACTIVITY 22   Seeing relationships among words

Each group of four words includes one word that does not belong. Draw an X through the odd word. AWL words from the reading passages have a dotted underline.

1. accumulating   collecting   amassing   ~~subsiding~~

2. adjust   transform   maintain   fluctuate

3. aid   loss   enable   benefit

4. commentator   reporter   analyst   economist

5. cycles   series   stable   phases

6. depression   expansion   decline   downturn

7. impact   influence   effect   predict

8. labor   goods   services   employment

9. offset   compensate   balance   deepen

10. recovery   recession   stabilize   restore

11. simultaneous   concurrent   prior   synchronized

12. subsided   receded   decreased   expanded

13. trend   tendency   exception   sustained

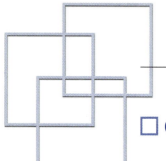

Reading Assignment 4

ECONOMICS IN ACTION

☐ Getting Ready to Read

ACTIVITY 23 **Adjusting reading strategies**

This last selection considers a specific event and uses that event to illustrate how economic theory can help us understand and predict effects and how economic theory influences policymakers. As you carry out Phase One of Muscle Reading (Preview, Outline, Question), notice how this selection is different from Selections 2 and 3. Think of a plan to adjust your reading strategies for this difference. Answer these questions.

1. Describe at least two ways that Selection 4 is different from Selections 2 and 3.

    _____

    _____

2. Describe how your reading process will change because of the differences.

    _____

    _____

☐ Reading for a Purpose

As you read Selection 4, keep in mind your own reaction to the ideas presented. Do you agree or disagree? What are your own thoughts about 9/11 and the current state of the economy? After reading this selection, you will be asked to write a short reaction paper.

Reading Selection 4

ECONOMICS IN ACTION

The Economic Impact of September 11

1   The tragic events of September 11, 2001, left a trail of human destruction that was hitherto almost unimaginable. In the days and months following September 11, people all over the United States tried to assess the human and economic toll of the events of that fateful day. The assessment that many macroeconomists were asked to make was to calculate the economic impact of the events of September 11. As the economist Paul Krugman, who is also a regular columnist for the *New York Times*, said in his Op-Ed column a few days after September 11, "It seems almost in bad taste to talk about dollars and cents after an act of mass murder. Nonetheless, we must ask about the economic aftershocks from Tuesday's horror." Macroeconomic theory can help us understand the long- and short-term economic impact of this and other such tragedies.

2   In the case of September 11, the most obvious short-term costs were the destruction of life and property in New York, Washington, D.C., and Pennsylvania; the disruption of financial markets, given that many large financial institutions were located in and around the World Trade Center; and the costs to airlines from disruptions in air travel in the days following the tragedy. However, the theory of economic fluctuations, presented in Chapters 23 and 24, tells us that spending shocks have feedback effects that aggravate the initial direct effects. In the case of New York, the disruption to the economy was substantially greater than the destruction of property and cleanup costs would indicate because of drastic cutbacks in tourism, which led to a sharp fall off in hotel stays, dining out in restaurants, and shopping for expensive goods in Manhattan. The lack of spending by consumers led firms in the hotel, restaurant, and retail industries to lay off thousands of workers. According to a study done by the New York City Chamber of Commerce in September 2001, the cost in terms of reduced economic activity was expected to be almost $40 billion, and the cost in terms of employment was expected to be almost 25,000 jobs. Financial markets were severely disrupted in the short run: they were closed for the remainder of the week, and when they opened the following week, the Dow Jones Industrial Average fell from 9605.5 to 8920.7,

a decline of about 7 percent; at the end of the first week of trading, the Dow had fallen to 8235.8, a decline of about 14 percent. The airline industry was hit hard: in the weeks following September 11, airlines announced plans to lay off tens of thousands of workers—20,000 apiece at American Airlines and United Airlines.

3   The theory of economic fluctuations states that when faced with an economic shock that reduces spending, policymakers can respond by putting into place specific measures designed not only to stop the fall in spending, but indeed to try to restore both confidence and spending by consumers and firms. The president promised $20 billion in federal aid to New York to help the city rebuild. As fears that one or more airlines would have to go into bankruptcy mounted, both Congress and the Senate sought to provide relief for the beleaguered airline industry by overwhelmingly approving a bill that provided $5 billion in federal funds and $10 billion in loan guarantees. The response of monetary policymakers to the events of September 11 was equally swift: on September 17, the Federal Reserve cut interest rates from 3.5 percent to 3 percent, making it cheaper for firms and individuals to borrow money, and also announced its willingness to take steps to restore normalcy to financial markets. Help was not offered only by the government and the Federal Reserve; millions of people all over the United States contributed hundreds of millions of dollars to charities that helped the victims and their families make payments on their rent, school tuition, and health care, doing their part to keep the negative effects from deepening.

4   The theory of economic growth tells us that the long-term growth of an economy depends on its ability to produce goods and services, which in turn depends on the economy's stocks of labor, capital, and technology. While the destruction of life and property in New York and Washington, D.C., was substantial—"more than we can bear," in the words of Mayor Giuliani—the loss of labor and capital was small relative to the size of the entire U.S. population and the entire U.S. capital stock. In the same Op-Ed piece mentioned earlier, Paul Krugman speculated that the long-term effects would not be substantial: "Nobody has a dollar figure for the damage yet, but I would be surprised if the loss is more than 0.1 percent of U.S. wealth—comparable to the material effects of a major earthquake or hurricane." While such calculations may seem a little too cold blooded at first glance, it is important that

macroeconomists make such assessments so that we can develop a more complete understanding of the impacts of such tragedies, and also so that we can come up with appropriate policy responses to these events.

5   The prediction that the events of September 11 would not have a long-term effect seems to have been vindicated by a reassessment of the situation six months later. In the weeks following September 11, the financial markets seemed to stabilize and then recover: by November 9 the Dow had reached the level it was at on September 10, and it ended the year almost 6 percent higher, at 10,178.7. GDP grew rapidly in the fourth quarter of 2001: it increased at a rate of 1.4 percent, signaling a possible return to the sustained positive growth rates experienced during the long expansion. Finally, the unemployment rate seemed to stabilize and then improve as well—after increasing from 5 percent to 5.8 percent over the last four months of 2001, it came back down to 5.4 percent in the first two months of 2002.

9/11/01 wreckage in New York City

Source: Taylor, J. (2004). *Economics* (4th ed.). Boston: Houghton Mifflin Company, pp. 34–35.

☐ Assessing Your Learning

Demonstrating Comprehension

EXERCISE **24** **Recognizing an author's purpose**

Each paragraph in Reading Selection 4 has a different purpose. Select the correct answer to identify the purpose of each paragraph.

1. Paragraph 1

    a. to describe

    b. to introduce

    c. to complain

2. Paragraph 2

    a. to list effects

    b. to list causes

    c. to list disruptions

3. Paragraph 3

    a. to identify policy actions

    b. to state theories

    c. to recommend actions

4. Paragraph 4

    a. to illustrate applied theory

    b. to support the use economic theory for interpreting events

    c. to explain long-term growth factors

5. Paragraph 5

    a. to conclude with a prediction

    b. to convince readers that 9/11 continues to affect the economy

    c. to list facts that illustrate recovery

EXERCISE 25 **Responding to the reading**

Reading Selection 4 includes opinion as well as theory. What are your thoughts about the author's ideas? Reaction papers are commonly assigned in college classes. Review Selection 4 and prepare to write a reaction paper on a piece of the selection that has caused you to think in a new way. Do you believe all the author's claims? Do they match your own observations? Do you have any doubts? Take time to write a one-page reaction paper. Remember to begin by referring to points the author has made, give the author credit, and then add your ideas or opinions.

☐ For Further Study

EXERCISE 26 **Reading a related article of interest**

Now that you are familiar with some macroeconomic theories, select an article from the business section of a current publication. Search for one that mentions any of the key concepts from this chapter. Make a copy of the article, or cut it out. Highlight relevant parts, and write a one-paragraph explanation about how the article relates to what you have learned in this chapter.

☐ Assessing Your Learning at the End of a Chapter

Revisiting Chapter Objectives

Return to the first page of this chapter. Think about the chapter objectives. Put a check mark next to the ones you feel secure about. Review material in the chapter you still need to work on. When you are ready, answer the chapter review questions below.

☐ **Practicing for a Chapter Test**

EXERCISE 27   **Reviewing comprehension**

Check your comprehension of main concepts, or ideas, in this chapter by responding to the following chapter review questions.

1. Compare and contrast your reading process for Exercise 26 with your reading process for Reading Selections 2 and 3 in this chapter.
2. Return to Figure 17.1. Explain GDP and the trend line as shown in the graph.
3. For this theory, state an assumption that may underlie the theory.

Theory	Situation	Possible inference	Assumption
Economic growth, as evidenced by increase in real GDP, provides lasting improvements in the well-being of people.	A country has a low real GDP.		

4. Demonstrate your ability to solve economic problems. Using the data from Canada and Britain shown in the table on the next page, plot a graph to illustrate the unemployment rate.

The graph below shows a business cycle that occurred in the United States in the 1970s. Label the peak, recession, trough, and recovery phases of this business cycle.

Rate of Unemployment 1990–2000

Rate of Unemployment (percent)

Year	Canada	Britain
1990	7.7	6.9
1991	9.8	8.8
1992	10.6	10.1
1993	10.8	10.5
1994	9.5	9.6
1995	8.6	8.7
1996	8.8	8.1
1997	8.4	7.0
1998	7.7	6.3
1999	7.0	6.0
2000	6.1	5.5

1990   1995   2000

Source: Taylor, J. (2004). *Economics* (4th ed.). Chapter 17, p. 42.

5. Recall the article you selected to share with your instructor and write about. Explain and justify your opinions about the article.
6. Define gross domestic product (GDP).
7. Contrast economic growth and economic fluctuations.
8. Return to Figure 17.4. How many periods of recession are shown on the graph? _____

   How many periods of expansion are shown on the graph? _____

9. Explain the relationship between recessions and . . .
   a. unemployment
   b. inflation
   c. interest

10. Discuss the economic impact of 9/11.

Academic Vocabulary

Here are some academic vocabulary words that were introduced in this chapter. Confirm the words that you know the meaning of. Identify the words that are not yet part of your active vocabulary. Relearn the words that you need to relearn.

accumulating	adjustment	aid	annual	appropriate
area	commentator	considerably	consists	consumers
contribute	cycles	debates	decline	depression
designed	emerging	enable	expansion	factor
feature	financial	fluctuations	funds	guarantees
illustrated	impact	implement	income	indicate
initial	institutions	investors	labor	margin
nonetheless	obvious	occurring	offset	percentage
persistently	phases	policies	prediction	previous
prior	purchases	reassessment	recovery	resources
response	restore	simultaneous	simultaneously	specified
speculated	stabilize	stable	subsided	sufficient
sustained	technical	technically	technology	theory
transform	trend	variable		

WEB POWER

Go to http://esl.college.hmco.com/students to view more economics readings, plus exercises that will help you study the selections and the academic words in this chapter.

World Roots of American Education

ACADEMIC FOCUS: EDUCATION

Academic Reading Objectives

After completing this chapter, you should be able to:

✓ Check here as you master each objective.

1. Clarify understanding of issues raised in texts ☐
2. Articulate plausible implications or consequences ☐
3. Develop perspectives through exploration of beliefs, arguments, and theories ☐
4. Evaluate the level or degree of credibility of sources ☐
5. Prioritize what to learn for test-taking purposes ☐
6. Apply effective study skills ☐

Education Objectives

1. Examine the global roots of U.S. education systems ☐
2. Recognize goals of schooling ☐
3. Contrast elements from key periods in educational history ☐
4. Examine personal and group rights to participate in schooling ☐
5. Summarize distinguishing features of certain ancient educational systems ☐
6. Explore personal beliefs about education ☐

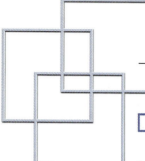

Reading Assignment 1

WORLD ROOTS OF AMERICAN EDUCATION

☐ Getting Ready to Read

Have you ever thought about becoming a teacher? Would you want to teach children, or adults? Which subject area would you want to specialize in? Teaching is a part of everyone's lives. Not only are educational theories applied in school settings with students and teachers, but teaching also occurs in work and home settings. Whether or not your career path involves teaching professionally, taking a course in education or human growth and development could help you in many ways.

EXERCISE 1 Writing self-reflections in a reading journal

Spend a few minutes thinking about **teaching** *in order to prepare for writing in your reading journal. Work with your classmates to generate a list of questions about teaching and education.*

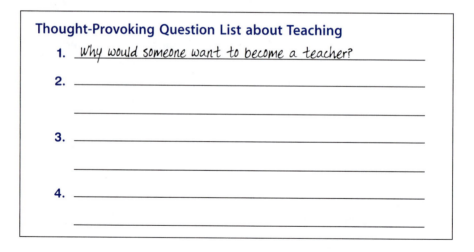

Thought-Provoking Question List about Teaching

1. Why would someone want to become a teacher? _____

2. _____

   _____

3. _____

   _____

4. _____

   _____

Now take **ten minutes** *to freewrite in your reading journal. Your instructor will time you. Write your thoughts about teaching and education.*

EXERCISE 2   Arranging for a class observation

It is important for advanced ESL students to have experiences in content-area classes. By working with this book, you have already become familiar with a variety of reading materials and vocabulary from different disciplines. If you are not already taking some non-ESL coursework, now is the time to arrange for a class observation. You could visit a class in your major or any popular course you might be interested in. Here is a list of some of the most popular courses at a typical college (excluding English and math courses):

- Introduction to Microcomputers
- Preparing for Student Success
- Humanities
- Human Growth and Development
- Psychology
- Principles of Economics—Macro
- General Education Biology
- Human Anatomy & Physiology
- Social Environment
- Natural Environment
- Critical Thinking/Ethics
- Music Appreciation
- Art Appreciation
- Philosophy
- Nutrition
- Financial Accounting
- Education
- Diverse Populations

Follow these steps to arrange for a class observation:[1]

1. Compare the list above with a course-offering schedule from your college. Try to find an introductory class at the 100 or 1000[2] level. This level indicates that it is for freshman; 200 or 2000 for sophomores; 300 or 3000 for juniors, and 400 or 4000 for seniors. Classes at the 500/5000 or above level can only be offered at universities with graduate-level programs.

2. Find out who is teaching the class you want to visit. Is this person a full-time or part-time faculty member? If he or she is full-time, locate his or her office to find out about office hours. Then stop by and ask permission to observe the class. Make sure the instructor will not be giving an exam on the day you want to visit. If the instructor is part-time, check with the department. This instructor probably has a mailbox where you could leave a note (with contact information) requesting to observe the class.

3. If possible, ask the instructor for a copy of the syllabus and take a look at the textbook in the bookstore before you go to the class.

4. Go to the class early. Sit in the back and just observe. Do not participate in the class. It is probably best to go to the class alone, but if two classmates want to go to the same class, be sure to run it by the professor. Stay for the complete period, and be sure to thank the faculty member after the class.

5. Have some blank paper with you, and take notes on the following:
   a. What teaching methods is the instructor using (e.g., lecture, discussion)?
   b. What materials is he or she using?
   c. How are the students responding and behaving?
   d. Do you think the students are learning?
   e. Are they taking notes?
   f. What are the most important concepts covered in this class?
   g. Compare how the students and instructor interact here with the way they interact in other classroom experiences you have had. Who does the talking here?

1. Note: If you cannot find time outside class time, consider using one reading class period as a field experience period, with students going to different classes at the same time.
2. Numbering systems such as these are the most common, but they may vary at your institution. Nevertheless, the course number will probably include some indicator of level.

h. Does anything surprise you, or is anything not clear?

i. Is homework assigned?

j. What impresses you the most about this class (positively or negatively)?

Assignment: Write a short reaction paper about your class observation. Use your notes. Briefly describe the class and teaching methods used. Then explain what you learned from this experience.

EXERCISE 3   Applying a reading strategy

Phase One of Muscle Reading includes three steps: Preview, Outline, and Question. Apply these steps to the passages in this chapter.

Muscle Reading Reminder

Phase One:
Preview
Outline
Question

To **preview**, look ahead for familiar concepts, facts, or ideas that catch your interest and are related to your goals. Look at visual elements including the history chart and section divisions. Determine your reading strategy. How will you use what you learn from your reading? How will you be tested on this material? How much time do you need?

To **outline**, mentally note the section titles.

To **question**, write down actual questions about possible content. You could transform section titles into question structures if other ideas do not come right to your mind.

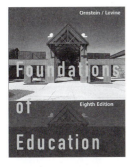

Cover of Ornstein, A. C., & Levine, D. U. (2003). *Foundations of Education* (8th ed.). Boston: Houghton Mifflin.

☐ Reading the Selection

The following reading passages were selected from a chapter found in a textbook written for pre-service teachers. *Pre-service* means it is written for education students who are learning about their profession before they become teachers. This chapter is designed to help education students learn about how schooling became part of human experience and how educational practices have evolved and influenced schooling practices in the United States. Only the first part of the chapter is included here. It considers influences from ancient China, India, and Egypt. The history chart summarizes points from additional time periods. To learn more, you can visit a useful site associated with this book by linking to it from the student website: http://college.hmco.com/education/students/.

Reading Selection 1

WORLD ROOTS OF AMERICAN EDUCATION

Education in Preliterate Societies

1   Our narrative begins in preliterate times before the invention of reading and writing when our ancestors transmitted their culture orally from one generation to the next. We can find the origins of informal learning in families and appreciate why it remains so powerful even today. Although we live in a time when information is electronically stored and retrieved in computers, an examination of preliterate education can help us understand why schools often tend to resist change as they train the young in essential "survival" skills.

2   Preliterate people faced the almost overwhelming problems of surviving in an environment that pitted them against the drought and floods, wild animals, and attacks from hostile groups. By trial and error, they developed survival skills that over time became cultural patterns. For culture to continue, it had to be transmitted deliberately from the group's adults to its children, a process called acculturation. As children learned the group's language, skills, and values, they inherited and perpetuated their culture.

3   Over time, the group developed survival skills that were inculcated as moral codes in the young. Marking the passage from childhood to adulthood, rituals used dancing, music, and dramatic acting to create a powerful supernatural meaning and evoke a moral response. Thus children learned the group's prescriptions (things they should do) as well as its proscriptions or taboos (behaviors that were forbidden).

4   Lacking writing to record their past, preliterate societies relied on oral tradition—storytelling—to transmit their cultural heritage. Elders or priests, often gifted storytellers, sang or recited narratives of the group's past. Combining myths and legends, the oral tradition informed the young about the group's heroes, victories, and defeats. The songs and stories helped young people to learn the group's spoken language and develop more abstract thinking about space and time. Today, storytelling remains an entertaining but important way for children to learn about their past and themselves.

5   As toolmakers, humans made and used spears, axes, and other tools, the earliest examples of human-made technology. Similarly, as language users, they created, used, and manipulated symbols. When these symbols came to be expressed in signs, pictographs, and letters, creating a written language, humans made the great cultural leap to literacy and then to schooling.

6   A global frame of reference helps to understand the worldwide movement to develop schools in literate societies. For that reason, our historical survey begins with the ancient empires of China, India, and Egypt.

Education in Ancient Chinese Civilization

7   Because of its long history and vast influence, Chinese civilization offers significant insights into education's evolution. With the world's largest population, modern China is an important global power. Historically it was a great empire whose civilization reached high pinnacles of political, social, and educational development. The empire was ruled by a series of dynasties spanning more than forty centuries from 2200 B.C. to A.D. 1912.[*] Many educational traditions that originated in imperial China still have an influence today. (See Overview 6.1 for key periods in China and other countries.)

[*] Shaughnessy, E. (2000). *China: Empire and Civilization*. New York: Oxford University Press.

8   Like many people, the Chinese were ethnocentric and believed their culture and language to be superior to all others* Scorning foreigners as barbarians, the Chinese were inward-looking, seeing little value in other cultures. Eventually, imperial China's reluctance to adapt technology from other cultures isolated and weakened it and, by the nineteenth century, made it vulnerable to foreign exploitation. The challenge of how to adapt to new ideas, especially in science and technology, and still maintain one's own culture remains an important educational issue in China today and in other countries as well.

9   The Chinese educational heritage reveals persistent efforts to maintain unbroken cultural continuity.[†] These efforts help us understand questions educators still ask: What is the relationship between cultural continuity and change, and how does education promote one or the other?

The Confucian Code

10   In imperial China, Confucian ethics regulated political, social, economic, and educational relationships. A philosopher and government official, **Confucius** (551–478 B.C.) feared violence and political unrest. Therefore, he devised an ethical system that stressed family values and political and social stability. Confucius used two important concepts—hierarchy and subordination—to guide human relationships.[‡] He envisioned the vast Chinese empire as one great extended family, paternalistically governed by the imperial father, the emperor. All the empire's subjects were to be compliantly subordinate and show deep piety toward their ruler.[∫] The *Getting to the Source* box presents some Confucian ideas about teaching.

---

* Prazniak, R. (1996). *Dialogues Across Civilizations: Sketches in World History from the Chinese and European Experiences.* Boulder, CO: Westview.

† Grossman, D. (1896, February). "Teaching About a Changing China." *Social Education*, p. 100.

‡ For primary sources on Confucius, see Confucius. (1979). *The Analects* (D. C. Lau, Trans.). New York: Penguin Books; see also Kai-wing Chow, On-cho No, & Henderson, J. B. Eds.). (1999). *Imagining Boundaries: Changing Confucian Doctrines, Texts, and Hermeneutics.* Albany: State University of New York Press.

∫ Fairbanks, J. K., Reischauer, E. O., & Craig, A. M. (1965). *East Asia: The Modern Transformation* (Vol. 2) London: Allen and Unwin, pp. 80–85.

GETTING TO THE SOURCE

A Confucian View of Teaching

Confucius

Confucius (551–479 B.C.) developed the ethical system that governed society, politics, and education in ancient China. Concerned with maintaining social and cultural harmony, Confucius's ideas on education emphasized the proper attitudes and relationships between teachers and students. Confucian philosophy has had and continues to exercise an important influence on culture and education in China, Japan, Korea, and other Asian countries. The following selection is from Confucius's "Record on the Subject of Education."

Record on the Subject of Education

When a superior man knows the causes which make instruction successful, and those which make it no effect, he can become a teacher of others. Thus, in his teaching, he leads and does not drag; he strengthens and does not discourage; he opens the way but does not conduct to the end without the learner's own efforts. Leading and not dragging produces harmony. Strengthening and not discouraging makes attainment easy. Opening the way and not conducting to the end makes the learner thoughtful. He who produces such harmony, easy attainment, and thoughtfulness may be pronounced a skillful teacher.

Among learners there are four defects with which the teacher must make himself acquainted. Some err in the multitude of their studies; some, in their fewness; some in the feeling of ease with which they proceed; and some, in the readiness with which they stop. These four defects arise from the difference of their minds. When a teacher knows the character of his mind, he can save the learner from the defect to which he is liable. Teaching should be directed to develop that in which the pupil excels, and correct the defects to which he is prone.

The good singer makes men able to continue his notes, and so the good teacher makes them able to carry out his ideas. His words are brief, but far-reaching; unpretentious, but deep; with few illustrations, but instructive. In this way he may be said to perpetuate his ideas.

When a man of talents and virtue knows the difficulty on one hand and the facility on the other in the attainment of learning, and knows also the good and bad qualities of his pupils, he can vary his methods of teaching. When he can vary his methods of teaching, he can be a master indeed. When he can be a teacher indeed, he can be the Head of an official department. When he can be such a Head, he can be the Ruler of a state. Hence, it is from the teacher indeed that one learns to be a ruler, and the choice of a teacher demands the greatest care; as it is said in the Record, "The three kings and four dynasties were what they were by their teachers."

Source: Ulich, R. (Ed.). (1954). *Three Thousand Years of Educational Wisdom.* Cambridge, MA: Harvard University Press, pp. 21–22.

Scholarships and Hierarchies

11   At the summit of the Chinese social hierarchy were the emperor and imperial court. Somewhat lower but still very prestigious and powerful were the scholar officials who governed China for the emperor. Next came the wealthy landowners, the gentry, and then the smaller landowning farmers, artisans, and merchants. At the bottom were the landless workers.

12   Like Plato's Republic (discussed later in the chapter), China's educational system was founded on the rationale that only intellectuals were capable of ruling. Since intellectual activity was valued more than applied and manual work, schools aimed to reproduce the intellectual elite by preparing ongoing generations of scholar-officials. Thus they emphasized learning the Confucian classics, especially the *Analects*, a collection of Confucius's lectures on society, government, and ethics. The works of Mencius (371–289 B.C.), a scholar who interpreted Confucius's philosophy, were also important.*

13   Dominating education in imperial China, Confucian ethics tried to develop personal virtue, morality, and loyalty. These values, in turn, would create a harmonious society. Informal education, carried on in kinship groups, emphasized the wisdom of elders, the desirability of maintaining traditional values, and the dangers of departing from custom. These traditional family relationships and values were the foundation of China's civic and social order. Confucianist ethical doctrines were also carried to Japan and Korea, which were influenced by Chinese culture.

Ancient Chinese scholars

* Schirokauer, C. (1991). *A Brief History of Chinese Civilization.* New York: Harcourt Brace Jovanovich, pp. 40–41.

China's Contribution to the World and Western Education

14   An important educational legacy from ancient China was its system of national examinations. Chinese educators developed comprehensive written examinations to assess students' academic competence. Students prepared for the examinations by studying ancient Chinese literature and Confucian texts with master teachers at imperial or temple schools. The examinations emphasized recalling memorized information rather than solving actual problems. The examination process, like the society, operated hierarchically and selectively. Students had to pass a series of rigorous examinations in ascending order; if they failed, they were dismissed from the process.* In imperial days, only a small number of finalists were eligible for the empire's highest civil service positions. The educational and examination systems were reserved exclusively for upper-class males. Ineligible for government positions, women were excluded from schools as well.

15   Currently, national examinations, especially for university entrance, dominate education in modern China and Japan. Other countries such as the United Kingdom have developed national tests. In the United States in 2001, the education act sponsored by the Bush administration required that states, in order to receive federal aid, administer a national test to students in the third through eighth grades. Although national tests contribute to uniform assessment throughout a country, they often force teachers to teach for the test rather than for students' interests and needs.

Source: Ornstein, A. C., & Levine, D.U. (2003). *Foundations of Education* (8th ed.). Boston: Houghton Mifflin, pp. 58–59, 62–63.

Muscle
Reading
Reminder

Phase Three:
Recite
Review
Review Again

* Fairbanks, J. K., Reischauer, E. O., & Craig, A. M. (1965). *East Asia: The Modern Transformation* (Vol. 2). London: Allen and Unwin, pp. 87–88.

☐ Assessing Your Learning

Demonstrating Comprehension

Paragraphs 14 and 15 at the end of Reading Selection 1 discuss the practice of national exams as a legacy from ancient China. From ancient times to the present, issues of assessment practices have often been debated among educators, politicians, and parents. Currently, many students at U.S. educational institutions are required to take standardized multiple-choice reading comprehension exams that include question items designed to show how well a student can apply specific reading skills. These tests are similar to tests a student might take in a content class, but are also different in a specific way. An example of a multiple-choice test that focuses on content can be found on the student website associated with the *Foundations of Education* textbook.

For Exercise 4, items have been written to test your comprehension and application of reading skills you have been working on with this book, *College Reading*. They have been written in a standard assessment style. (Visit our website at http://esl.college.hmco.com/students for a list of the reading skills tested on two common standardized reading tests for college students: the CPT and TASP.) Answering correctly demonstrates that you comprehend the material in Reading Selection 1 and that you have developed critical reading skills.

Master Student Tip

▼ **Tips for Making Strategic Choices**

Sometimes you really do not know which answer to choose on a multiple-choice test. The following strategies might help you when you need to guess.

EXERCISE 4 Answering multiple-choice questions

Refer to Reading Selection 1, World Roots of American Education, to answer the questions that follow.

1. Which of the following best expresses the main idea of the "**Education in Preliterate Societies**" section? (¶ 1–6)
   a. Oral traditions of transmitting knowledge and cultural heritage began in preliterate times and remain a part of schooling practices today.
   b. A global frame of reference helps us understand the worldwide movement to develop schools in literate societies.
   c. Our preliterate ancestors transmitted their culture orally from one generation to the next.

■ For the ones you have no clue about, always select the same letter. If there are four choices, consistently stick with either B or C. This gives you a 25 percent chance of getting the answer right. Sometimes test writers do not use A so often because it is first, or D because it is last.

■ Look at length. Does one answer stand out because it is much longer or shorter than the others? Could this be the one?

■ Are there language clues that could help you?

■ Make educated guesses. Try to eliminate an option or two to improve your chances.

2. The writer's main purpose in writing this section (¶ 1–6) is to:
   a. persuade the reader that storytelling is important for children.
   b. cause the reader to examine how children learned in preliterate societies.
   c. classify for the reader various teaching methods used in preliterate times.

3. Which of the following best defines the concept of <u>acculturation</u> as it is used in paragraph 2?
   a. A process of transmission of language, skills, and values.
   b. A trial-and-error process to develop survival skills.
   c. The passage from childhood to adulthood.

4. According to what is stated or implied in Part 1 of the passage, oral tradition in preliterate societies included all of the following except:
   a. Myths with messages about morals.
   b. Legends about heroes and accomplishments.
   c. Songs with recorded notes.

5. Which set of topics best organizes the information from the second section, "**Education in Ancient Chinese Civilization**"?
   a. China's superiority   b. China's long history   c. China's long history
      Challenge of change   Challenge of change   China's superiority
      China's long history   China's superiority   Challenge of change
      Confucian ethics   Confucian ethics   Confucian ethics

6. In which categories is Confucius recognized as a credible authority?
   a. As an economist and social scientist.
   b. As an ethicist and philosopher.
   c. As an anthropologist and historian.

7. Which hierarchical model best illustrates power relationships in ancient China?
   a. • Emperor & Court   b. • Emperor & Court   c. • Emperor & Court
      • Gentry & Landowners   • Scholar officials   • Scholar officials
      • Artisans & Merchants   • Gentry & Landowners   • Artisans & Merchants
      • Scholar officials   • Artisans & Merchants   • Gentry & Landowners

8. Which assumption reflects the author's depiction of education in ancient China?
   a. Intellectual pursuits had more value than manual labor.
   b. All wealthy citizens were wise and powerful.
   c. Social order was harmonious.

9. Paragraph 13 begins with the following sentences:

   > Dominating education in imperial China, Confucian ethics tried to develop personal virtue, morality, and loyalty. These values, in turn, would create a harmonious society.

   What does the second sentence do?
   a. It provides a factual detail.
   b. It compares historical periods.
   c. It identifies an effect.

10. Paragraph 15 addresses the use of national exams. The last sentence of this paragraph reveals a bias. Which of the following assumptions most influenced the views expressed by the writer in this selection?
    a. Teachers should "teach for the test."
    b. Teachers should base their teaching on student needs and interests.
    c. Teachers should support national tests.

☐ Linking Concepts

EXERCISE 5 **Practicing with more tests**

Will you be taking a standardized multiple-choice test soon? Visit our website at http://esl.college.hmco.com/students for links to practice tests for the CPT and the TASP exams. These tests assess basic skills in reading, writing, and mathematics.

☐ Focusing on Education

EXERCISE 6   Understanding issues raised in texts

Throughout the passages in this chapter, several themes emerge. From your reading so far, use your own words to summarize the authors' major or primary theme. Paraphrase their ideas.

According to Ornstein and Levine, _____

_____

_____

_____

     After having read about educational practices in preliterate times and in ancient China, you should be able to ask questions. Academic questions reveal that you are a thoughtful reader who has paid attention to keywords, facts, and details and can remember them. Academic questions go beyond the surface. They reveal your ability to explore new ideas and make connections with your own experiences and knowledge.

Look back at Reading Selection 1 to find at least two areas where you could ask academic questions. Annotate the passage location, and then write complete questions here. The first one is done for you as an example.

1. Academic question(s): When I read about storytelling in preliterate times, I really started thinking about ways teachers and parents use stories and anecdotes to help us learn. Why do stories help us learn? How is storytelling as a teaching method different from other methods?

2. Academic question(s): _____

_____

_____

_____

_____

3. Academic question(s): _____

_____

_____

_____

_____

EXERCISE 7 Developing perspectives

Turn to the "Getting to the Source" box in Reading Selection 1. The source in this case is a look at Confucius's "Record on the Subject of Education."

Contrast the first paragraph that begins "Confucius . . ." with the next paragraphs that begin "When a superior . . .", "Among learners . . .", "The good singer . . .", and "When a man . . ."

1. Which verb tenses do you see in the first paragraph?
2. Which verb tenses do you see in the next paragraphs?
3. Underline subjects in the first paragraph.
4. Underline subjects in the next paragraphs. How are they different?
5. What do you notice about the gender of pronouns used?
6. Who wrote the first paragraph?
7. Who wrote the next paragraphs?
8. Is Robert Ulich, ed., a primary source or secondary source?

POWER GRAMMAR

Language Use Transitions

Take time to analyze pattern changes in subjects, verb tenses, and pronouns as you read. These changes signal transitions in purpose, tone, or expectations for the reading audience. Noticing when the grammar changes as you read can aid your comprehension.

EXERCISE 8 Sharing words of wisdom

Take a look again at the words of Confucius about education. He provides a perspective on four points about teaching. Work creatively with Confucius's words of advice. Prepare a visual illustration to help others learn about the ideas of Confucius. You could choose just one of his ideas, or work with more than one. Be creative! You can prepare your visual illustration by hand or with a computer.

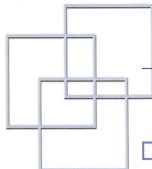

Reading Assignment 2

☐ Getting Ready to Read

Reading Selection 2 is a chart that provides a historical overview of ten influential periods. Ideas from these times and places continue to affect our educational practices here and now. Learning about them can provide a foundation of important understanding.

Think about this: What is the best way to read a chart? Should you read everything? Should you just scan? Should you read up and down, or should you read across from left to right? It depends on your purpose!

☐ Reading for a Purpose

When you read the chart that follows, your primary purpose is to get a global understanding of the ten influential periods from 7000 BC to AD 1600. You will need to read carefully for this purpose. A second purpose is to select one period to teach your classmates about. A third purpose is to prioritize what to learn for test-taking purposes. Keep all three purposes in mind while you read.

EXERCISE 9   Reading strategy: Focusing on categories

To get a global understanding, first read the chart title and the seven categories from left to right. An indication that these are important to read first is the fact that they are in bold print. Take a few minutes to list the seven categories here.

1. Historical Group or Period _____

2. _____

3. _____

4. _____

5. _____

6. _____

7. _____

Next read up and down, just the first column on the left. This column shows the historical group or period. Think about places and time frames.

Now read across. Read about preliterate societies in the six topic categories. Does the information help you recall material from Reading Selection 1? Continue to read across, period by period.

Notice how your reading purpose changes when you read about India and Egypt. Here you are building schema to help you understand later, when you read Reading Selections 3 and 4. Building schema is like putting hangers in the closet of your mind; you are storing ideas. Later, you will be able to attach new information to the hangers. Storing these ideas in a graphic form can help you read, understand, and learn. Finally, notice that when you read about the eras from Greek to Reformation, you will only learn from the chart because the passages about them are not included in this reading book.

Next, scan the chart in an up and down manner. Look for points of comparison and contrast.

Finally, imagine you will be tested on the material in this chart. Visualize different question content and question types a teacher might use (multiple-choice, true-false, fill-in-the-blanks, short answer, or essay).

Reading Selection 2

OVERVIEW: KEY PERIODS IN EDUCATIONAL HISTORY, TO A.D. 1600

Overview *Key Periods in Educational History, to A.D. 1600*			
Historical group or period	**Educational goals**	**Students**	**Instructional methods**
Preliterate societies 7000 B.C.–5000 B.C.	To teach group survival skills and group cohesiveness	Children in the group	Informal instruction; children imitating adult skills and values
China 3000 B.C.–A.D.1900	To prepare elite officials to govern the empire according to Confucian principles	Males of gentry class	Memorization and recitation of classic texts
India 3000 B.C.–present	To learn behavior and rituals based on the Vedas	Males of upper castes	Memorizing and interpreting sacred texts
Egypt 3000 B.C.–300 B.C.	To prepare priest scribes to administer the empire	Males of upper classes	Memorizing and copying dictated texts
Greek 1600 B.C.–300 B.C.	*Athens*: To cultivate civic responsibility and identification with city-state and develop well-rounded persons *Sparta*: To train soldiers and military leaders	Male children of citizens; ages 7–20	Drill, memorization, recitation in primary schools; lecture, discussion and dialogue in higher schools
Roman 750 B.C.–A.D. 450	To develop civic responsibility for republic and then empire; to develop administrative and military skills	Male children of citizens; ages 7–20	Drill, memorization, recitation in *ludus*; declamation in rhetorical schools

Overview *Key Periods in Educational History, to A.D. 1600* (cont.)			
Historical group or period	**Educational goals**	**Students**	**Instructional methods**
Preliterate societies 7000 B.C.–5000 B.C.	Survival skills of hunting, fishing, food gathering; stories, myths, songs, poems, dances	Parents, tribal elders, and priests	Emphasis on informal education to transmit skills and values
China 3000 B.C.–A.D.1900	Confucian classics	Government officials	Written examinations for civil service and other professions
India 3000 B.C.–present	Vedas and religious texts	Brahmin priest scholars	Cultural transmission and assimilation; spiritual detachment
Egypt 3000 B.C.–300 B.C.	Religious or technical texts	Priests and scribes	Restriction of educational controls and services to priestly elite; use of education to prepare bureaucrats
Greek 1600 B.C.–300 B.C.	*Athens*: reading, writing, arithmetic, drama, music, physical education, literature, poetry *Sparta*: drill, military songs and tactics	*Athens*: private teachers and schools, Sophists, philosophers *Sparta*: military officers	*Athens*: the concept of the well-rounded, liberally educated person *Sparta*: the concept of serving the military state
Roman 750 B.C.–A.D. 450	Reading, writing, mathematics, Laws of Twelve Tables, law, philosophy	Private schools and teachers; schools of rhetoric	Emphasis on education for practical administrative skills; relating education to civic responsibility

Overview *Key Periods in Educational History, to A.D. 1600* (cont.)			
Historical group or period	**Educational goals**	**Students**	**Instructional methods**
Arabic A.D. 700–A.D. 1350	To cultivate religious commitment to Islamic beliefs; to develop expertise in mathematics, medicine, and science	Male children of upper classes; ages 7–20	Drill, memorization, recitation in lower schools; imitation and discussion in higher schools
Medieval A.D. 500–A.D. 1400	To develop religious commitment, knowledge, and ritual; to prepare persons for appropriate roles in hierarchical society	Male children of upper classes or those entering religious life; girls and women entering religious communities; ages 7–20	Drill, memorization, recitation, chanting in lower schools; textual analysis and disputation in universities and higher schools
Renaissance A.D. 1350–A.D. 1500	To cultivate a humanist expert in classics (Greek and Latin); to prepare courtiers for service to dynastic leaders	Male children of aristocracy and upper classes; ages 7–20	Memorization, translation, and analysis of Greek and Roman classics
Reformation A.D. 1500–A.D. 1600	To instill a commitment to a particular religious denomination; to cultivate general literacy	Boys and girls, ages 7–12, in vernacular schools; young men, ages 7–12, of upper class backgrounds in humanist schools	Memorization, drill, indoctrination, catechetical instruction in vernacular schools; translation and analysis of classical literature in humanist schools

Overview *Key Periods in Educational History, to A.D. 1600* (cont.)			
Historical group or period	**Educational goals**	**Students**	**Instructional methods**
Arabic A.D. 700–A.D. 1350	Reading, writing, mathematics, religious literature, scientific studies	Mosques; court schools	Arabic numerals and computation; reentry of classical materials on science and medicine
Medieval A.D. 500–A.D. 1400	Reading, writing, arithmetic, liberal arts; philosophy, theology; crafts; military tactics and chivalry	Parish, chantry, and cathedral schools; universities; apprenticeship; knighthood	Establishment of the structure, content, and organization of universities as major institutions of higher education; the institutionalization and preservation of knowledge
Renaissance A.D. 1350–A.D. 1500	Latin, Greek, classical literature, poetry, art	Classical humanist educators and schools such as lycée, gymnasium, Latin school	An emphasis on literary knowledge, excellence, and style as expressed in classical literature: a two-track system of schools
Reformation A.D. 1500–A.D. 1600	Reading, writing, arithmetic, catechism, religious concepts and ritual; Latin and Greek; theology	Vernacular elementary schools for the masses; classical schools for the upper classes	A commitment to universal education to provide literacy to the masses; the origins of school systems with supervision to ensure doctrinal conformity; the dual-track school system based on socioeconomic class and career goals

Source: Ornstein, A.C., & Levine, D.U. (2003). *Foundations of Education* (8th ed.). Boston: Houghton Mifflin, pp. 60–61.

☐ Assessing Your Learning

Demonstrating Comprehension

EXERCISE 10 Clarifying the historical frame

Create a timeline to illustrate the actual chronological space covered by Ornstein & Levine's overview of the global roots of U.S. educational systems. The chart shows the groups in chronological order, but period time spans vary.

Timeline Example

7000 BC–5000 BC   3000 BC   1000 BC   X   AD 500   AD 1660

Preliterate   AD 2000

Write three observations about the historical frame that became apparent from your timeline.

1. _____

_____

_____

_____

2. _____

_____

_____

_____

3. _____

_____

_____

_____

EXERCISE 11   Recognizing educational purposes

Each period/group valued different types of knowledge. Match the group on the left with primary goals listed on the right. Draw a line to show the correct match. The first one is done for you as an example.

	Group or period		Educational purposes
K	**1.** Preliterate		**A.** Administrative knowledge
	2. Ancient China		**B.** Civic responsibility, administrative & military
	3. Ancient India		**C.** Civic responsibility & general knowledge base
	4. Ancient Egypt		**D.** Confucian principles for government
	5. Greek—Athens		**E.** Humanists, Greek & Latin classics, elitist
	6. Greek—Sparta		**F.** Islamic beliefs, mathematics, medicine & science
	7. Roman		**G.** Military knowledge
	8. Arabic		**H.** Practices from the Vedas
	9. Medieval		**I.** Religious & general literacy
	10. Renaissance		**J.** Religion, rituals, & roles
	11. Reformation		**K.** Survival skills and group membership

Matching chart

EXERCISE 12 **Summarizing educational features**

Divide the class into nine groups. Each group is responsible for preparing an oral summary about one key period. Each summary should answer the following questions:

1. Who were the students?

2. What did they have to study?

3. What did they have to do in order to learn?

4. Who were the teachers?

5. How do the practices from then affect us now?

Be prepared to check for dictionary definitions of unfamiliar terms to teach your classmates.

EXAMPLE:

In preliterate societies, all children were students. They studied skills they needed to survive such as hunting, fishing, food gathering and they learned about traditions and values. They listened to their parents, tribal elders, and priests. Tribes are groups of people who lived together in those days—now we still have Native American Indian tribes, for example. Elders are older people. The children heard stories and myths. According to the American Heritage dictionary, myths are traditional stories dealing with supernatural beings, ancestors, or heroes. Teaching also included songs, poems, and dances. Today we still use some of these forms as part of our teaching practices. For example, U.S. students learned the alphabet in the form of a song.

Write out your summaries before you present them to the class orally. Consider using index cards to help you memorize your part.

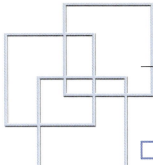

Reading Assignment 3

EDUCATION IN ANCIENT INDIAN CIVILIZATION

☐ Reading for a Purpose

The following passage describes education in India, another country with a long history of formal education. As you read, allow your mind to make connections with what you recently learned about education in China and what you know from experience here in the United States or in your native country.

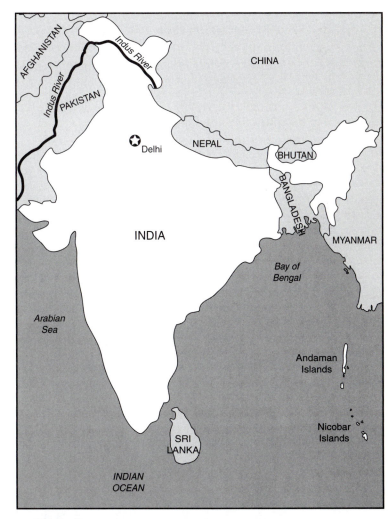

Ancient India

Reading Selection 3

Education in Ancient Indian Civilization

16   Like China, India is an ancient civilization. River valley civilizations flourished on the banks of India's Indus River at Mohenjo-daro and Harrapa from 3000 B.C. to 1500 B.C. These civilizations developed an elaborate urban culture with well-plotted brick houses, copper tools, and drainage and sanitation systems.

17   India's educational history reveals a general pattern of intrusion by invaders, followed by a cultural clash with the indigenous people, and then the restoration of sociocultural equilibrium. In this cultural equilibrium, the invaders were absorbed in India's culture while at the same time indigenous people borrowed some of the invader's ideas.*

18   Among the early invaders were the Ayrans, ancestors of India's Hindi-speaking majority who conquered India in 1500 B.C. and imposed their rule over the indigenous Dravidian inhabitants. They were followed by the Muslims, who established the Mughul dynasty in the thirteenth century. Then, in the eighteenth century, the British gained control over India.

19   Cultural changes introduced by India's earliest invaders, the Ayrans, had powerful social and educational influences that continue even today. The Ayrans introduced their religion, Hinduism, and their highly stratified social order, the **caste system**.

20   Hinduism, a powerful central force in India, incorporates a wide range of religious beliefs and elaborate rituals. Believing in the transmigration of souls, Hinduism emphasizes that a person's soul experiences a series of reincarnations. A person's position in the cosmic scale depends on how well he or she performs duties and rituals. Reincarnation ends only when a soul reaches the highest spiritual level and is reabsorbed in Brahma, the divine power.†

21   The four original castes were ***Brahmins***, priest-educators; ***Kshatriyas***, rulers, judges, and warriors; ***Vaishyas***, merchants; and ***Shudras***, the farmers. At the bottom of the caste system were the

---

* For India's history and culture, see Vohra, R. (1997). *The Making of India: A Historical Survey*. Armonk, NY: M. E. Sharpe; and Kulke, H., & Rothermund, D. (1998). *A History of India*. New York: Routledge.

† Mulhern, J. (1959). *A History of Education: A Social Interpretation*. New York: Ronald Press, pp. 80–128; and Nakosteen, M. (1965). *The History and Philosophy of Education*. New York: Ronald Press, pp. 23–40.

untouchables, who performed the most menial work. There was no social mobility. People stayed in the caste into which they were born. Based on their caste, people learned their duties and roles by imitating parents and other adults. Schooling was reserved for the upper castes, primarily the Brahmins. Outlawing caste-based discrimination, modern India has an "affirmative action" for lower caste members. However, like racism in the United States, discrimination still exists.

Evolution and Indian Education

22   The development of education in India is closely linked to general historical pattern of assimilating different cultures. The earlier schools reflect the cultural changes brought by the Ayrans. Ancient India had the following types of schools:

- Brahmanic schools, for the priestly caste, stressed religion, philosophy, and the **Vedas**. The **Vedas**, the ***Bhagavad Gita***, and the ***Upanishads***, Hinduism's sacred religious books, portray the goal of life as a search for universal spiritual truths. The quest for truth, Indian educators believe, requires disciplined meditation. Contemporary transcendental meditation and yoga follow these ancient Indian principles for finding inner spiritual truth and serenity.
- *Tols* were one-room schools where a single teacher taught religion and law.
- Court schools, sponsored by princes, taught literature, law, and administration.

23   Hindu educational philosophy, emphasizing religious purposes, prescribed appropriate student-teacher relationships. The teacher, an *ayoha*, was to encourage students to respect all life and to search for truth. Students were to respect teachers as a source of wisdom, and teachers were to refrain from humiliating students.*

24   The Mughul dynasty, established after the Muslim invasions, introduced the Islamic religion and Persian and Arabic philosophy, science, literature, astronomy, mathematics, medicine, art, music, and architecture.

* Patel, N. (1994). "A Comparative Exposition of Western and Vedic Theories of the Institution of Education," *International Journal of Educational Management*, 8, pp. 9–14.

25   By the time the English entered India in the late eighteenth century, India's schools were conducted either by Hindus or Muslims or by smaller sects such as Buddhists, Jains, and Parsis. Only about 10% of India's children, mostly boys, attended. Hindu higher schools, conducted by Brahmins, emphasized religious literature, mathematics, astronomy, and Sanskrit grammar. Muslim schools, called *madrassahs*, were attached to mosques and emphasized grammar and the Koran.*

26   When the English established their colonial rule in India, they encountered an ancient civilization with many languages and religions. Placing a greater value on their own language than on those spoken in India, the English imposed their own language as the official one for government and commerce. Therefore, they established English-language schools to train Indians for positions in the British-controlled civil service.

India's Contribution to the World and Western Education

27   Ancient India's legacy to the world demonstrates how education helped a civilization to endure over centuries. Through the processes of cultural assimilation and readaptation, Indian civilization has survived to the present. In today's climate of rising ethnic and religious tensions, India still faces profound challenges in assimilating and respecting diverse cultures. The United States and other culturally pluralistic nations face similar challenges. Finally, the Indian situation reveals how caste, like racism in the United States, was once perpetuated by society and indoctrination but is now being corrected through educational process.

Source: Ornstein, A. C., & Levine, D. U. (2003). *Foundations of Education* (8th ed.). Boston: Houghton Mifflin, pp. 64–65.

* Edwards, M. (1967). *Raj; The Story of British India*. London: Pan Books, p. 133.

☐ Assessing Your Learning

Demonstrating Comprehension

EXERCISE 13 **Specifying the theme**

In your own words, state the authors' main point about education in India.

_____

_____

_____

_____

EXERCISE 14 **Organizing information about influential groups**

Complete the chart below with information from Reading Selection 3. Identify details about the three primary groups that invaded and influenced India.

TITLE:			
Time period	Invading group & leaders	Religious influence	Social/Educational influence
1500 BC			
	■ Muslims ■ Mughul dynasty		

EXERCISE 15   **Organizing information about groups in a chart**

As stated in paragraph 19, "The Ayrans introduced their religion, Hinduism, and their highly stratified social order, the **caste system**."

Complete the chart below with information from the reading selection. See paragraph 21 for details.

TITLE:	
Column Title:	Column Title:
1. Brahmins	
	Menial workers

EXERCISE 16   **Explaining beliefs**

On separate paper, write a one-paragraph response for the following items. Write the explanation as if this were a short-answer essay exam.

1. Explain Hindu beliefs about souls.
2. Explain Hindu beliefs about teachers and students.

☐ Linking Concepts

As you were reading Selection 3, you were asked to allow your mind to make connections with what you recently learned about education in China and what you know from experience here in the United States or in your native country. Thinking actively about relationships among ideas can deepen your comprehension.

EXERCISE 17   Contrasting elements from key periods

Complete these statements of contrast and comparison about ancient China and India and the United States. Refer back to the reading selections.

1. Chinese students learned from the texts of _____,

    whereas, Indian students read _____.

2. Spiritual and religious studies were most important in _____.

3. Both Chinese and _____ societies respected teachers as

    a source of _____, and teachers were to refrain

    from _____ students.

4. Indian schools reflect assimilation of different _____.

    Similarly, the United States is a _____

    pluralistic nation.

5. The Indian situation reveals how _____ like

    _____ in the United States was once perpetuated by

    society and _____, but is now being

    corrected through educational process.

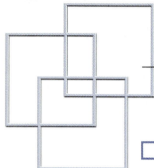

Reading Assignment 4

EDUCATION IN ANCIENT EGYPTIAN CIVILIZATION

☐ Reading for a Purpose

This is the last reading passage. Read actively. Think about all the different reading strategies you have learned and used this semester. Put them into practice!

Education in ancient Egypt

Reading Selection 4

Education in Ancient Egyptian Civilization

28   Like other early civilizations, ancient Egypt—one of the world's earliest—developed as a river valley culture. Because of the Nile River's life-sustaining water, agricultural groups established small village settlements on the Nile's banks that were first organized into tribal kingdoms. About 3000 B.C. these kingdoms consolidated into a large empire, which eventually became a highly organized and centralized political colossus.

29   An important Egyptian religious and political principle affirmed that the pharaoh, the emperor, was of divine origin. The concept of divine emperorship gave social, cultural, political, and educational stability to the Egyptian empire by endowing it with supernaturally sanctioned foundations. Knowledge and values were seen as reflecting an orderly, unchanging, and eternal cosmos. The concept of king-priest also gave the priestly elite high status and considerable power in Egyptian society. The educational system reinforced this status and power by making the priestly elite guardians of the state culture.

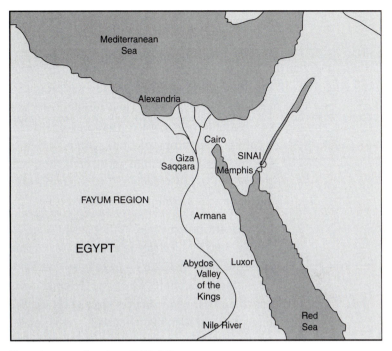

Egyptian empire circa 2700 BC

Religious and Secular Concerns

30   Educationally, the Egyptians were both otherworldly and this-worldly. Although preoccupied with the supernatural, they were also concerned with the technologies needed to navigate the Nile Valley and to design and build massive pyramids and temples. To administer and defend their vast empire, they studied statecraft, and their concern with mummification led them to study medicine, anatomy, and embalming. The Egyptians also developed a system of writing, hieroglyphic script, that enabled them to create and preserve religious, political, and medical literatures.

31   The Egyptian empire required an educated bureaucracy to collect and record taxes. By 2700 B.C., the Egyptians had in place an extensive system of temple and court schools. One of the school system's basic functions was to train scribes, many of whom were priests, in skills of reading and writing. Schools were often built as part of the temple complex, and there was a close relationship between formal education and religion.* After receiving some

---

* Mulhern, J. (1959). *A History of Education: A Social Interpretation.* New York: Ronald Press, pp. 55–79.

preliminary education, boys studied the literature appropriate to their future professions. Special advanced schools existed for certain kinds of priests, government officials, and physicians.

32   In the scribal schools, students learned to write the hieroglyphic script by copying documents on papyrus, sheets made from reeds growing along the Nile. Their teachers' basic method was dictating to the students, who copied what they heard. The goal was to reproduce a correct, exact copy of a text. Often students would chant a short passage until they had memorized it thoroughly. For those who proceeded to advanced studies, the curriculum included mathematics, astronomy, religion, poetry, literature, medicine, and architecture.

Historical Controversies About Egypt

33   Ancient Egypt's role in shaping Western civilization has become controversial. In 332 B.C., Egypt was conquered by Alexander the Great and incorporated into the Helenistic civilization, which in turn had been shaped by ancient Greek culture. The conventional historical interpretation was that ancient Egyptian civilization was a highly static despotism and that its major cultural legacy was its great architectural monuments. This interpretation saw Greek culture, especially Athenian democracy, as the cradle of Western civilization.

34   A highly controversial interpretation by Martin Bernal argues that the Greeks borrowed many of their concepts about government, philosophy, the arts, and sciences from Egypt. Furthermore, the Egyptians, geographically located in North Africa, were African people, and the origins of Western culture are therefore African.* Though they recognize that there were interactions between the Egyptians and the Greeks, Bernal's critics contend that he greatly overemphasizes Egypt's influence on ancient Greece. While historians continue to debate the matter, tentative findings indicate that Egyptian-Greek contacts, particularly at Crete, introduced the Greeks to Egyptian knowledge, such as mathematics, and to Egyptian art forms.

35   This intriguing historical controversy has important ideological significance. Whoever interprets the past gains the power of illuminating and shaping the present. In particular, the controversy relates to current debate about Afrocentrism and Afrocentric

---

* Bernal, M. (1987). *Black Athena: The Afroasiatic Roots of Classical Civilization: The Fabrication of Ancient Greece 1785–1985.* New Brunswick, NJ: Rutgers University Press, pp. 2–3.

curriculum. It also show how contemporary multicultural issues are stimulating new historical interpretations.

   In the next section we turn to the ancient Greeks. Whether influenced directly or indirectly by the Egyptians, the Greeks continue to hold an important place in the history of education. Keep in mind, however, that most historical cultures have borrowed from one another in many ways, and the roots of Greek thought may indeed be traceable to Egypt or elsewhere.

Source: Ornstein, A. C., & Levine, D. U. (2003). *Foundations of Education* (8th ed.). Boston: Houghton Mifflin, pp. 66–67.

☐ Assessing Your Learning
Demonstrating Comprehension

EXERCISE 18   Articulating implications and consequences

We have seen that policy decisions in the area of education affect many aspects of society. Complete each sentence below with a possible implication or consequence.

   1. The Egyptians believed their pharaohs were divine. As a result,

   _____

   _____

   2. The Egyptian empire was vast and centered along the Nile River. As a

   consequence, _____

   3. Their concern with mummification led them to _____

   _____

   4. Their development of hieroglyphic script enabled them to _____

   _____

   5. Schools were often built as part of the temple complex, revealing

   _____

For extra practice in articulating consequences and implications, revisit the historical overview chart (Reading Selection 2). Write cause-effect sentences about the different groups. Also consider how past practices have affected current practices in the United States.

☐ Questions for Discussion

EXERCISE 19   **Evaluating sources and exploring theories**

Prepare short answers for the following questions about Reading Selection 4. Then discuss your ideas with the whole class.

1. Who is the author of *Black Athena: The Afroasiatic Roots of Classical Civilization: The Fabrication of Ancient Greece 1785–1985*?
2. State his theory.
3. What do his critics believe?
4. What do recent findings show?
5. What do you believe?
6. How can you evaluate Bernal's credibility?
7. In paragraph 35, Ornstein and Levine state, "Whoever interprets the past gains the power of illuminating and shaping the present." Explain in your own words what this means.

EXERCISE 20   **Examining rights to participate in schooling**

Prepare short answers for the following additional questions related to Reading Selection 4. Then discuss your ideas with the whole class.

1. How has access to education affected your life?
2. If you could study anywhere right now, where would you want to be earning a degree?
3. Think about the different educational systems described in this chapter. Who had access to education, and who was excluded? What do you think about this?
4. The U.S. educational system values **inclusion**. A consciousness that certain groups have had limited educational opportunities has resulted in laws, policies, practices, and planning to make education accessible for all. For example, the following groups have fought for and won educational rights: women, Native Americans, African Americans, Americans with disabilities, and non-English speakers. How does **inclusion** affect educational experiences? How does it affect society? What kind of cultural changes result from **inclusion**?

☐ Learning Vocabulary

EXERCISE 21   Reviewing word parts

The charts below include academic words from the reading selections in this chapter. Remember, as you encounter vocabulary, noticing word forms contributes to accurate comprehension. Fill in the correct forms for each blank.

Word families and related word forms				
Headword	*-ed*	*-s*	*-ing*	
A. Verbs	**Past, perfect, passive voice**	**Present, 3rd person singular**	**Gerund as a noun**	**Noun formed with suffix or modification**
1. assess	assessed	assesses	assessing	assessment
2. conduct				
3. create				
4. emphasize				
5. establish				
6. interpret				
7. proceed				
8. require				
9. survive				
10. transmit				

Word families and related word forms		
Headword	*-al*	*-s*
B. Nouns	**Adjective**	**Plural**
1. controversy		
2. convention		
3. culture		
4. hierarchy		
5. ethic		
6. tradition		

EXERCISE 22   **Using correct word parts**

Complete each of the sentences below with the correct form of the academic words from the boxes. These sentences come from the reading passages in this chapter.

1. Our ancestors _____ their

   _____ orally from one generation to the next.

2. They trained their children in _____ skills.

3. Preliterate people faced almost overwhelming problems of

   _____ in an environment that pitted them against droughts, floods, and attacks.

4. In imperial China, Confucian _____ regulated political, social, economic, and educational relationships.

5. Confucius developed an _____ system of governance.

6. Confucius's ideas on education _____ the proper attitudes and relationships between teachers and students.

7. At the summit of the Chinese social _____ were the emperor and imperial court.

8. Mencius was an important scholar who _____ Confucius' philosophy.

9. Chinese educators developed comprehensive written examinations to _____ students' academic competence.

10. The quest for truth, Indian educators believed, _____ disciplined meditation.

11. Hindu educational philosophy, _____ religious purposes, prescribed appropriate student-teacher relationships.

12. By the time the English entered India in the late eighteenth century, India's schools were _____ either by Hindus or Muslims or by smaller sects.

13. Through processes of _____ assimilation and readaptation, Indian civilization has _____ to the present.

14. In Egypt agricultural groups _____ small village settlements along the banks of the Nile River.

15. For those who _____ to advanced studies, the curriculum included mathematics, astronomy, religion, poetry, literature, medicine, and architecture.

16. Ancient Egypt's role in shaping Western civilization has become _____ .

17. The _____ historical _____ was that ancient Egypt was highly despotic and that its major legacy was its great architectural monuments.

☐ Assessing Your Learning at the End of a Chapter
Revisiting Chapter Objectives

Return to the first page of this chapter. Think about the chapter objectives. Put a check mark next to the ones you feel secure about. Review material in the chapter you still need to work on. When you are ready, answer the chapter review questions below.

☐ Practicing for a Chapter Test

EXERCISE 23 **Reviewing comprehension**

Check your comprehension of main concepts, or ideas, in this chapter by responding to the following chapter review questions.

1. Flip through the pages of this chapter to locate something you have a question about. Write your question on separate paper to hand in to your instructor. Do not put your name on the paper. Your instructor can collect all questions and review common points that need to be clarified.[3]

2. We have seen that policy decisions in the area of education affect many aspects of society. Complete each sentence below with a possible implication or consequence.

   a. In ancient China, the educational and examination systems were reserved exclusively for upper-class males; as a result, _____

   _____

   b. Although national tests contribute to uniform assessment, such tests also sometimes cause teachers to _____

   _____

3. Chinese, Indian, and Egyptian societies all valued memorization as a technique for learning. Discuss your own beliefs about memorization as a method for education.

4. Identify a credible source for a specific content area. Explain why the public can truly trust and value this person's opinion.

5. Describe your study plan for your final exam for this class. How will you prepare? Identify your steps one-by-one.

---

3. This idea is based on a feedback technique called "The Muddiest Point" by Cross, K. P., & Angelo, T. A. (1993). *Classroom Assessment Techniques.*

6. Discuss which steps listed above for question 5 you actually applied when you studied for the quiz on the last chapter. What effect did they have?
7. Identify a specific ancient civilization that has influenced U.S. educational practices. Discuss the custom and its influence.
8. Describe the purposes of schooling in ancient Egypt.
9. Contrast schooling during two key historical periods.
10. Discuss your own beliefs based on personal experience with respect to educational opportunities for people from different groups.
11. Summarize the distinguishing features of one key period in the history of education.
12. Explain the most important thing you have learned about education from this chapter.

Academic Vocabulary

Here are some academic vocabulary words that were introduced in this chapter. Confirm the words you know the meaning of. Identify the words that are not yet part of your active vocabulary. Relearn the words you need to.

abstract	academic	administration	adulthood	aid
appreciate	assessment	attached	attainment	attitudes
brief	capable	challenges	civil	classics
codes	comprehensive	conduct	considerable	contacts
contemporary	contribute	conventional	debate	discrimination
diverse	documents	dominate	dramatic	emphasized
enabled	error	established	ethical	evolution
excluded	exclusively	facility	foundation	founded
functions	furthermore	generations	goal	grades
hence	hierarchy	ideological	illustrations	imposed

incorporated	indicate	insights	instructive	interpret
lectures	manipulated	manual	methods	ongoing
philosopher	philosophy	preliminary	primarily	principles
proceed	promote	range	regulated	reinforced
relied	reluctance	restoration	reveals	roles
stratified	selectively	somewhat	status	stimulating
subordinate	superior	symbols	tensions	tentative
traceable	tradition	transmit	uniform	urban
vary	vast			

WEB POWER

Go to **http://esl.college.hmco.com/students** to view more readings about education, plus exercises that will help you to study the selections and the academic words in this chapter.

Text Credits

All pronunciations throughout this text and the definitions of stray, mutter, idiom, pushove pithy, kibitz(ing), crème de la crème, hybrid, zeal, protagonist, antipathy, paranoia, spy, gene, billboard, pogo stick, organism, encompass, catastrophe, canopy, crevices, stand, theory, assumption, and inference. Copyright © 2000 by Houghton Mifflin Company. Adapted and reproduced by permission from *The American Heritage Dictionary of the English Language*, Fourth Edition; Copyright © 1998 by Julia Alvarez. From *Something to Declare*, published by Plume, an imprint of Penguin Group (USA), in 1999 and originally in hardcover by Algonquin Books of Chapel Hill, 1998. Reprinted by permission of Susan Bergholz Literary Services, New York. All rights reserved, pp. 3, 5, 8–18; "My Mother Juggling Bean Bags" from *From a Three-Cornered World: New & Selected Poems* by James Masao Mitsui. Copyright © 1997 by James Masao Mitsui. Reprinted by permission of the University of Washington Press, pp. 38, 42–43; "Textbook Reconnaissance" from Dave Ellis, *Becoming a Master Student*, Ninth Edition, p. 1. Copyright © 2000 by Houghton Mifflin Company. Reprinted with permission, p. 53; "The Discovery Wheel" from Dave Ellis, *Becoming a Master Student*, Ninth Edition, pp. 14–17. Copyright © 2000 by Houghton Mifflin Company. Reprinted with permission, pp. 57–58; "Muscle Reading" from Dave Ellis, *Becoming a Master Student*, Ninth Edition, pp. 108 –115. Copyright © 2000 by Houghton Mifflin Company. Reprinted with permission, pp. 73–68; From Chapter One: Introducing Psychology from Douglas A. Bernstein, Alison Clarke-Stewart, Louis A. Penner, Edward J. Roy, and Christopher D. Wickens, *Psychology*, Fifth Edition, p. 3. Copyright © 2000 by Houghton Mifflin Company. Reprinted with permission, pp. 93–94; Chapter 7 Outline from Douglas A. Bernstein, Alison Clarke-Stewart, Louis A. Penner, Edward J. Roy, and Christopher D. Wickens, *Psychology*, Fifth Edition, p. 213. Copyright © 2000 by Houghton Mifflin Company. Reprinted with permission, p. 98; From Chapter 7: Memory from Douglas A. Bernstein, Alison Clarke-Stewart, Louis A. Penner, Edward J. Roy, and Christopher D. Wickens, *Psychology*, Fifth Edition, pp. 214–218. Figures 7.1 and 7.2 based on data in E. Tulving, D. L. Schacter, and H. A. Stark (1982). Priming Effects in Word-Fragment Completion Are Independent of Recognition Memory. *Journal of Experimental Psychology: Learning, Memory, and Cognition*, Vol. 8, No. 4, 336–342. From Douglas A. Bernstein et al., *Psychology*, Fifth Edition. Copyright © 2000 by Houghton Mifflin Company. Reprinted with permission, p. 100–111; A Serial-Position Curve. Figure 7.9 from Douglas A. Bernstein, Alison Clarke-Stewart, Louis A. Penner, Edward J. Roy, and Christopher D. Wickens, *Psychology*, Fifth Edition, p. 226. Copyright © 2000 by Houghton Mifflin Company. Reprinted with permission, p. 123; "Our Changing Environment" from Chapter 1 of Peter H. Raven and Linda R. Berg, *Environment*, Third Edition. Copyright © 2000 by John Wiley & Sons, Inc. This material is used by permission of John Wiley & Sons, Inc, pp. 129–130; "Old-Growth Forests of the Pacific Northwest" from Peter H. Raven and Linda R. Berg, *Environment*, Third Edition, pp. 55–57. Copyright © 2000 by John Wiley & Sons, Inc. This material is used by permission of John Wiley & Sons, Inc, pp. 140–145; "Environmentalists at Work—Case in Point: Lake Washington" from Peter H. Raven and Linda R. Berg, *Environment*, Third Edition, pp. 31–36. Copyright © 2000 by John Wiley & Sons, Inc. This material is used by permission of John Wiley & Sons, Inc, pp. 155–165; Macroeconomics: The Big Picture—Introduction from John B. Taylor, *Economics*, Fourth Edition. Copyright © 2004 by Houghton Mifflin Company. Reprinted with permission, pp. 180–181; "Real GDP over Time" from John B. Taylor, *Economics*, Fourth Edition. Copyright © 2004 by Houghton Mifflin Company. Reprinted with permission, pp. 189–197; "Unemployment, Inflation, and Interest Rates" from John B. Taylor, *Economics*, Fourth Edition. Copyright © 2004 by Houghton Mifflin Company. Reprinted with